Lecture Notes in Computer Science 9410

Commenced Publication in 1973
Founding and Former Series Editors:
Gerhard Goos, Juris Hartmanis, and Jan van Leeuwen

More information about this series at http://www.springer.com/series/8379

Maciej Koutny · Jörg Desel
Serge Haddad (Eds.)

Transactions on
Petri Nets
and Other Models
of Concurrency X

Springer

Editor-in-Chief

Maciej Koutny
Newcastle University
Newcastle upon Tyne
UK

Guest Editors

Jörg Desel
FernUniversität in Hagen
Hagen
Germany

Serge Haddad
École Normale Supérieure de Cachan
Cachan
France

ISSN 0302-9743   ISSN 1611-3349   (electronic)
Lecture Notes in Computer Science
ISBN 978-3-662-48649-8   ISBN 978-3-662-48650-4   (eBook)
DOI 10.1007/978-3-662-48650-4

Library of Congress Control Number: 2015951658

Printed on acid-free paper

Springer-Verlag GmbH Berlin Heidelberg is part of Springer Science+Business Media
(www.springer.com)

Preface by Editor-in-Chief

The 10th Issue of LNCS Transactions on Petri Nets and Other Models of Concurrency (ToPNoC) contains revised and extended versions of a selection of the best papers from the workshops held at the 35th International Conference on Application and Theory of Petri Nets and Concurrency (Petri Nets 2014, Tunis, Tunisia, 23–27 June 2014), and the 14th International Conference on Application of Concurrency to System Design (ACSD 2014, Tunis, Tunisia, 23–27 June 2014). It also contains one paper submitted directly to ToPNoC.

I would like to thank the two guest editors of this special issue: Jörg Desel and Serge Haddad. Moreover, I would like to thank all authors, reviewers, and the organizers of the Petri Nets 2014 and ACSD 2014 satellite workshops, without whom this issue of ToPNoC would not have been possible.

July 2015   Maciej Koutny

LNCS Transactions on Petri Nets and Other Models of Concurrency: Aims and Scope

ToPNoC aims to publish papers from all areas of Petri nets and other models of concurrency ranging from theoretical work to tool support and industrial applications. The foundations of Petri nets were laid by the pioneering work of Carl Adam Petri and his colleagues in the early 1960s. Since then, a huge volume of material has been developed and published in journals and books as well as presented at workshops and conferences.

The annual International Conference on Application and Theory of Petri Nets and Concurrency started in 1980. The International Petri Net Bibliography maintained by the Petri Net Newsletter contains over ten thousand entries, and the International Petri Net Mailing List has close to two thousand subscribers. For more information on the International Petri Net community, see: http://www.informatik.uni-hamburg.de/TGI/PetriNets/

All issues of ToPNoC are LNCS volumes. Hence they appear in all main libraries and are also accessible on SpringerLink (electronically). It is possible to subscribe to ToPNoC without subscribing to the rest of LNCS.

ToPNoC contains:

- revised versions of a selection of the best papers from workshops and tutorials concerned with Petri nets and concurrency;
- special issues related to particular subareas (similar to those published in the *Advances in Petri Nets* series);
- other papers invited for publication in ToPNoC; and
- papers submitted directly to ToPNoC by their authors.

Like all other journals, ToPNoC has an Editorial Board, which is responsible for the quality of the journal. The members of the board assist in the reviewing of papers submitted or invited for publication in ToPNoC. Moreover, they may make recommendations concerning collections of papers for special issues. The Editorial Board consists of prominent researchers within the Petri net community and in related fields.

Topics

System design and verification using nets; analysis and synthesis, structure and behavior of nets; relationships between net theory and other approaches; causality/partial order theory of concurrency; net-based semantical, logical and algebraic calculi; symbolic net representation (graphical or textual); computer tools for nets; experience with using nets, case studies; educational issues related to nets; higher level net models; timed and stochastic nets; and standardization of nets.

Applications of nets to: biological systems; defence systems; e-commerce and trading; embedded systems; environmental systems; flexible manufacturing systems; hardware structures; health and medical systems; office automation; operations research; performance evaluation; programming languages; protocols and networks; railway networks; real-time systems; supervisory control; telecommunications; cyber physical systems; and workflow.

For more information about ToPNoC see: www.springer.com/lncs/topnoc

Submission of Manuscripts

Manuscripts should follow LNCS formatting guidelines, and should be submitted as PDF or zipped PostScript files to ToPNoC@ncl.ac.uk. All queries should be addressed to the same e-mail address.

LNCS Transactions on Petri Nets and Other Models of Concurrency: Editorial Board

Preface by Guest Editors

This volume of ToPNoC contains revised and extended versions of a selection of the best workshop papers presented at the 35th International Conference on Application and Theory of Petri Nets and Other Models of Concurrency (Petri Nets 2014) and the 14th International Conference on Application of Concurrency to System Design (ACSD 2014).

We, Jörg Desel and Serge Haddad, are indebted to the Program Committees of the workshops and in particular to their chairs. Without their enthusiastic work, this volume would not have been possible. Many members of the Program Committees participated in reviewing the new versions of the papers selected for this issue. We asked for the strongest contributions of the following workshops:

- PNSE 2014: International Workshop on Petri Nets and Software Engineering (chairs: Daniel Moldt, Heiko Rölke)
- FMS 2014: International Workshop on Formal Methods for Security (FMS) (chairs: Véronique Cortier, Riadh Robbana)
- BioPPN 2014: International Workshop on Biological Processes and Petri Nets (chairs: Alia Benkahla, Monika Heiner)

The best papers of these workshops were selected in close cooperation with their chairs. The authors were invited to improve and extend their results where possible, based on the comments received before and during the workshops. The resulting revised submissions were reviewed by three referees. We followed the principle of asking for fresh reviews of the revised papers, i.e., from referees who had not been involved initially in reviewing the original workshop contributions. All papers went through the standard two-stage journal reviewing process, and eventually seven were accepted after rigorous reviewing and revising. This volume contains a variety of high-quality contributions, covering specification, validation, verification, and synthesis of Petri nets and other models of concurrency.

The paper "Verification of Logs - Revealing Faulty Processes of a Medical Laboratory" by Robin Bergenthum and Joachim Schick presents a case study showing a systematic approach to revealing faulty processes in a medical laboratory. This approach consists in (1) extracting a sample of the data, (2) formalizing it with the language of the information system, (3) distinguishing between valid and faulty words, and (4) building a Colored Petri net that accepts the valid words. In addition, this Colored Petri net is translated into a PL/SQL-program.

The paper "An Everlasting Secure Non-interactive Timestamping Scheme in the Bounded Storage Model" by Assia Ben Shil and Kaouther Blibech Sinaoui provides a non-interactive timestamping scheme for models where an adversary has limited memory but potentially unlimited computing power. Thus, the security of their timestamping scheme does not depend on the lifetime of any cryptographic technique. More precisely, the authors prove that this timestamping scheme is eternally secure, even against an adversary with unlimited computing power.

The paper "Timed Aggregate Graph: A Finite Graph Preserving Event- and State-Based Quantitative Properties of Time Petri Nets" by Kais Klai defines an abstraction of the behavior of Time Petri nets in the form of a finite graph. The author proves that this graph preserves timed traces and reachable states of a Time Petri net and provides an algorithm that maps abstract runs of Timed Aggregate Graphs to explicit runs of the corresponding Time Petri net. The graph can also be used to check event- and state-based properties as well as the Zenoness property, i.e., the existence of a run with infinitely many events in finite time.

The paper "SMT-based Abstract Parametric Temporal Planning" by Atur Niewiadomski and Wojciech Penczek extends the abstract planning phase of an approach to solve the web service composition problem, as implemented in the Planics tool. In this phase, the tool composes service types. The paper provides a theory for this phase and a new module for parametric temporal planning. For applying this module, the user query is extended with object variables and with a $PLTL^{\alpha}_{-X}$ formula, specifying temporal aspects of world transformations in a plan. The paper not only provides the theory and the implementation, but also experimental results.

The paper "Kleene Theorems for Synchronous Products with Matching" by Ramchandra Phawade and Kamal Lodaya studies relations between subclasses of Petri nets, products of automata, and syntactic expressions. The authors define a specific composition of automata such that the corresponding Petri nets are live and one-bounded labelled free-choice nets. For the converse direction, a particular property of the nets is necessary, roughly stating that conflicts of the net are deterministic, i.e., that every two transitions in conflict are labelled differently. The behavior of these composed automata (nets, respectively) in terms of expressions requires the Kleene operator, which refers to the repetitive behavior of the models. The main results are so-called Kleene Theorems for a subclass of free-choice Petri nets.

The paper "Symbolic Model Checking of Security Protocols for Ad Hoc Networks on Any Topologies" by Mihai Lica Pura and Didier Buchs presents the use of AlPiNA, a symbolic model checker based on Algebraic Petri nets, for modeling ad hoc networks and for verifying security protocols designed for this type of networks. More precisely, the authors study the ARAN secure routing protocol and manage to find all the attacks that were previously reported for this protocol.

The paper "Symbolic Search of Insider Attack Scenarios from a Formal Information System Modeling" by Amira Radhouani, Akram Idani, Yves Ledru, and Narjes Ben Rajeb deals with internal attacks on information systems, i.e., attacks by people from inside the organization. The authors propose to model functional requirements and their Role Based Access Control (RBAC) policies using B machines, and then to formally reason on both models. Combining an analysis of symbolic behaviors with a model-checking tool allows us to find an observable concrete sequence of operations that can be performed by an attacker.

As guest editors, we would like to thank all authors and referees who have contributed to this issue. The quality of this volume is the result of the high scientific value of their work. Moreover, we would like to acknowledge the excellent cooperation throughout the whole process that has made our work a pleasant task.

We are also grateful to the Springer/ToPNoC team for the final production of this issue.

June 2015

Jörg Desel
Serge Haddad

Organization of This Issue

Guest Editors

Jörg Desel   FernUniversität in Hagen, Germany
Serge Haddad   ENS Cachan, France

Co-chairs of the Workshops

Alia Benkahla   Institut Pasteur de Tunis, Tunisia
Véronique Cortier   LORIA, France
Monika Heiner   Brandenburg University of Technology, Germany
Daniel Moldt   University of Hamburg, Germany
Riadh Robbana   INSAT-University of Carthage, Tunisia
Heiko Rölke   DIPF, Germany

Referees

Gianfranco Balbo   Simon Hardy
Chistel Baier   Lom M. Hillah
Hanifa Boucheneb   Lucca Hirschi
Jens Brandt   Yasir Imtiaz Khan
Didier Buchs   Robert Lorenz
Josep Carmona   Patrice Moreaux
Vincent Cheval   Franck Pommereau
José-Manuel Colom   Jean-François Pradat-Peyre
Stéphanie Delaune   Maximilian Schlund
Raymond Devillers   Mark-Oliver Stehr
Frédéric Gervais   Lilia Sfaxi
Stefan Haar   Karsten Wolf

Contents

Verification of Logs - Revealing Faulty Processes of a Medical Laboratory

Robin Bergenthum and Joachim Schick[✉]

Department of Software Engineering and Theory of Programming,
FernUniversität in Hagen, Hagen, Germany
{robin.bergenthum,joachim.schick}@fernuni-hagen.de

Abstract. If there is suspicion of Lyme disease, a doctor sends a blood sample of the patient to a medical laboratory. The laboratory performs a number of different blood examinations, testing for antibodies against the Lyme disease bacteria. The total number of performed examinations depends on the intermediate results of the blood count. Of course, the number of performed examinations is important since the cost of each examination needs to be covered by the health insurance companies. In order to control and restrict the number of performed examinations, the health insurance companies provide a so called charges regulation document. If some health insurance company disagrees with the charges of a laboratory, it is the job of the public prosecution service to validate the charges according to this document.

In this paper we present a case study showing a systematic approach to revealing faulty processes in a medical laboratory. Different files produced by the information system of the respective laboratory are analyzed, consolidated, and stored in a database. An excerpt of this data is translated into an event log, providing a list of all events performed by the information system. This list is further compressed and translated into the language of the information system. Compared to the size of the data and the size of the event log, the size of the language is small. With the help of the regulation document this language can be split in two sets - the set of valid and the set of faulty words. In a next step, we build a colored Petri net model corresponding to the set of valid words in a sense that only the valid words are executable in the Petri net model. In a last step we translate the colored Petri net into a PL/SQL-program. This program can automatically reveal all faulty processes stored in the database.

1 Introduction

Many information systems are used in the healthcare sector and each system produces some kind of log-data. This is particularly true in the domain of medical laboratories where all samples, materials and examination results have to be stored. Making extensive use of a well-adapted information system is their most important method for quality management. It is a big part of "good laboratory

© Springer-Verlag Berlin Heidelberg 2015
M. Koutny et al. (Eds.): ToPNoC X, LNCS 9410, pp. 1–18, 2015.
DOI: 10.1007/978-3-662-48650-4_1

practice" and for this reason medical laboratories own records of several millions of processed orders.

Every examination performed by a medical laboratory is paid for by a health insurance company. The cost of each examination is rated by a fixed scale of charges given in a so-called charges regulation document. Of course, the correct application of the regulations has to be proven to the health insurance companies. If any suspicion about incorrect application of the regulations arises, the public prosecution service has to validate the billed charges according to the regulation document. Usually, the prosecution service orders an expert to investigate and report on the issue.

In this case study we present an approach of using colored Petri nets, inspired by the methods in process mining, process discovery, and conformance checking to reveal faulty processes in log-files of a medical laboratory. The files contain data recorded over a period of five years with 1500 to 2000 orders a day. Each order consists of 20 to 30 events, examinations and results. Altogether, there are about 100 million lines of log that need to be analyzed and verified. Each line of the given log describes an event or a sub-process of the medical laboratory. Each event refers to a performed action recorded by the information system. Each event carries the time stamp, order ID, and may carry additional variables. Typical actions of the system are *register order*, *register requirements*, *register examination results*, *validate results*, *make invoice*, *archive order*, etc.. In addition to these basic actions, a medical laboratory is able to perform a large number of different examinations. In this case study, the prosecution service ordered a report revealing all faulty processes concerned with Lyme disease.

To reveal all faulty processes in a set of log-files we choose a four step approach. We call the first step *consolidation step*. The goal is to develop a schema to integrate and load all recorded files into a single relational database. In our case study, this results in a database with a total number of about 100 million lines. Using the same schema, it is easy to implement a query on the data to subtract any redundant or superfluous information. This results in a list of all recorded events related to processes regarding Lyme disease. In the area of process mining, such a list is called an event log, i.e. a sequence of events carrying information about order-numbers, time-stamps and results. In our case study, in contrast to the enormous total number of lines in the database, the number of events regarding Lyme disease diagnostic in the event log is only 500,000.

The second step of our approach is called *formalization step*. We re-sort the event log by order ID of each event. In other words, we gather sequences of events from the event log, with each sequence describing the treatment of a single patient. Each sequence of events corresponds to a sequence of actions. Each sequence of actions is called a word. The set of words is called the language of the event log. Obviously, since most of the processes of the laboratory are standardized, a lot of sequences in the event log correspond to the same words. Thus, the number of words is much smaller than the number of processes performed. In our case study, the total number of Lyme disease patients is 20,000 although the language of the event log consists of only 300 words. The next task in the formalization step is to split the language into two sublanguages, the set of valid and the set of faulty words. This has to be done manually with the help of the charges regulation document. This is a time consuming task, but it is very easy and quite error-proof to classify single words. A main advantage of our approach is that there is no need to formalize or model the regulation document from scratch. One could try to directly build a model of regulations, but the regulations are given as plain text. Starting from such a description is highly error-prone and easily yields a model that does not fit the recorded event log regarding names, values and level of abstraction. In our approach, we only need to answer yes or no for each of the 300 words. This is a straightforward task and can easily be done by domain experts on the regulations with no knowledge about the information system or modelling techniques. Of course we only classify the set of words; we do not classify the complete event log. Altogether, we produce a set of valid sequences of actions. We call this set the language of regulations.

The third step of our approach is called *integration step*. The language of regulations is integrated into a colored Petri net model. Such integration can be supported by synthesis or workflow mining algorithms. In our case study, the language of regulations is already highly compressed and settled, so that we construct a corresponding colored Petri net model manually, using the editor CPN-Tools [1]. The constructed colored Petri net model is a formalization of the charges regulation document using the language of the recorded files. Only valid process instances of the Lyme disease diagnostic are executable in this Petri net model. A big advantage of such a Petri net model is that it can be analyzed, simulated and verified using numerous algorithms well-known in the area of Petri nets. During the case study, it turned out to be very beneficial that one can modify the model to realize a stricter or looser application of the given regulations. Of course, once the model is constructed it can also be re-used to verify other laboratories.

The fourth step of our approach is called *implementation step*. Colored Petri nets are easily readable and have an intuitive and formal semantic. Petri nets are executable, but nevertheless we translate the colored Petri net model into a PL/SQL-program. We translate transitions to functions, places to tables and arcs to delete or insert statements. The main advantage of having a PL/SQL-program is that we can replay and check all stored sequences directly in the database. There is no need to transfer the recorded data from the database to CPN-Tools. If a replay fails, the sequence corresponds to the occurrence of a faulty process of the medical laboratory.

Figure 1 depicts our approach. The whole approach is built on a chain of formal models. First, we consolidate the initially recorded data files and store them in the database with the help of a schema. We implement a query on the data and produce the event log. Second, we extract the language of the event log and deduce the language of regulations. Third, we build the colored Petri net. Finally, we translate the Petri net into a PL/SQL-program. The chain of constructed models documents the complete inspection procedure. All results

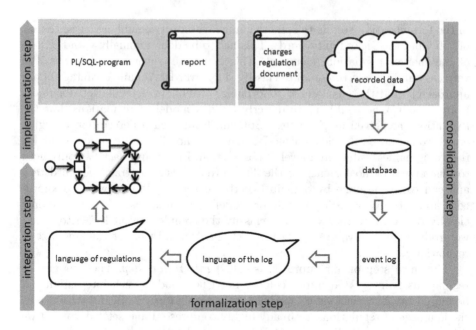

Fig. 1. Approach to revealing faulty processes

can easily be reconstructed and models can be re-used when inspecting other laboratories. Furthermore, going in small steps from one formal model to another highly supports the validity of the produced investigation report. Furthermore, we are able to support each step by algorithms and tools. Some of the steps can even run fully automated. For example, it is possible to use synthesis algorithms for the construction of the Petri net model or an automated translation from this model to the PL/SQL-program.

Using our approach we are able to contract the recorded data files to a small set of valid words. In our case study, the initial 1,800 files contain 100 million lines of code. 2 million of these lines deal with Lyme disease diagnostic. The produced event log contains 500,000 lines of events while the language of the log consists of only 300 different words. Many words have the same set of actions, but permute the order of simultaneously performed tests. Other words are almost identical and only differ in the results of comparable tests. The 300 words form 22 different equivalence classes of words. It is easy to build a colored Petri net model from these 22 classes of words.

The chosen approach is inspired by techniques well-known in the area of process mining, where some recorded behavior is merged into a formal model of the underlying process [2–4]. Note that in our case it is of great importance to choose an appropriate process mining algorithm that does not introduce additional behavior to the model. There are language-based discovery algorithms [5–7] or even synthesis algorithms [8–11] that meet this requirement. The approach is also inspired by work done in the field of business process modelling and requirements engineering, where the starting point of the discovery phase is the construction of a formal and valid specification [12–16]. Nevertheless, there are two major aspects that distinguish our approach from other approaches known in literature. First, we use colored Petri nets to model the processes in the laboratory. The reason for this is that these processes highly depend on values, i.e. the intermediate results of different blood examinations. Second, the formal language of the event logs needs to be filtered by hand according to the charges regulation document. This step cannot be automated and is crucial for the quality of the produced report.

The paper is organized as follows: Sect. 2 provides formal definitions. Section 3 presents the approach and our case study. In Sect. 4, we sum up the results to prove the applicability of the developed approach.

2   Preliminaries

In this section we briefly recall the basic notions of languages, event logs and colored Petri nets.

An alphabet is a finite set A and we denote A^* the set of words over A. We denote λ the empty word and call a subset $L \subseteq A^*$ a language over A. Business processes describe the flow of work within an organization [17]. Each process consists of a set of activities that needs to be performed. We denote T the set of all activities and call the execution of an activity an event. Each event is labelled with the name of the corresponding activity. Furthermore, events carry a time stamp and may carry a value. The time stamp denotes the time the activity was performed. The value can store additional information on the execution of the activity. We denote V the set of values. A set of events corresponding to the occurrence of a process is called a case. Recording the behavior of a system yields a set of interleaved cases we call an event log.

Definition 1. *Let T be a finite set of activities, V be a finite set of values, and let C be a finite set of cases. An element $\sigma \in (T \times V \times C)^*$ is called an event log. Fix a case $c \in C$ we define the function $p_c : (T \times V \times C) \to (T \times V)$ by*

$$p_c(t, v, c') = \begin{cases} (t, v), & \text{if } c = c' \\ \lambda, & \text{else.} \end{cases}$$

Let $\sigma = e_1 \ldots e_n \in (T \times V \times C)^*$ be an event log, we define the language $L(\sigma)$ by $L(\sigma) = \{p_c(e_1)...p_c(e_i) | i \leq n, c \in C\} \subseteq (T \times V)^*$.

The language of an event log is finite and prefix-closed. It reflects the control flow between activities given by the events of the log.

In this paper we use colored Petri nets to model valid behavior of a medical laboratory. The underlying Petri net models the control flow between actions and variables control the examination results. The following definition of colored Petri nets is given in [1].

Definition 2. *A colored Petri net is a tuple* $CPN = (\Sigma, P, T, A, N, K, G, E, I)$, *where:*

Σ *is a finite set of non-empty types, called color sets.*
P *is a finite set of places.*
T *is a finite set of transitions so that:* $P \cap T = \emptyset$ *holds.*
A *is a finite set of arcs so that:* $P \cap A = T \cap A = \emptyset$ *holds.*
N *is a node function. It is defined from* A *into* $(P \times T) \cup (T \times P)$.
K *is a color function. It is defined from* P *into* Σ.
G *is a guard function. It is defined from* T *into expressions so that: for all* $t \in T$
   the type of $G(t)$ *is boolean and the set of types of variables in* $G(t)$ *is subset*
   of Σ.
E *is an arc expression function. It is defined from* A *into expressions so that:*
   for all $a \in A$ *the type of* $E(a)$ *is multi-sets over the color set of the place*
   connected to a and the set of types of variables in $E(a)$ *is subset of* Σ.
I *is an initialisation function. It is defined from* P *into closed expressions so*
   that: for all $p \in P$ *the type of* $I(p)$ *is multi-sets over* $K(p)$.

In contrast to low-level Petri nets, each place of a colored Petri net has a type called color set. According to this type, each place carries values called tokens. Arcs carry expressions over variables and if an arc is connected to a place, the tokens of the place can bind to the variables of the arc expression. A so called binding of a transition maps variables to tokens of related places. A transition is executable if there is a binding where the transition guard evaluates to *true*. When the transition occurs, as for low-level Petri nets, it removes the bound tokens from the input places and produces tokens in the output places (see [1] for a formal definition).

The initialization function of a colored Petri net assigns tokens to places describing an initial marking. Given a colored Petri net CPN, a sequence of sequential enabled transitions is called an occurrence sequence of CPN. For our case study, we add the values of the occurred bindings to the events of an occurrence sequence. The language $L(CPN)$ of CPN is defined as the set of all occurrence sequences. Let $log \in (T \times V \times C)^*$ be an event log, log is executable in CPN if $L(log) \subseteq L(CPN)$ holds.

3   Verification of Logs

In this section we present an approach to validating a set of given recorded files with the help of a regulation document. In the following case study, on behalf of the public prosecution service, we reviewed recorded data of an information system of a medical laboratory. The laboratory records one file each day and we inspected files recorded over a period of five years. Altogether, we analyzed and verified 1,800 files with a total of 100 million lines of logged data using our approach.

We verified the recorded data according to the regulations given by the so called charges regulation document provided by health insurance companies. The goal was to identify faulty processes by the medical laboratory in all processes related to Lyme disease diagnostic. An overview of our approach is depicted in Fig. 1 in the introduction. The following four subsections reflect the four steps of our approach.

3.1   Consolidation Step

The first step of our approach is called consolidation step. As illustrated in Fig. 1, we build an entity-relationship diagram and load the recorded files into a database. With the help of the diagram we build a query on the data. Using this query, we build an event log. This event log is a formal description of all executed processes considering Lyme disease diagnostic.

In our case study we use the commercial Oracle Database to store and process the recorded data. This database system provides the procedural programming language PL/SQL for the implementation of the so-called stored procedures. To set up our database, we review the recorded files. Figure 2 depicts a very small excerpt from a recorded data file of the medical laboratory. All files of the laboratory's information system have a hierarchical structure with a flexible record length of up to 1024 characters. Each file is a sequence of different types of blocks. Each type corresponds to a set of different actions of the system. The first line of each block is the header of the block and all following lines are indented.

The excerpt depicted in Fig. 2 starts with a block corresponding to the registration of a new order for a blood count. The header of this block reads as follows: The first integer 727980834 is a registration-ID automatically generated by the system to identify orders. This ID perfectly caters for the need to identify different cases in our given files. In our case study, each registration-ID corresponds to a case in the system. The next two integers indicate the time the registration occurred, i.e. 25 January 2011, 11:49:54 in our example. The next two strings indicate that the action was triggered manually. The last integer of the header encodes the type of the respective block. In this particular information system, the integer 10 encodes a so called *registration block*. The inner lines of the registration block carry the values of an *order blood count* action. Values are the name, birthday and address of the registered patient.

The second block depicted in Fig. 2 corresponds to the scheduling of examinations. The header refers to the same case as the first registration block since both IDs match. Note that both recorded actions occurred within the same second. The difference between both headers is only in the integer at the end of the line. In this block, the integer 20 marks a so called *schedule examination* block. This block consists of two sub-blocks; both sub-blocks are marked by the keyword BORR. The keyword BORR abbreviates Lyme disease and indicates that the scheduled examinations are part of a Lyme disease diagnosis. Again, the inner lines of both sub-blocks carry additional values of the schedule examination block where BORG and BORM are again abbreviations of two different blood examinations. In this example the block corresponds to the occurrence of two different actions: a BORG-examination and a BORM-examination are scheduled.

```
727980834          250111  114954  SF        erfass  10
        NAME       ██████████████
        GEBDAT     06.01.1979
        ...
727980834          250111  114954  SF        erfass  20
        BORR       BORG            0000
                   RESTYPE W
                   ST_BA[1]        X
                   ST_BA[4]        X
                   MVALBER LA
                   UNTVERS 0000
        BORR       BORM            0000
                   RESTYPE W
                   ST_BA[1]        X
                   ST_BA[4]        X
                   MVALBER LA
                   UNTVERS 0000
702673748          250111  115004  SF        erfass  10
        NAME       ...
        ...
702673748          250111  164235  MB        onlval  21
        JB         FT3
                   WERT    2.8
        ...
702984083          250111  174847  MB        onlval  21
        TSH1       TSH1
                   WERT    0.63
        ...
727980834          270111  123344  US        onlval  21
        BORR       BORG            0000
                   WERT    < 10.0
                   ST_RES  J
                   ST_BA[1]        R
                   ST_BA[4]        R
                   ST_MVAL J
        BORR       BORM            0000
                   WERT    < 18.0
                   ST_RES  J
                   ST_BA[1]        R
                   ST_BA[4]        R
                   ST_MVAL J
        ...
727980834          270111  195346  AB        abschl  13
        ...
727980834          280111  071406  HW        rechdr  11
        RNR        KV110128
        ROK        OK
```

Fig. 2. An excerpt of a recorded file of the medical laboratory.

The sixth block shown in Fig. 2 corresponds to the recording of results of a scheduled examination. The integer 21 marks a *receive result* block. This block matches the schedule examination block apart from two important differences. First, the keyword ONLVAL indicates that this event was automatically triggered by the information system as soon as the results of examinations were received. Second, the inner lines of the block carry the results of these examinations. In this example, the results of the BORG- and the BORM-examinations were received. The value of the BORG-examination is smaller than 10.0 and the value of the BORM-examination is smaller than 18.0. Both values show the absence of the relevant antibodies, i.e. both examinations are negative and no further examinations need to be scheduled.

After reviewing the recorded files, we built an entity-relationship diagram. In our case study we used the Oracle SQL Developer Data Modeler to construct this model. We produced the entity-relationship diagram depicted in Fig. 3.

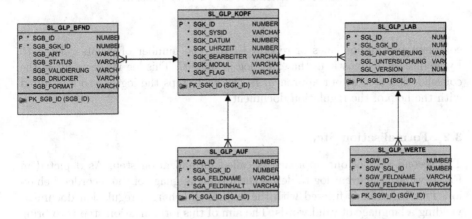

Fig. 3. Entity-relationship diagram of our Oracle Database.

Figure 3 depicts a schema showing five entities. The names are: SL GLP KOPF (header), SL GLP LAB (lab), SL GLP WERTE (values), SL GLP AUF (order), and SL GLP BFND (findings). With the help of this schema, we write a PL/SQL-program to load all the files into the Oracle Database. After all the data is stored, we extract a consolidated and formal event log from this database. The event log only contains events and values corresponding to processes that have to fulfill the regulations set out in the charges regulation document concerning Lyme disease diagnostic. With the entity-relationship diagram, it is easy to implement a query to receive an appropriate event log.

In our example, the excerpt depicted in Fig. 2 only contains four blocks corresponding to Lyme disease diagnostic. In the first and in the third block, two new orders have arrived and both patients are registered. In the second block, a BORG- and a BORM- examination for the first order are scheduled. The sixth block shows the results of both examinations. We are able to discard all other blocks shown in Fig. 2. If we apply the constructed view to this excerpt, we get the event log shown in Table 1. This event log is free of additional events and values. It shows the six events corresponding to the four blocks concerned with Lyme disease of Fig. 2.

With the help of the Oracle database and the implemented query, arbitrary extracts from the recorded files can be shown as event logs. If we consider the

Table 1. Event log of the file depicted in Fig. 2.

ID	Action	Value	Stamp
727980834	10		25.01.11, 11:49:54
727980834	20 BORG		25.01.11, 11:49:54
727980834	20 BORM		25.01.11, 11:49:54
702673748	10		25.01.11, 11:50:04
727980834	21 BORG	<10	27.01.11, 12:33:44
727980834	21 BORM	<18	27.01.11, 12:33:44

complete 100 million lines of recorded data, the number of events related to Lyme disease diagnostic in the event log is 500,000. This log is the result of the consolidation step of our approach. In the next steps the log has to be filtered with the help of the regulation document.

3.2 Formalisation Step

The second step of our approach is called formalization step. As depicted in Fig. 1, we use the event log to define the formal language of the recorded behavior. This behavior is filtered with the help of the charges regulation document yielding a language of valid words. The aim of this formalization step is to bring together the recorded behavior and the regulation document given as plain text. Note that it is much easier to merely evaluate the recorded language with the help of the regulations rather than to build a second independent model of regulations and hope it will fit the language of the recorded behavior.

To deduce a formal language from the event log, we identify the actions of the system. In our case study the list of significant actions reads as follows:

$$T = \{10, 20BORG, 20BORM, 20BVLSEG, 20BP39G, 20BP83, 20BIV1,$$
$$20BIV2, 20BIV3, 20BIV4, 20BOSPC, 20BVLSEM, 20BP39M,$$
$$21BORG, 21BORM, 21BVLSEG, 21BP39G, 21BP83, 21BIV1,$$
$$21BIV2, 21BIV3, 21BIV4, 21BOSPC, 21BVLSEM, 21BP39M\}$$

As described above, the integers 10, 20 and 21 indicate if a blood count for a patient is registered, an examination is scheduled or if a result is received. The attached letters are the abbreviations of the corresponding examinations. There are 12 different tests related to Lyme disease diagnostic leading to 25 different actions in total. Every action with a name starting with 21 carries a value of the type *boolean*. An examination is either negative or positive. We are able to omit all other values given in the files and all other actions occur without additional data. As stated above, all events with the same registration ID belong to the same case in our information system. Events of the same case can be ordered by their time stamp and therefore every case yields a sequence of actions. Each of these sequences is called a word of the event log. Of course, different cases of the event log can be described by the same word. The set of all words is called the language of this event log. In our case study, the number of cases given in the event log is 20,000, while the language of the event log consists of 300 different words.

The following table shows three example words given by the event log of our case study:

Table 2. The language of the event log.

$L(log) = \{$10 20BORG 20BORM (21BORG,false) (21BORM,false),

   10 20BORG 20BORM 20BVLSEG 20BP39G 20BP83 20BIV1 20BIV2
   20BIV3 20BIV4 20BOSPC 20BVLSEM 20BP39M (21BORG,true)
   (21BORM,true) (21BVLSEG,false) (21BP39G,false) (21BP83,false)
   (21BIV1,false) (21BIV2,false) (21BIV3,false) (21BIV4,false)
   (21BOSPC,false) (21BVLSEM,false) (21BP39M,false),

   10 20BORG 20BORM 20BVLSEG 20BP39G 20BP83 20BIV1 20BIV2
   20BIV3 20BIV4 20BOSPC 20BVLSEM 20BP39M (21BORG,false)
   (21BORM,false) (21BVLSEG,false) (21BP39G,false) (21BP83,false)
   (21BIV1,false) (21BIV2,false) (21BIV3,false) (21BIV4,false)
   (21BOSPC,false) (21BVLSEM,false) (21BP39M,false),

  . . .$\}$

It is easy to automatically process the language from the given event log. This language is a complete and formal description of the set of processes executed in the information system of the medical laboratory. Any sequence of actions and values drawn from the events of a case corresponds to a word in the language of the log. Obviously, the language of the log is much smaller than the event log since cases with the same process are not distinguished.

Once the language of the log is obtained, the next step is to distinguish valid and faulty words. This is a major task in the presented approach which cannot be automated. The charges regulation document is given as plain text. It is absolutely necessary to understand the regulations and apply them to the set of words. However, the main advantage of this approach is that the set of words is given in a very compact and formal style. There is no room for interpretation or ambiguities. The rules of the charges regulation document do not need to be modelled explicitly, they just need to be applied to the language. As stated in [13,16], a single word is much easier to understand than a whole system. Single words can be evaluated by experts on the regulation document. There is no need for these experts to know how to model a system or know how the information system works.

In our case study, we have to answer yes or no for each of the 300 words. This is a major but simple task. Note that some of the words are almost identical and only differ in the results of comparable tests. According to the regulation document, the blood count needs to be performed in two steps. First, the BORG and BORM-examination results have to be evaluated. Only if one of these results is positive, a more detailed set of examinations is performed. It directly follows that there is no need to distinguish identical sequences of actions where either 21BORM or 21BORG carries the value *true*. Furthermore the validity of a word does not change if the order of the BORG and BORM actions is permuted. The same deductions apply for the other 10 examinations. Thus, the set of 300 words comes down to a set of 50 different equivalence classes of words and for each such class we checked one representative. Altogether, we found 22 valid and 28 non valid equivalence classes of words in our language of the recorded event log.

In the example shown in Table 2, the first two words are valid. The third word is faulty since the set of examinations {BVLSEG, BP39G, BP83, BIV1, BIV2, BIV3, BIV4, BOSPC, BVLSEM, BP39M} may only be performed if one of the BORG- and BORM-examinations is positive.

The result of the formalization step is the set of valid words. This set is a formal model of the charges regulation document given in the language of the information system. In other words, the set of valid words perfectly fits the recorded data in terms of abstraction, names of activities, values and so on. By constructing this language, the most challenging task of the investigation process is completed. In the next steps, this set is integrated into an executable model.

3.3   Integration Step

The third step of our approach is called integration step. As illustrated in Fig. 1, we build a Petri net modelling the language of the charges regulation document. We add colors to formalize the results of the different examinations processed by the medical laboratory in a well readable and compact manner. Valid process instances of the Lyme disease diagnostic process reported in the event log are executable in this colored Petri net model. Of course, our Petri net model can be analyzed, simulated and verified using numerous algorithms well-known in the area of Petri nets.

As suggested in [18], it is possible to skip the integration step and filter the event log with the help of the set of valid words obtained in the earlier step, but there are important reasons to build an integrated model first. A model provides a more compact representation of the set of words so that the model can be more easily simulated and analyzed. A lot of well-known Petri net algorithms and Petri net tools (CPN-Tools in our example) exist for this purpose. Furthermore, it is easy to translate the executable Petri net model into executable code in the next step of our approach.

Integrating a set of words into a Petri net is a familiar problem. A lot of research tackling this problem in the areas of both process mining [2,7,19,20] and language based synthesis [6,8,9,11,21] exists. It is possible to apply algorithms from both areas to support the integration step. In the presented case study, we build the corresponding model by hand. The constructed language of the charges regulation document is already highly compressed, so that there is no need for automated integration. After the formalization step this language contains only

22 valid words that have to be included in our Petri net model. This is quite an improvement compared to the 22,000 cases contained in the initial event log.

We build the Petri net model using a straight forward approach with all the information gathered in the preceding formalization step. First, a transition is constructed for every action occurring in the language of regulations. In our case study we identified 25 actions in the formalization step yielding 25 transitions in the constructed Petri net. According to the set of valid words, we add places to this set of transitions, so that firing sequences of the net correspond to valid sequences of actions described by the words of the language of regulations. If an action carries a value, we add additional variables to the arcs connected to the respective transition. We adjust the Petri net so that each pair of an action and a value given in the language corresponds to a transition and a binding. In a last step, as is common for colored Petri nets, it is possible to merge transitions. Similar parts of the Petri net are folded yielding additional colored tokens representing the different parts of the low-level net.

For modeling, we use CPN-Tools [22,23]. CPN-Tools has been developed at the AIS group of the Technische Universiteit Eindhoven and supports all editing and simulation features for colored Petri nets. In our case study, our initial low-level Petri net contains 25 transitions corresponding to the 25 actions of our process identified in the formalization step. The control flow is rather simple and we just add the relevant places. First, a blood count has to be registered, and then an arbitrary number of the 12 examinations related to Lyme disease can be scheduled. The execution of these 12 examinations must follow a simple rule: perform the BORG- and BORM- examination before the other examinations. The control flow of the initial low-level net is independent from the values given in the language. Rules and regulations concerning values are added in the next step. All actions that correspond to an examination result carry a value. For this reason, we introduced a boolean colorset called RES and allow each transition to be executed while binding to *true* or *false*. At this point, we are able to require that a BORG- or BORM-examination must be positive before any other examination can be executed. In a last step we fold transitions if possible. The resulting net is depicted in Fig. 4.

In Fig. 4, the transition named 10 is enabled in the initial marking. If transition 10 fires, a BORG- and a BORM-token are produced in the place *search test* and tokens corresponding to all other examinations are produced in the place *western blot test*. In such a marking, only the upper transition 20 is enabled. If transition 20 fires, a BORG- or a BORM- examination is scheduled. As soon as an examination is scheduled, transition 21 is enabled. If transition 21 fires, it consumes a token from the place *investigation* and moves this token to the place *results*. While the token is moved, a random boolean value is attached. The lower transition named 20 is enabled if the western blot tests are scheduled and if there are at least two tokens in the place *results*. Note that the arc inscription $1'y + +1'z$ denotes a pair of tokens. One token is assigned to the variable y and another token is assigned to the variable z. The guard $[fb(z)]$ ensures that the token called z carries the value *true*. Thus follows that in the model shown in

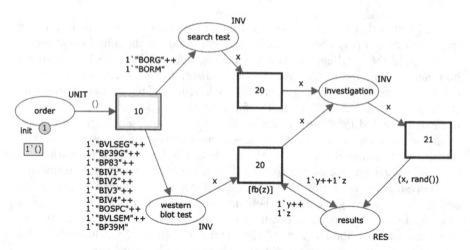

Fig. 4. Coloured Petri net representing the charges regulation document (Color figure online).

Fig. 4, the western blot tests can only be performed if the results of the BORG- and BORM-examination are present and at least one of these examinations is evaluated as *true*.

The model shown in Fig. 4 is able to reproduce single runs of the information system. In a way, it is a model of valid words, not a model of the running information system. Our goal is to replay each case of the event log in this model. There is no need to construct a model which is able to handle multiple cases at once. Besides the possibility to validate the produced model by simulation, CPN-Tools provides some model checking algorithms (see [1] for details). Table 3 depicts a small part of the CPN-Tools state space report of the model shown in Fig. 4.

The integration step yields an integrated model of the valid language produced during the formalization step of our approach. Of course, if analyzing this model uncovers faults or additional requirements, the language produced in the formalization step needs to be adapted according to the change made in the model. If the model matches the language and describes the valid behavior of the charges regulation document, the model is translated into executable PL/SQL-code in the last step of our approach.

Table 3. CPN-Tools state space report of the model shown in Fig. 4.

Liveness Properties ——————————
Dead Transition Instances: None
Live Transition Instances: None
Fairness Properties ——————————
No infinite occurrence sequences

3.4 Implementation Step

The fourth step of our approach is called implementation step. As depicted in Fig. 1, we translate the produced colored Petri net into PL/SQL-code. Although the colored Petri net model is executable itself, the PL/SQL is a proprietary programming language integrated in the Oracle Database. Using PL/SQL-code, we are able to execute SQL statements directly in our database where our event log is stored. This is more suitable than using Java, C++ or the Petri net itself in our approach. The aim of our fourth step is to get an executable program running next to the recorded data. With the help of such a program, faulty processes performed by the medical laboratory can automatically be revealed.

During our case study we transformed the colored Petri net depicted in Fig. 4 to PL/SQL code using the following ideas:

 (i) Each place of the colored Petri net corresponds to a table in the database. Tables are able to store records representing tokens and their values.
 (ii) Each transition of the colored Petri net corresponds to a parameterized function in our database. A function returns *true* only if the corresponding transition is executable. To check if a transition is executable, arcs of the Petri net are translated into SQL-statements. Roughly speaking, these statements check whether appropriate values exist in the tables that correspond to places in the preset of the transition.
(iii) Each arc of the colored Petri net yields an SQL-statement in the database. Arcs leading from a place to a transition correspond to DELETE-statements consuming tokens from tables. Arcs leading from a transition to a place correspond to INSERT-statements producing tokens in tables.
(iv) Each guard or function of the colored Petri net yields a function in the database. The SML-functions given in the colored Petri net can easily be translated.

A table of transformation patterns is depicted in Table 4. To verify the event log with the help of the PL/SQL-program, we replay the set of cases of the event log. Whenever it is not possible to replay a given case, the corresponding

Table 4. Transformation patterns form a CPN into a PL/SQL-program.

CPN	PL/SQL-program
COLOR	a list of attributes
PLACE	a table having a COLOR
TOKEN	a record in PLACE
PT-Arc	DELETE from PLACE return TOKEN
TP-Arc	INSERT into PLACE values TOKEN
EXPRESSION	a WHERE expression
TRANSITION	a function using ARCS
GUARD	a sub-function of TRANSITION

registration-ID is stored. With the help of this procedure, faulty processes can easily be revealed. The set of faulty processes is the basis of the report produced for the prosecution service. The results produced in our case study are presented in the next section.

4   Results and Conclusion

In the presented case study, we verified a huge set of files recorded by a medical laboratory. The files contained records of all actions undertaken by the laboratory over a period of five years. In that period, the laboratory performed 22,432 orders related to Lyme disease diagnostic. Following the presented approach, we produced a PL/SQL program and calculated the following results:

Table 5. Results of the presented case study.

Recorded processes	Valid	Faulty	Runtime
22,432	3311	19121	11 min

As shown in Table 5, only 15 % of the recorded behavior is valid according to the charges regulation document. It turned out that in almost every case the laboratory in question performed the complete set of 12 examinations. Yet, the regulations require that the BORG- and BORM-examinations precede all other examinations. Only if one of the two examinations is positive, the set of all examinations can be charged.

In order to obtain more information on the recorded data, we adjusted our colored Petri net model. We removed the transition guard requiring a positive result from one of the BORG- or BORM-examinations, assuming a more perfunctory interpretation of the regulation document. We repeated the validation procedure and found that still 50 % of all recorded processes were faulty even under this more liberal model. In other words, even if we allow that all 12 examinations can be performed at once, 50 % of all processes still contain additional faults such as unnecessary actions or manual changes to examination values.

In this paper, we presented an approach and a related a case study to verifying logs to reveal faulty processes of a medical laboratory. The produced PL/SQL program can directly be applied to any medical laboratory using the same information system. The main advantage of the presented approach is that it is based on a chain of formal models. With the help of these models, it is easy to keep track of the validity of the produced report. Most of the steps can be supported using algorithms or tools common in the area of Petri nets. Furthermore, experts on the regulation document can support the formalization step without any knowledge of modeling techniques. They merely give a yes- or no- answer to a small set of words obtained from the recorded event log. If a model is produced, it also can be verified, adapted, and reused. This can help to support different criteria regarding only parts of the regulation document.

Of course, all calculated results can be reproduced at any time if this is required by the public prosecution service. The approach provides well documented and traceable results. In the future, we will test this approach on a larger regulation document yielding a larger regulation model and will try to automate each step of the approach.

References

1. Jensen, K., Kristensen, L.M.: Coloured Petri Nets - Modelling and Validation of Concurrent Systems. Springer, Heidelberg (2009)
2. van der Aalst, W.M.P.: Process Mining - Discovery, Conformance and Enhancement of Business Processes. Springer, Heidelberg (2011)
3. van der Aalst, W.M.P., Adriansyah, A., van Dongen, B.F.: Replaying history on process models for conformance checking and performance analysis. Wiley Interdisc. Rev. Data Min. Knowl. Discov. **2**(2), 182–192 (2012)
4. Rozinat, A.: Process Mining: Conformance and Extension. Ph.D thesis, TU Eindhoven (2010)
5. van Dongen, B.F., van der Aalst, W.M.P.: Multi-phase process mining: building instance graphs. In: Atzeni, P., Chu, W., Lu, H., Zhou, S., Ling, T.-W. (eds.) ER 2004. LNCS, vol. 3288, pp. 362–376. Springer, Heidelberg (2004)
6. Bergenthum, R., Mauser, S.: Mining with user interaction. In: Desel, J., Yakovlev, A. (eds.) Proceedings of the Workshop Applications of Region Theory, Petri Nets 2011. CEUR Workshop Proceedings, vol. 725, pp. 79–84. Newcastle University, Newcastle upon Tyne (2011)
7. Bergenthum, R., Mauser, S.: Folding partially ordered runs. In: Desel, J., Yakovlev, A. (eds.) Proceedings of the Workshop Applications of Region Theory, Petri Nets 2011. CEUR Workshop Proceedings, vol. 725, pp. 52–62. Newcastle University, Newcastle upon Tyne (2011)
8. Badouel, E., Darondeau, P.: Theory of regions. In: Reisig, W., Rozenberg, G. (eds.) APN 1998. LNCS, vol. 1491, pp. 529–586. Springer, Heidelberg (1998)
9. Bergenthum, R., Desel, J., Mauser, S., Lorenz, R.: Construction of process models from example runs. Petri Nets Other Models Concurrency **2**, 243–259 (2009)
10. Darondeau, P.: Synthesis and control of asynchronous and distributed systems. In: Basten, T., Juhás, G., Shukla, S.K. (eds.) ACSD, pp. 13–22. IEEE Computer Society, Bratislava (2007)
11. Bergenthum, R., Desel, J., Kölbl, C., Mauser, S.: Experimental results on process mining based on regions of languages. In: Proceedings of the Workshop CHINA, Petri Nets 2008, China, pp. 73–87 (2008)
12. Glinz, M.: Improving the quality of requirements with scenarios. In: Second World Congress on Software Quality, Yokohama, pp. 55–60 (2000)
13. Desel, J.: From human knowledge to process models. In: Kaschek, R., Kop, C., Steinberger, C., Fliedl, G. (eds.) Information Systems and e-Business Technologies. LNBIP, vol. 5, pp. 84–95. Springer, Heidelberg (2008)
14. Weske, M.: Business Process Management - Concepts, Languages, Architectures, 2nd edn. Springer, Heidelberg (2012)
15. Mayr, H.C., Kop, C., Esberger, D.: Business process modeling and requirements modeling. In: ICDS, p. 8. IEEE Computer Society (2007)

16. Mauser, S., Bergenthum, R., Desel, J., Klett, A.: An approach to business process modeling emphasizing the early design phases. In: Proceedings of the Workshop Algorithmen und Werkzeuge für Petrinetze. CEUR Workshop Proceedings, vol. 501, pp. 41–56 (2009)

17. van der Aalst, W.M.P., Stahl, C.: Modeling Business Processes - A Petri Net-Oriented Approach (Cooperative Information Systems series). MIT Press, Cambridge (2011)

18. Harel, D.: Come, Let's Play - Scenario-Based Programming Using LSCs and the Play-Engine. Springer, Heidelberg (2003)

19. van der Werf, J.M.E.M., van Dongen, B.F., Hurkens, C.A.J., Serebrenik, A.: Process discovery using integer linear programming. Fundam. Inform. **94**(3–4), 387–412 (2009)

20. van der Aalst, W., Adriansyah, A., de Medeiros, A.K.A., Arcieri, F., Baier, T., Blickle, T., Bose, J.C., van den Brand, P., et al.: Process mining manifesto. In: Daniel, F., Barkaoui, K., Dustdar, S. (eds.) BPM Workshops 2011, Part I. LNBIP, vol. 99, pp. 169–194. Springer, Heidelberg (2012)

21. Bergenthum, R., Desel, J., Lorenz, R., Mauser, S.: Process mining based on regions of languages. In: Alonso, G., Dadam, P., Rosemann, M. (eds.) BPM 2007. LNCS, vol. 4714, pp. 375–383. Springer, Heidelberg (2007)

22. Vinter Ratzer, A., Wells, L., Lassen, H.M., Laursen, M., Qvortrup, J.F., Stissing, M.S., Westergaard, M., Christensen, S., Jensen, K.: CPN tools for editing, simulating, and analysing coloured Petri Nets. In: van der Aalst, W.M.P., Best, E. (eds.) ICATPN 2003. LNCS, vol. 2679, pp. 450–462. Springer, Heidelberg (2003)

23. Westergaard, M.: CPN tools 4: multi-formalism and extensibility. In: Colom, J.-M., Desel, J. (eds.) PETRI NETS 2013. LNCS, vol. 7927, pp. 400–409. Springer, Heidelberg (2013)

An Everlasting Secure Non-interactive Timestamping Scheme in the Bounded Storage Model

Assia Ben Shil[1,3]([✉]) and Kaouther Blibech Sinaoui[2,3]

[1] Faculty of Sciences of Bizerte, University of Carthage, Tunis, Tunisia
essia.benshil@gmail.com
[2] ISTEUB, University of Carthage, Tunis, Tunisia
kaouther.blibech@gmail.com
[3] LIP2 Laboratory, Tunis, Tunisia

Abstract. Digital timestamping is a cryptographic technique allowing to affix a reliable date to a digital document in order to prove that it exists and its integrity is kept since this date. However, there is a good chance that a lot of current timestamping systems will not be secure in the coming years. In fact, the security of most of the existing timestamping systems is based on the security of the used cryptographic techniques as hash functions. However, a hash function has a limited lifetime. In this context, we provide a non-interactive timestamping scheme in the bounded storage model (BSM). In this model, we assume that an adversary has a limited memory but his computing power can be unlimited. Thus, the security of our timestamping scheme does not depend on the lifetime of any cryptographic technique. We prove, in fact, that our timestamping scheme is eternally secure even against an adversary with unlimited computing power.

Keywords: Timestamping · Bounded storage model · Computing power · Eternal security

1 Introduction

Timestamping [16] is an important technique for proving the existence of digital documents and detecting their alterations. It is also important for the long-term preservation of some cryptographic tools as encryption keys and digital signatures.

Generally, a timestamping system provides a proof-of-existence of a document. This proof is called timestamp. To provide a timestamp for a given document there are two phases: a timestamping phase, and a verification phase. The timestamping phase allows one or more Timestamping Authority (TSA) to affix a reliable date to a document and generate the associated timestamp using a timestamping protocol. The verification phase allows any verifier to verify that the document was correctly timestamped by the TSA with respect to the used timestamping protocol.

© Springer-Verlag Berlin Heidelberg 2015
M. Koutny et al. (Eds.): ToPNoC X, LNCS 9410, pp. 19–33, 2015.
DOI: 10.1007/978-3-662-48650-4_2

Most of the existing timestamping systems [2,3,7–14,16] are secure under the assumption that the cryptographic techniques they use are secure. However, with the evolution of computing power, there is a good chance that what is secure today will not be secure some years later. Therefore, since most of the existing schemes are based on some hash functions they assume to be one-way and without collisions, they cannot be considered secure forever. In fact, hash functions are not secure all the time [21].

To provide timestamping systems producing timestamps whose validity cannot be challenged, we decided to place our research work within the Bounded Storage Model (BSM) [17,18]. In this model, instead of assuming that the users' computing power is limited, Maurer assumes that their memory is limited. Thus, the ciphers in this model are eternally secure [1].

The idea is that a very long random string called randomizer is transmitted at every round t^1. When the randomizer is transmitted, no participant has sufficient storage space to entirely store it. Even if later their storage space becomes sufficient to entirely store the randomizer transmitted at the round t, the users would have already lost the access to this string. Thus, the performed encryptions are always valid.

In [19], Moran proved that timestamping is possible in the BSM and proposed a non-interactive timestamping scheme in this model. In this scheme, each stamper can timestamp his document locally without communicating with any other party [19]. Thus, the non-interactive timestamping ensures the confidentiality of the timestamped document and hides even the fact that a timestamping occurred. For these reasons, we consider that the system of Moran is very interesting, but it suffers from a lack of precision and practical details. In this context, we presented in [4] a non-interactive timestamping scheme in the BSM. In this paper, we provide a formal representation of our timestamping scheme and we prove that it is eternally secure.

This paper is organized as follows: In the following section, we present the existing timestamping systems and their weaknesses. Then, we introduce the BSM and we present Moran's timestamping system. In Sect. 5, we present Shamir's secret sharing scheme. Then, we present our non-interactive timestamping scheme [4] based on Shamir's secret sharing scheme. In Sect. 7, we detail more formally our timestamping scheme [5]^2. Finally, we prove the eternal security of our timestamping solution [5].

2   Existing Timestamping Schemes and their Weaknesses

There are two classes of timestamping systems described in [10]:

Simple timestamping systems [16] are centralized systems requiring a single TimeStamping Authority (TSA) and having an absolute trust in the TSA.

---

[1] A round t is the interval between the time t and the time $t + 1$.

[2] Notice that [5] is a short version of this paper that has been published in FMS: the Formal Methods for Security Workshop co-located with the PetriNets-2014 Conference.

In fact, the TSA receives a document's hash value and sends to the stamper a timestamp created within a dedicated timestamping protocol. In such a system, we cannot verify the timestamp reliability.

Secure timestamping systems are systems reducing the trust in the TSA. In fact, the latter has to provide a timestamping correctness proof. There are two kinds of secure timestamping systems:

- Centralized secure timestamping systems [2,3,7–10,13,14] requiring a single authority which has to prove the correctness of the generated timestamps. There are many techniques for doing that. For example, linking schemes [10] are used to link a set of timestamps. These links can be used as proofs at verification time.
- Distributed secure timestamping systems [11,12] are based on duplication. In fact, each request is timestamped by n independent TSAs. Each TSA returns a timestamp fragment that the stamper uses to create the final timestamp.

The above timestamping systems are all based on some cryptographic techniques as digital signatures and hash functions. However, the lifetime of digital signatures is limited. In addition, if a document must be securely represented by its hash value, the used hash function has to be irreversible and collision-resistant. However, these properties cannot be proven for practical hash functions and many ones have been broken [21] (e.g. SHA-0[3] in 2004 and SHA-1[4] and MD5[5] in 2005, which have been suggested as practical hash functions in several timestamping schemes).

To overcome the problems of the existing timestamping systems, we propose to adopt the secret sharing techniques [6,22] whose security does not rely on the lifetime of any cryptographic technique. In [4], we provided a timestamping scheme in the bounded storage model. This scheme is based on Shamir's secret sharing scheme [22]. The aim of this paper is to prove the security of the mentioned timestamping scheme. In the following section, we introduce the bounded storage model since our timestamping scheme is conceived in this model.

3   The Bounded Storage Model

Generally, in cryptography, the proposed systems and the used functions are secure under the assumption that it exists a limit for the computational power of any user or adversary. However, there is no limit for his storage space. Thus, he can be able to store the whole of a transmitted chiphertext and decrypt it later when his computing power increases. In the bounded storage model, the proposed systems must be secure even against an adversary with an unlimited computational power. In fact, the adversary has a limited memory and is, consequently, not able to store all the transmitted ciphertext to try to decrypt it later.

---

[3] Secure Hash Algorithm 0 published in 1993.
[4] Secure Hash Algorithm 1 published in 1995.
[5] Message-Digest Algorithm 5 published in 1992.

The BSM was proposed by Maurer in 1992 [17] for the development of encryption keys. It aims to generate, from a short secret key K, a key with a larger size X [15] that can be used as encryption key. The system operates as follows: In this model, it is assumed that the storage capacity is limited, and there is no assumption about the computing power. Let s be the assumed limit on a user's storage capacity. Ciphers in the BSM use a very long string R called randomizer. The latter may for example be a random sequence of bits transmitted by a satellite. If R is a random string of r bits, the space of R is $\{0,1\}^r$. Notice that "$r \gg s$" is required to ensure that no user can fully store R. Having a secret key K of size k in the space $\{0,1\}^k$, we can use a known function F to generate the derived key $X = F(R,K)$ of size x bits. The function F must use only a small part of R so that we do not need to fully read R.

Example: Suppose that the adversary storage capacity is $s = 10^{15}$ bits, Alice and Bob share a secret key of 6000 bits and they (with the adversary Eve) access to a random source emitting 100 Gigabits per second (10^{11} bits/s) for about one day and a half ($1,25.10^{16}$ s), then they can derive a key length of 10 Gigabits ($x = 10^{10}$) and the adversary has absolutely no information about it. Alice and Bob do only need to read 10^{12} bits of the random source.

Maurer's system has been the subject of intensive studies. Indeed, many key generation systems have been proposed in the BSM [18]. The BSM was used for timestamping by Moran in [19]. In [4], we proposed an improvement of Moran's timestamping system. In the following section, we present the timestamping system of Moran and then our proposition is presented.

4 Timestamping Solutions in the BSM

In the BSM, we assume that a long random string R of r bits is transmitted during the round t (between t and $t+1$). If s is the maximum storage capacity of any entity in t, then $s \ll r$. Notice the space of R is $\{0,1\}^r$ where r is the size of the string R. Similarly, we consider that a document D of size d bits has a value in $\{0,1\}^d$. In the timestamping scheme proposed by Moran, to timestamp a document D, its content is used to select a few blocks from R whose values will be inserted in the timestamp T of D.

For example, in practice, we can suppose that a randomizer emits at a fixed rate about 100 Gigabits/s (10^{11} bits/s) during a round of approximatively an hour (3600 s). Therefore the maximum size r of the string transmitted during a round t is about $r = 3600.10^{11}$ bits. This string will be divided into blocks of equal size in order to index the string. The block size is chosen so that its maximum value is adapted to the usual arithmetic calculations. Thus, we can define a maximum number of blocks for the transmitted string. For example, we can use blocks of 3072 bits.

On the other hand, any verifier must save randomly some blocks of R (using a function named $Sketch(R)$) in order to verify, later, the validity of any timestamp made during the round t. Verifying the validity of a timestamp associated with a document D is performed at a later date by a verifier who has simply to check that there are no conflicts between his sketch and the timestamp of D. However, in this solution, a timestamp includes some additional values of R. If the verifier cannot store during the round t more than s bits of R, he may at the verification time store s' with $s' > s$. Each verification of a timestamp generated in the round t can lead him to discover new blocks of R. After a number of verification processes, he can reconstruct partially, if not entirely R and backdate any document.

To overcome this problem, we propose a timestamping protocol allowing to verify the timestamp of a document D without learning additional values of R. To this aim, instead of inserting the blocks of R in the timestamp, these blocks will be the secret of the stamper. The verifier must then prove that he has the value of a given block in his sketch and the stamper has to prove that he has used this value to create the timestamp. In the verification process of this scheme, a verifier may accept or reject a timestamp without discovering any additional information about the string R transmitted during the round t.

Our timestamping scheme is presented with more details in the following sections. But, first of all, we will present Shamir's secret sharing scheme [22].

5   Shamir's Secret Sharing Scheme

Secret sharing allows sharing a secret S among the set of n participants such that a coalition of the n participants is required to determine the secret S. Threshold secret sharing [6,22] allows sharing a secret S among a set of n participants such that a coalition of at most k-1 participants cannot determine the secret S, while any coalition of at least k participants can find out S.

Shamirs secret sharing scheme [22] is a k-out-of-n threshold secret sharing scheme based on polynomial interpolation. Shamir's secret sharing scheme is the most used one and most of the proposed secret sharing schemes are based on it. In this scheme, to share a secret among n participants P_1, P_2, ..., P_n, the dealer:

- Sets the polynomial: $f(x) = S + \sum_{j=1}^{k-1} f_j x^j$ mod p where p is a prime $(p > n+1)$
  and the f_j are values chosen randomly and secretly in Z_p. He randomly selects n distinct elements of Z_p denoted x_i for $i = 1 \ldots n$.
- For $i = 1 \ldots n$, he secretly sends the point $(x_i, f(x_i))$ to the participant P_i.

Given only k points $(x_i, f(x_i))$, with x_i distinct values, there is only one polynomial $f(x)$ of degree $k-1$, which graphic representation passes through all these points. This polynomial can be effectively obtained from the points $(x_i, f(x_i))$. We can use the following interpolation formula for that purpose:

$$f(x) = \sum_{i=1}^{k} [f(x_i) \prod_{j=1, j \neq i}^{k} [(x - x_j)/(x_i - x_j)]]$$

Then, we compute the secret S as follows $S = f(0)$.

Notice that, this scheme is information theoretically secure. In fact, at least k participants have to pool their shares in order to discover the secret S. In the following section, we will describe our timestamping scheme conceived on the BSM and based on Shamir's secret sharing scheme.

6   Our Timestamping Scheme

The idea is to timestamp the document D locally using the secret sharing scheme of Shamir [22] in order to divide D into n shares D_i. Notice that this set of coefficients f_i of the polynomial f used to split D into n shares is public ($1 \leq i \leq k-1$)[6]. So, the stamper of a document D has to consider that D is his secret and compute the set of shares $D_i = f(i)$ for $1 \leq i \leq n$. Note $Share(D)$ the set of shares D_i. Assuming that the blocks of R are indexed by a number beginning from 1 till the number of blocks, the values R_{D_i}, indexed by the shares D_i for $1 \leq i \leq n$ are recovered. The polynomial that passes through the points $P_i(R_{D_i}, D_i)$ for $1 \leq i \leq n$ represents the timestamp of D. Note here that we choose to use the polynomial that passes through the points $P_i(R_{D_i}, D_i)$ and not the polynomial that passes through the points $P_i(D_i, R_{D_i})$. The idea is to hide the set of couples (index, value) of R used by the stamper. The fact of using a polynomial that passes through the "reverses" points allows to hide this association. This process is described in Fig. 1.

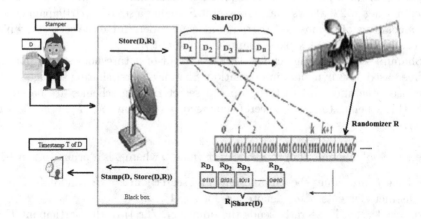

Fig. 1. Timestamping process

Any user of the system saves a random subset of R named $Sketch(R)$ formed by a number of couples of values (index of block, value of the block). This process is described in Fig. 2.

To verify the validity of the timestamp T of D for a random string R, the verifier who stored $Sketch(R)$ proceeds as follows: For each index in both $Share(D)$

---

[6] The fact that the set of f_i is public allows us to detect some kinds of attacks (see Theorem 3).

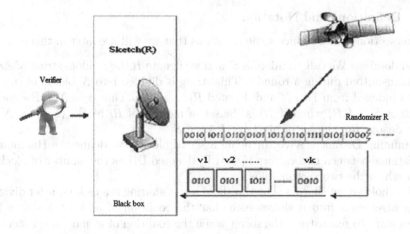

Fig. 2. Storage of a sketch of R

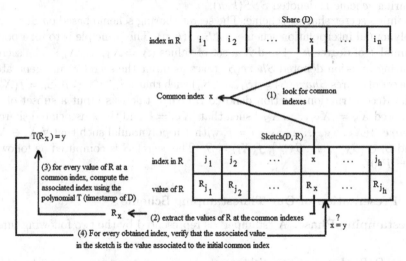

Fig. 3. Verification process

and $Sketch(R)$ he extracts the associated value R_i from $Sketch(R)$, computes its associated index by the polynomial given in the timestamp and checks that the computed index and the one of $Sketch(R)$ match. The verification process is described in Fig. 3.

In the following section we provide a more formal description of our scheme.

7   Formal Description of Our Timestamping Scheme

In the following sections we provide some definitions and notations and then we use them in order to prove the security of our timestamping scheme.

7.1 Definitions and Notations

In this section, we introduce some notations that we will use later in this paper.

- Randomizer: We call "randomizer" and we denote R the random string of size r transmitted during a round t. This string is divided into N blocks of size b bits indexed from 1 to N and denoted $R_1, \ldots, R_N$. Thus, $r = N.b$. For each subset $S \subseteq I(R)$ where $I(R)$ is the set of indexes of R_i blocks ($1 \leq i \leq N$), we denote $R_{|S}$ the set of blocks of $R \ \forall \ i \in S$.
- Hamming Distance: A vector being a set of blocks, we define the Hamming Distance between two vectors V_1 and V_2 denoted DH as the number of blocks for which the two vectors differ.
- Threshold secret sharing: The threshold secret sharing is a technique for dividing a secret S into n shares such that the coalition of at least k shares is necessary to reconstruct the secret while the coalition of at most $k-1$ shares does not reveal even partially the secret ($k < n$). A k-out of-n threshold secret sharing scheme is denoted $SSS(k,n)$.
- Shamir's secret sharing scheme: The secret sharing scheme based on Shamir's polynomial interpolation scheme is a $SSS(k,n)$. The principle is to fix a polynomial f of degree $k-1$ and X a set of values ($X = X_1, \ldots, X_n$). The secret sharing function denoted $Share(S)$ takes as input the secret S and generates the set of shares $Share(S) = (S_1, \ldots, S_n)$ such that $\forall \ i, 1 \leq i \leq n, S_i = f(X_i)$. The Reconstruction function denoted $Share^{-1}$ takes as input a subset of X denoted $X_S = [X_{S_1}, \ldots, X_{S_k}]$ such that $|X_S| = k$ and the k associated shares: $Share^{-1}(X_S, S_{X_{S_1}}, \ldots, S_{X_{S_k}}) = f$, with f a polynomial such that $\forall \ X_i \in X_S$ and $S_i \in [S_{X_{S_1}}, \ldots, S_{X_{S_k}}], f(X_i) = S_i$. The secret S is computed as follows: $S = P(0)$.

7.2 Presentation of Our Timestamping Scheme

Timestamping Phase. A "stamper" is represented by the two following functions:

- $Store(D, R)$ that uses Shamir's secret sharing process to compute $Share(D)$ for a given document D. Then, It computes the vector $R_{|Share(D)}$ and stores it. More formally, $Store(D, R)$ consists in computing $Share(D) = (D_1, \ldots, D_n)$, where D_i is the ith index specified by D and the vector $(R_{D_1}, \ldots, R_{D_n})$ where R_{D_i} is the block of R indexed by D_i. We call this vector $R_{|Share(D)}$, where the notation $R_{|I}$ means the values of blocks of R indexed by $I_1, \ldots, I_n$, with $I = I_1, \ldots, I_n$.

Definition 1. $Store(D, R) = R_{|Share(D)}$.

- $Stamp(D, Store(D, R))$ applies the interpolation formula to find the unique polynomial passing through the points $P_i(x, y)$ where x is a block of the vector $R_{|Share(D)}$ and y the associated index in $Share(D)$. This polynomial is the timestamp T.

Definition 2. $T = Share^{-1}(R_{|Share(D)}, Share(D)) = Stamp(D, Store(D, R))$.

Verification Phase. A "verifier" is represented by the two following functions:

- $Sketch(R)$ allows choosing, randomly, a set of indexes denoted H with $H \subset I(R)$, computing $R_{|H}$ and storing this vector.

Definition 3. $Sketch(R) = (H, R_{|H})$.

- $Verify(Sketch(R), D, T)$ allows to verify that there are no conflicts between $Sketch(R)$ and T (which is the timestamp of D, namely a polynomial).

Definition 4. $Verify(Sketch(R), D, T) = success$ only if

$$DH(T(R_{|H} \cap R_{|Share(D)}), H \cap Share(D)) = 0$$

for a document D and a timestamp T.

The Behavior of an Adversary. An "adversary" consists in the two following functions:

- $Store^*(R)$ which saves a subset of R called C. The difference between $Sketch(R)$ and $Store^*(R)$ is that $Sketch(R)$ is computed randomly and "on line" while $Store^*(R)$ function may not be.

- $Stamp^*(D, C)$ that given a document D and a string C tries to produce a timestamp T^* of D.

Definition 5. $Stamp^*(D, C) = T^* = Share^{-1}(R^*_{|Share(D)}, Share(D))$.

Where $R^*_{|Share(D)}$ is the vector of blocks associated with $Share(D)$ according to T^*. If an adversary A produces for a document D and a randomizer R, a timestamp T^* that is equal to the timestamp T produced by $Stamp(D, Store(D, R))$, we say that he backdates "correctly" the document. More formally:

Definition 6. *An adversary backdates a document D with a success probability γ for a given randomizer R if:*

$$Pr[Verify(Sketch(R), D, Stamp^*(D, Store^*(R))) = success] \geq \gamma.$$

Definition 7. *An adversary backdates "correctly" a document D for a given randomizer R if $DH(V_1, V_2) = 0$ with $V_1 = R^*_{|Share(D)}$ and $V_2 = R_{|Share(D)}$.*

Definition 8. *An adversary backdates "correctly" a document D for a given randomizer R with at most err errors, if $DH(V_1, V_2) \leq err$, with $V_1 = R^*_{|Share(D)}$ and $V_2 = R_{|Share(D)}$.*

8 Security Proofs of Our Timestamping Scheme

Given the following parameters:

- s: the storage capacity of the most powerful adversary.
- r: the size of the random string R transmitted during a round t.
- b: the size of a block of the random string R transmitted during a round t.
- n: the number of indexes specified by a given document.
- N: the number of blocks of the random string R transmitted during a round t.
- $|H|$: the number of blocks of a sketch.

We assume that:

(1) $r \gg s$: The size of the random string R transmitted during a round t is greater than the storage capacity of the most powerful user of the system.
(2) $1 < N/|H|$: The number of blocks of R transmitted during a round t is greater than the number of blocks in a sketch saved by a potential user.
(3) $2^b \gg r/b$: The number of possible values for a block of size b bits is greater than the number of blocks of the string R transmitted during a round t.
(4) $r/b > n$: The number of blocks of the string R transmitted during a round t is greater than the number of shares used in the adopted Shamir's secret sharing scheme.
(5) $b \gg 1$: The size of a block of R is much greater than 1 bit.

In our security study we demonstrate mainly two important characteristics of our non-interactive timestamping scheme. First, we prove that backdating documents in our timestamping scheme has a negligible[7] probability. Second, we prove that the timestamps provided by our timestamping scheme have an eternal validity.

8.1 Negligible Probability of Backdating Documents

In our timestamping scheme, the probability that an adversary backdates a document D for a string R already transmitted using his stored blocks of R is negligible. This proof is established in two steps. In the first step, we show that if an adversary A wants to backdate "successfully" a document D for a random string R, then he must backdate it "correctly" for this string R with an error err negligible. In the second step, we show that the probability of backdating "correctly" a document D for a random string R is negligible.

First Step. Given a correct timestamp T and a forged timestamp T^* produced by an adversary A for the document D and the random string R, A succeeds in backdating D for R if the vector of blocks associated with $Share(D)$ according to T^* denoted $R^*_{|Share(D)}$ is close in Hamming distance to $R_{|Share(D)}$. In this

---

[7] An event that occurs with a negligible probability can be safely ignored.

case, we say that the adversary backdates "correctly" the document D for the random string R with err errors, where err is an integer very close to zero. More formally, let A be an adversary. Denote $R_{successful(D)} = R^{\gamma}_{successful(D)}$ the set of strings R for which A has the necessary storage to try to backdate the document D with a probability of success greater than γ.

Lemma 1 ([20]). *If an adversary backdates a document D for a random string R with a probability of success γ then he backdates it "correctly" with at most $(N/|H|)ln(1/\gamma)$ errors.*

Proof. Let us suppose that the adversary provides a timestamp for the document D for the string R such that the timestamp is made with $err^* > err$ incorrect indexes. Denote $INCORRECT(D,R)$ the set of incorrect indexes for D and R. If $H \cap INCORRECT(D,R) \neq \emptyset$ the verifier will reject the timestamp of the adversary.

Let i be an index of H, the probability that i be in $INCORRECT(D,R)$ is:

$$Pr[i \in INCORRECT(D,R)] = err^*/N.$$

The probability that i does not belong to $INCORRECT(D,R)$ is

$$1 - Pr[i \in INCORRECT(D,R)] = 1 - err^*/N.$$

The probability that all the elements of $|H|$ do not belong to $INCORRECT(D,R)$ is:

$$Pr[\forall i \in H, i \notin INCORRECT(D,R)] = (1 - err^*/N)^{|H|} \leq e^{-(err^*|H|)/N}.$$

If an adversary backdates a document D for a random string R with a probability of success $\gamma \leq e^{-(err^*|H|)/N} \leq e^{-(err|H|)/N}$ then he backdates it correctly with at most $err \leq (N/|H|)ln(1/\gamma)$. □

Denote $R_{correct}(D)$ the set of strings R for which A can "correctly" backdate D with at most $(N/|H|)ln(1/\gamma)$ errors.

Theorem 1. *If $err \leq (N/|H|)ln((1/\gamma))$ then, $R_{successful}(D)$ is a subset of $R_{correct}(D)$ [20].*

Proof. According to Lemma 1, if an adversary backdates a document D for a random string R with a probability of success γ then he backdates it correctly with at most $err \leq (N/|H|)ln(1/\gamma)$. So, if a random string R belongs to $R_{successful}(D)$ then it belongs to $R_{correct}(D)$. Thus, $R_{successful}(D) \subseteq R_{correct}(D)$. In addition, the more the probability of success γ becomes close to 1, the more this error becomes close to 0. So, successfully backdating means "correctly" backdating with a "negligible" error. We prove, in the second step, that the probability that the random string R chosen by the adversary to backdate a document D be in $R_{correct}(D)$ is negligible. □

Second Step. We now prove that for an adversary A, a document D and a string R: $Pr[R \in R_{correct}(D)]$ is negligible.

Theorem 2. *If $n \gg 1$ and $b \gg 1$ then $Pr[R \in R_{correct}(D)]$ is negligible, with b the size of a block of R and n the number of indexes in $Share(D)$.*

Proof. We proved in the first step, that if an adversary backdates a document "successfully", he backdated it "correctly" with at most a negligible error. Then we proved in the second stage that the probability that the string R for which the adversary tries to backdate the document D be in $R_{correct}(D)$ is negligible.

In fact, knowing that the size of blocks of a random string R is b and the number of these blocks is N, the number of possible random strings is $\left(2^b\right)^N$.

Moreover, to backdate a document D, the adversary has to create a timestamp T^* for D such that at least $n - err$ blocks of R indexed by D are used to generate T^*.

In other words, he can try to backdate D only for random strings for which he knows the values of at least $n - err$ blocks from the n blocks indexed by D. Thus, since the adversary tries to correctly backdate D with at most err errors, the number of random strings he can use is at most $\left(2^b\right)^{N-n}$.

So, the probability that a random string R belongs to $R_{correct}(D)$ is:

$Pr[R \in R_{correct}(D)] \leq \left(2^b\right)^{N-n} / \left(2^b\right)^N \leq 1/2^{nb}$. Since $n \gg 1$ and $b \gg 1$, this probability is negligible.   □

Theorem 3. *Given a sketch H, an adversary is not able to find a document D^* which is correctly timestamped within our timestamping system.*

Proof. If an adversary owns a sketch H, he could use the interpolation formula on H in order to find the polynomial that associated the blocks of H with their indexes. He has then a forged timestamp T^*. What he has to do later is to find a document D^* whose shares match those present in H and used to compute T^*. To do that, he has to use the interpolation formula to find a polynomial that matches a document D^* to H. But, since the sharing polynomial, in our scheme, is fixed and public he will not be able to correctly timestamp D^*.   □

8.2   The Eternal Security of Our Timestamping Scheme

In [20], Moran proves that in his non-interactive timestamping scheme, an adversary with a storage s can easily backdate $\delta = s/|T|$ documents by running the timestamping process on some δ documents and storing the generated timestamps (each of them has length of at most $|T|$). However, the probability that an adversary backdates more than δ documents is negligible. We show here that, in our timestamping scheme, after the transmission of R, it is very difficult to forge a fake timestamp for a given document. Moreover, we show that an adversary having a document D and δ correct timestamps can forge a fake timestamp for D only with a negligible probability. Thus, we prove the following theorem:

Theorem 4. *If $2^b \gg r/b$ and $r/b > n$ then the probability to forge a fake timestamp for a document D and a string R using δ correct timestamps related to R is negligible.*

Proof. The inequality $2^b \gg r/b$ means that the number of values for a block of size b bits is greater than the number of blocks of the string R transmitted during a round t.

n is the number of indexes specified by a given document, this number must always be less than the number of blocks of R. So, $r/b > n$.

It follows that $2^b \gg n$, which means that the number of possible values for a block of R is much greater than the number of indexes specified by the document D.

For each timestamp T_j $(1 \leq j \leq \delta)$, if the adversary gives any value v from the 2^b possible values of a block of R, it will recover a given index i.

However, the fact that $i = T_j(v)$ does not mean that $R_i = v$. This means that i is the value associated with v by the polynomial T_j but the couple (i, v) does not necessarily belong to the string R. In other words, the string R may not associate the value v to the block indexed by i. Moreover, it may exist i such that $R_{i'} = v$ and there is no way to verify if $i = i'$. The only points of T_j for which the adversary knows that they belong to R are the points whose indexes are specified by the document associated with T_j. The probability that the adversary chooses one of these points is $n/2^b \ll 1$.

To obtain the k points required to forge a fake timestamp, the probability is negligible since it is the product of the probabilities of selecting each of the points belonging to a valid timestamp.

So, the adversary can obtain the k points needed to forge a fake timestamp for a document D for a random string R with a negligible probability. $\square$

Thus, we proved that our non-interactive timestamping system is secure and that it produces timestamps with eternal validity. As improvement to our system, we can provide a multi-documents timestamping system. The idea is simple. To timestamp a set of n documents, we have just to give an index to every document. The couple (index, document) will then be represented as a point. By interpolation, we find out the unique polynomial passing through the set of points (eg. the set of documents). We sample the set of n other points of the obtained polynomial. These points will represent the shares of the set of documents to timestamp. Finally, we apply our timestamping system as presented in Sect. 6 of this paper. Thus, we reduce the cost of timestamping n documents one by one and we obtain shares and timestamps having the same size as in the timestamping system described in Sect. 6 of this paper.

9   Conclusion

In this paper, we have formally presented a non-interactive timestamping solution in the bounded storage model. Our solution is non-interactive and hides even the fact that a timestamping occurred. It also ensures total confidentiality of the provided timestamps. In addition, our solution provides eternal security for the provided timestamps. In fact, neither increasing the storage capacity of an adversary or the evolution of his computing power will compromise a provided timestamp. Thus, our solution is more secure than existing systems whose timestamps can be challenged when the computing power or storage capacity of users increases. In this context, we studied the security of our solution and proved that the possibility of cheating is negligible. In our future works, we plan to adopt new secret sharing schemes for timestamping.

References

1. Aumann, Y., Ding, Y.Z., Rabin, M.O.: Everlasting security in the bounded storage model. IEEE Trans. Inf. Theory **48**(6), 1668–1680 (2002)
2. Bayer, D., Haber, S., Stornetta, W.S.: Improving the efficiency and reliability of digital timestamping. In: Capocelli, R., Santis, A.D., Vaccaro, U. (eds.) Sequences91: Methods in Communication, Security and Computer Science, pp. 329–334. Springer, New York (1992)
3. Benaloh, J.C., de Mare, M.: One-Way accumulators: a decentralized alternative to digital signatures. In: Helleseth, T. (ed.) EUROCRYPT 1993. LNCS, vol. 765, pp. 274–285. Springer, Heidelberg (1994)
4. Ben Shil, A., Blibech, K., Robbana, R.: A new timestamping schema in the bounded storage model. In: Proceedings of the 3rd Conference on Risks and Security of Internet and Systems, CRiSIS (2008)
5. Ben Shil, A., Blibech, K., Robbana, R.: A timestamping scheme with eternal security in the bounded storage model. In: Proceedings of the Formal Methods for Security Workshop co-located with the PetriNets-2014 Conference (2014)
6. Blakley, G.R.: Safeguarding cryptographic keys, International Workshop on Managing Requirements Knowledge., 313–317 (1979)
7. Blibech, K., Gabillon, A.: A new timestamping scheme based on skip lists. In: Gavrilova, M.L., Gervasi, O., Kumar, V., Tan, C.J.K., Taniar, D., Laganá, A., Mun, Y., Choo, H. (eds.) ICCSA 2006. LNCS, vol. 3982, pp. 395–405. Springer, Heidelberg (2006)
8. Blibech, K., Gabillon, A.: A new totally ordered timestamping scheme. In: 5th Conference on Security and Network Architectures SAR (2006)
9. Blibech, K., Gabillon, A.: CHRONOS: an authenticated dictionary based on skip lists for timestamping systems. In: SWS, pp. 84–90 (2005)
10. Blibech, K., Gabillon, A., Bonnecaze, A.: Etude des systèmes d'horodatage. Tech. et Sci. Informatiques **26**(3–4), 249–278 (2007)
11. Bonnecaze, A., Liardet, P., Gabillon, A., Blibech, K.: A distributed time stamping scheme, 4th Conference on Security and Network Architectures SAR 2005 (2005)
12. Bonnecaze, A., Trebuchet, P.: Threshold signature for distributed time stamping scheme. Ann. des Telecommun. **62**(11–12), 1353–1364 (2007)
13. Buldas, A., Laud, P., Lipmaa, H., Villemson, J.: Time-stamping with binary linking schemes. In: Krawczyk, H. (ed.) CRYPTO 1998. LNCS, vol. 1462, p. 486. Springer, Heidelberg (1998)
14. Budas, A., Laud, P.R., Schoenmakers, B.: Optimally efficient accountable timestamping. In: Public Key Cryptography (2000)
15. Dziembowski, S., Maurer, U.M.: On generating the initial key in the bounded-storage model. In: Cachin, C., Camenisch, J.L. (eds.) EUROCRYPT 2004. LNCS, vol. 3027, pp. 126–137. Springer, Heidelberg (2004)

16. Haber, S., Stornetta, W.S.: How to time-stamp a digital document. J. Cryptology **3**(2), 99–111 (1991)
17. Maurer, U.: Conditionally-perfect secrecy and a provably-secure randomized cipher. J. Cryptology **5**(1), 53–66 (1992)
18. Maurer, U.: Secret key agreement by public discussion. IEEE Trans. Inf. Theory **39**, 733–742 (1993)
19. Moran, T., Shaltiel, R., Ta-Shma, A.: Non-interactive timestamping in the bounded storage model. In: Franklin, M. (ed.) CRYPTO 2004. LNCS, vol. 3152, pp. 460–476. Springer, Heidelberg (2004)
20. Moran, T., Shaltiel, R., Ta-Shma, A.: Non-interactive timestamping in the bounded storage model. J. Cryptology **22**(2), 189–226 (2009)
21. National Institute of Standards and Technology (NIST), Announcement of Weakness in the Secure Hash Standard, Technical report (1994)
22. Shamir, A.: How to share a secret. ACM Commun. **22**(11), 612–613 (1979)

Timed Aggregate Graph: A Finite Graph Preserving Event- and State-Based Quantitative Properties of Time Petri Nets

Kais Klai[⊠]

LIPN, CNRS UMR 7030, Université Paris 13, Sorbonne Paris Cité,
99 avenue Jean-Baptiste Clément, 93430 Villetaneuse, France
kais.klai@lipn.univ-paris13.fr

Abstract. In this paper, we propose a new finite graph, called Timed Aggregate Graph (TAG), abstracting the behavior of bounded Time Petri Nets (TPN) with strong time semantics. The main feature of this abstract representation compared to existing approaches is the used criterion to encapsulate the elapsing of time within each node of the TAG (called aggregate), and how to maintain the relative differences between the firing times of enabled transitions. We prove that the TAG preserves timed traces and reachable states of the corresponding TPN. Another interesting and novel feature of the TAGs is the possibility of extracting an explicit run from any of its traces. Thus, we supply an algorithm that maps an abstract run of the TAG to an explicit timed trace (involving a relative elapsed time before each fired transition) of the corresponding TPN. Moreover, the fact that the TAG preserves the timed behavior of the corresponding TPN makes it directly usable in order to check both event- and state-based timed properties as well as the Zenoness property. Zenoness is a pathological behavior which violate a fundamental progress requirement for timed systems stating that it should be possible for time to diverge. A TPN is said to be Zeno when it admits a run where an infinity of transitions are fired in a finite amount of time. We give an algorithm allowing to detect the Zenoness of bounded TPNs and compare the size of the TAG to two well known approaches namely the state class graph and the zone-based graph methods.

1 Introduction

In real-time systems, it is often required to verify real-time constraints in addition to functional or qualitative temporal properties. Together with timed automata [1], Time Petri Nets [17] (TPN for short) are one of the most powerful formalisms for the specification and the verification of such systems. They are considered as a good tradeoff between modeling power and verification complexity. Time Petri nets extend Petri nets [19] with temporal intervals associated with transitions, specifying firing delays ranges for transitions. Other extensions of Petri nets with time exist such as timed Petri nets [21] but they are less expressive [20]. There are two ways of letting the time elapse in a time Petri net.

© Springer-Verlag Berlin Heidelberg 2015
M. Koutny et al. (Eds.): ToPNoC X, LNCS 9410, pp. 34–54, 2015.
DOI: 10.1007/978-3-662-48650-4_3

The first way, known as the *Strong Time Semantics* (STS), is defined in such a manner that time elapsing cannot disable a transition. Hence, when the upper bound of a firing interval is reached, the transition must be fired. In contrast to that, the *Weak Time Semantics* (WTS) does not make any restriction on the elapsing of time.

For real-time systems, dense time model (where time is considered in the domain $\mathbb{R}_{\geq 0}$) is the unique possible option, raising the problem of handling an infinite number of reachable states. In fact, the set of reachable states of a time Petri net is generally infinite due to the infinite number of time successors a given state could have. We focus in this paper on the time Petri nets model, and propose a new finite abstraction of the underlying (infinite) state space.

Several abstractions of the TPN state space have been proposed in the literature which preserve different kinds of properties (reachability of markings, timed/untimed temporal properties, linear/branching temporal properties,...). They all aim at constructing, by removing some irrelevant details, a contraction of the state space of the model, which preserves properties of interest. They mainly differ in the state agglomeration criterion, the characterization of states (interval states or clock states) and the kind of preserved properties. Two main abstraction approaches exist in the literature: region graphs [1] and the state class approach [3]. The other methods [2,4–6,10,11,16,24] are either refinements, improvements or are derived from these basic approaches. The objective of these representations is to yield a state-space partition that groups concrete states into sets of states presenting similar behaviors with respect to the properties to be verified. These sets of states must cover the entire state space and must be finite in order to ensure the termination of the verification process. In addition to specific timed (or untimed) temporal properties, the Zenoness property is considered as an important pathological behavior a timed system should avoid. It is a behavior which violate a fundamental progress requirement for timed systems stating that it should be possible for time to diverge. This requirement is justified by the fact that timed systems cannot be infinitely fast. A TPN is said to be zeno if it admits a zeno-run i.e., an infinite execution that takes only finite time.

In order to check a given property on a TPN, most of the existing approaches do not exploit the obtained abstraction directly. In [7] the authors propose to translate a TPN into an equivalent timed automata which can be used to detect zenoness (using [13]) or to check timed properties (using tools like UPPAAL, KRONOS,...). The drawback of such a method is to interpret back the obtained results on the original TPN. An other indirect method consists in the use of observers [22] which are TPNs expressing some timed properties and which will be synchronized with the TPN of the system. The problem of this approach comes, on one hand, from the size the state space of the synchronized product compared to the size of the state space of the system model only, and, on the other hand, from the difficulty of expressing properties on markings of the TPN with observers [8].

In this work, we propose a new finite graph, called Timed Aggregate Graph (TAG), abstracting the behavior of bounded TPNs with strong time semantics.

The particular encoding of time information within each node of the TAG (called aggregate) allows to ensure the verification of timed properties on-the-fly and directly by exploring the TAG. The key idea behind the TAG approach presented in this paper is then the fact that the time information associated with each node is related to the current path leading to this node. In particular, given a node of the TAG, for each couple of enabled transitions $\langle t, t' \rangle$, the value of the earliest and latest firing times of t (reps. t') the last time, in the current path, t "met" t' (resp. t' met t) is stored in the node. This allows to maintain the relative differences between the firing times of enabled transitions (diagonal constraints) and to easily determine the fireable transitions at each node. In addition to this information, the earliest and the latest firing time of each enabled transition is computed dynamically for each node of the TAG. This allows to compute the minimum and maximum elapsed time through every path of the graph, to preserve the timed traces of the underlying TPN and to compute, on-the-fly, the minimum an the maximum time a given run can take. Moreover, we show how the TAG can be used, on-the-fly, in order to check some usual event-based time properties (e.g., is some transition fireable between d and D time units), and how each path of the TAG can be mapped to an explicit *timed* run of the TPN.

A preliminary version of this work has been published in [14], where a we proved that the TAG is a finite abstraction of the infinite reachable state space of a bounded TPN and that it preserves reachable states and timed traces. We established that the TAG can be used directly to check state-based timed properties. Here, we extend the TAG approach to event-based timed properties, we supply an algorithm to extract an explicit run from any path of the TAG, and we consider the problem of detecting zenoness on TAGs.

This paper is organized as follows: In Sect. 2, some preliminaries about TPNs and the corresponding semantics are recalled. In Sect. 3, we define the Timed Aggregate Graph (TAG) associated with a TPN and we illustrate its construction through several simple examples. In Sect. 4, which represents the core of this paper, we first show how the maximum (resp. minimum) time taken to reach a given marking (resp. to fire a given transition) can be obtained by the analysis of the TAG's paths. Then, we prove that each path of the TAG can be mapped to an explicit run of the corresponding TPN and vice versa. Section 5 is dedicated to the analysis of a TPN through its TAG. We show how the verification of some usual event-based timed reachability properties, as well as the detection of Zenoness, can be accomplished by exploring TAGs. In Sect. 6, we discuss the experimental results obtained with our implementation compared to two well-known tools, namely Romeo [9] and TINA [5]. Finally, a conclusion and some perspectives are given in Sect. 7.

2   Preliminaries and Basic Notations

A t-time Petri net (TPN for short) is a P/T Petri net [19] where a time interval $[t_{min}; t_{max}]$ is associated with each transition t.

Definition 1. *A* TPN *is a tuple* $\mathcal{N} = \langle P, T, Pre, Post, I \rangle$ *where:*

- $\langle P, T, Pre, Post \rangle$ *is a* P/T *Petri net*
- $I : T \longrightarrow \mathbb{N} \times (\mathbb{N} \cup \{+\infty\})$ *is the* time interval function *such that:* $I(t) = (t_{\min}, t_{\max})$, *with* $t_{\min} \leq t_{\max}$, *where* $t_{\min}$ *(resp.* $t_{\max}$*) is the earliest (resp. latest) firing time of transition* t.

A *marking* of a TPN is a function $m : P \longrightarrow \mathbb{N}$ where $m(p)$, for a place p, denotes the number of tokens in p. A *marked TPN* is a pair $\mathcal{N} = \langle \mathcal{N}_1, m_0 \rangle$ where $\mathcal{N}_1$ is a TPN and m_0 is a corresponding *initial marking*. A transition t is enabled by a marking m iff $m \geq Pre(t)$ and $Enable(m) = \{t \in T : m \geq Pre(t)\}$ denotes the set of enabled transitions in m. If a transition t_i is enabled by a marking m, then $\uparrow(m, t_i)$ denotes the set of newly enabled transitions [2]. Formally, $\uparrow(m, t_i) = \{t \in T \mid t \in Enable(m - Pre(t_i) + Post(t_i)) \wedge (t \notin Enable(m - Pre(t_i)) \vee (t = t_i))\}$. If a transition t is in $\uparrow(m, t_i)$, we say that t is newly enabled by the successor of m by firing t_i. Dually, $\downarrow(m, t_i) = Enable(m - Pre(t_i) + Post(t_i)) \setminus \uparrow(m, t_i)$ is the set of oldly enabled transitions. The possibly infinite set of reachable markings of $\mathcal{N}$ is denoted $Reach(\mathcal{N})$. If the set $Reach(\mathcal{N})$ is finite we say that $\mathcal{N}$ is bounded.

The semantics of TPNs can be given in terms of Timed Transition Systems (TTS) [15] which are usual transition systems with two types of labels: discrete labels for events (transitions) and positive real labels for time elapsing (delay). States (configurations) of a TTS are pairs $s = (m, V)$ where m is a marking and $V : T \longrightarrow \mathbb{R}_{\geq 0} \cup \{\bot\}$ a time valuation. In the following, $s.m$ and $s.V$ denote the marking and the time valuation respectively of a state s. If a transition t is enabled by a marking m then $V(t)$ is the elapsed time since t became enabled, otherwise $V(t) = \bot$. Given a state $s = (m, V)$ and a transition t, t is said to be fireable in s iff $t \in Enable(m) \wedge V(t) \neq \bot \wedge t_{\min} \leq V(t) \leq t_{\max}$.

Definition 2 (Semantics of a TPN). *Let* $\mathcal{N} = \langle P, T, Pre, Post, I, m_0 \rangle$ *be a marked TPN. The semantics of* $\mathcal{N}$ *is a TTS* $\mathcal{S}_{\mathcal{N}} = \langle Q, s_0, \rightarrow \rangle$ *where:*

1. *Q is a (possibly infinite) set of states*
2. $s_0 = (m_0, V_0)$ *is the initial state such that:*

$$\forall t \in T,\ V_0(t) = \begin{cases} 0 & \text{if } t \in Enable(m_0) \\ \bot & \text{otherwise} \end{cases}$$

3. $\rightarrow \subseteq Q \times (T \cup \mathbb{R}_{\geq 0}) \times Q$ *is the discrete and continuous transition relations:*
   (a) *the discrete transition relation:*
      $\forall t \in T : (m, V) \xrightarrow{t} (m', V')$ *iff:*

$$\begin{cases} t \in Enable(m) \wedge m' = m - Pre(t) + Post(t) \\ t_{\min} \leq V(t) \leq t_{max} \\ \forall t' \in T : V'(t') = \begin{cases} 0 & \text{if } t' \in \uparrow(m, t) \\ V(t') & \text{if } t' \in \downarrow(m, t) \\ \bot & \text{otherwise} \end{cases} \end{cases}$$

   (b) *the continuous transition relation:* $\forall d \in \mathbb{R}_{\geq 0},\ (m, V) \xrightarrow{d} (m', V')$ *iff:*

$$\begin{cases} \forall t \in Enable(m),\ V(t) + d \leq t_{max} \\ m' = m \\ \forall t \in T : \\ V'(t) = \begin{cases} V(t) + d\ if\ t \in Enable(m); \\ V(t) \quad otherwise. \end{cases} \end{cases}$$

The above definition requires some comments. First, the delay transitions respect the STS semantics: an enabled transition must fire within its firing interval unless disabled by the firing of others. Second, a state change occurs either by the firing of a transition or by time elapsing: The firing of a transition may change the current marking while the time elapsing may make some new transitions fireable. When a deadlock marking is reached, then only elapsing time is possible and the system remains in the same state.

Given a TPN $\mathcal{N}$ and the corresponding TTS $\mathcal{S_N}$, a path $\pi = s_0 \xrightarrow{\alpha_1} s_1 \xrightarrow{\alpha_2} \ldots$, where $\alpha_i \in (T \cup \mathbb{R}_{\geq 0})$, is a run of $\mathcal{S_N}$ iff $(s_i, \alpha_i, s_{i+1}) \in \rightarrow$ for each $i = 0, 1, \ldots$. The length of a run π can be infinite and is denoted by $\mid \pi \mid$. The possibly infinite set of runs of $\mathcal{S_N}$ is denoted $[\mathcal{S_N}]$. Without loss of generality, we assume that for each non empty run $\pi = s_0 \xrightarrow{\alpha_1} s_1 \xrightarrow{\alpha_2} \ldots$ of an STS corresponding to a TPN, there is no two successive labels α_i and α_{i+1} belonging both to $\mathbb{R}_{\geq 0}$. Then, π can be written, involving the reachable markings of $\mathcal{N}$, as $\pi = m_0 \xrightarrow{(d_1,t_1)} m_1 \xrightarrow{(d_2,t_2)} \ldots$ where d_i is the time elapsed at marking m_{i-1} before firing t_i. In order to associate a run $\pi = s_0 \xrightarrow{\alpha_1} s_1 \xrightarrow{\alpha_2} \ldots$ of $\mathcal{S_N}$, where $\alpha_i \in (T \cup \mathbb{R}_{\geq 0})$, with a run of $\mathcal{N}$, denoted $\mathcal{P}(\pi)$, we define the following projection function, where . denotes the concatenation operator between paths and π^i, for $i = 0, 1 \ldots$, denotes the suffix of π starting at state s_i.

$$\mathcal{P}(\pi) = \begin{cases} s_0.m & if\ \mid \pi \mid = 0 \\ s_0.m \xrightarrow{(0,\alpha_1)} . \mathcal{P}(\pi^1) & if\ \alpha_1 \in T \\ s_0.m \xrightarrow{(\alpha_1,\alpha_2)} . \mathcal{P}(\pi^2) & if\ \alpha_1 \in \mathbb{R}_{\geq 0} \wedge \mid \pi \mid \geq 2 \\ s_0.m \xrightarrow{\alpha_1} . \mathcal{P}(\pi^1) & if\ \alpha_1 \in \mathbb{R}_{\geq 0} \wedge \mid \pi \mid = 1. \end{cases}$$

3   Timed Aggregate Graph

In this section, we present the basis of our contribution which is a finite abstraction of the TPN's behavior, namely Timed Aggregate Graphs (TAGs). The key idea behind TAGs is the way the time information is encoded inside aggregates. In addition to the marking characterizing an aggregate, the time information is composed of two parts:

- The first part of the time information characterizing an aggregate is a dynamically updated interval, namely (α_t, β_t), associated with each enabled transition t. This interval gives the earliest and the latest firing times of any enabled transition starting from the aggregate. Either the corresponding transition is fireable at the current aggregate and the system must remain within the aggregate at least α_t time units and at most β_t time units (as long as the other enabled transitions remain fireable) before firing t, or t is not possible from the current aggregate (e.g. because of some diagonal constraint), in which case the system must move to an other aggregate by firing other transitions until t become fireable. In the latter case, the system must take at least α_t time units, and can take at most β_t time units to make t fireable in the future.

- The second part of the time information characterizing an aggregate is a matrix, namely *Meet*, allowing to dynamically maintain the relative differences between the firing times of enabled transitions (diagonal constraints). Given two enabled transitions t_1 and t_2, $Meet(t_1, t_2)$ is an interval $[\alpha_{t_1}^{m(t_1,t_2)}, \beta_{t_1}^{m(t_1,t_2)}]$ representing the earliest and the latest firing times of t_1 the last time both t_1 and t_2 were enabled (through the current paths leading to the aggregate).

Before we formally define the TAG and illustrate how the attributes of an aggregate are computed dynamically, let us first formally define aggregates.

Definition 3 (Timed Aggregate). *Let $\mathcal{N} = \langle P, T, Pre, Post, I \rangle$ be a TPN. A timed aggregate associated with $\mathcal{N}$ is a tuple $a = \langle m, E, Meet \rangle$, where:*

- *m is a marking*
- *$E = \{ \langle t, \alpha_t, \beta_t \rangle \mid t \in Enable(m), \alpha_t \in \mathbb{N} \wedge \beta_t \in \mathbb{N} \cup \{+\infty\} \}$ is a set of enabled transitions each associated with two time values.*
- *Meet is a matrix s.t. $\forall t, t' \in Enable(m)$, $Meet(t, t') = \langle \alpha, \beta \rangle$ where α (resp. β) represents the earliest (resp. latest) firing time of t the last time t and t' are both enabled before reaching the aggregate a.*

As for the states of a TTS, the attributes of an aggregate a are denoted by $a.m$, $a.E$ and $a.Meet$. Moreover, $a.Meet(t, t').\alpha$ (resp. $a.Meet(t, t').\beta$) is denoted by $a.\alpha_t^{m(t,t')}$ (resp. $a.\beta_t^{m(t,t')}$), or simply $\alpha_t^{m(t,t')}$ (resp. $\beta_t^{m(t,t')}$) when the corresponding aggregate is clear from the context. We use also $\alpha^{m(t,t')}$ (resp. $\beta^{m(t,t')}$) to denote $\alpha_t^{m(t,t')}$ (resp. $\beta_t^{m(t,t')}$) when the involved transition t is clear from the context.

The E attribute of an aggregate a allows to compute the minimum and the maximum time the system can elapse when its current state is within a. The following predicates (δ and Δ) compute these information for a given aggregate.

Definition 4 (Minimum and Maximum Stay Times). *Let $a = \langle m, E, Meet \rangle$ be an aggregate, the minimum and maximum time the system can stay at a are denoted by $\delta(a)$ and $\Delta(a)$ respectively, and are defined by the two following predicates:*

- $\delta(a) = \min_{\langle t, \alpha_t, \beta_t \rangle \in E} (\alpha_t)$
- $\Delta(a) = \min_{\langle t, \alpha_t, \beta_t \rangle \in E} (\beta_t)$

Given an aggregate $a = \langle m, E \rangle$ and an enabled transition t (i.e., $\langle t, \alpha_t, \beta_t \rangle \in E$), two primordial issues must be achieved to define the semantics of the TAG: (1) is t fireable from a?, and (2) if it is the case, how do we obtain the successor aggregate by firing t from a. In the following, we answer these issues.

Definition 5. *Let* $a = \langle m, E, Meet \rangle$ *be an aggregate and let* $\langle t, \alpha_t, \beta_t \rangle \in E$. *Then,* t *is fireable at* a, *denoted by* $a \overset{t}{\leadsto}$, *iff* $\forall \langle t', \alpha_{t'}, \beta_{t'} \rangle \in E$, $\alpha_t^{m(t,t')} \le \beta_{t'}^{m(t',t)}$

A transition t is fireable at an aggregate a iff there is no transition t', that is enabled by a, whose latest firing time was strictly smaller than the earliest firing time of t the last time both transitions were enabled.

Now that the fireability condition is formally defined, the following definition computes the successor aggregate obtained by the firing of a given transition. In this definition, the notion of newly (and oldly) enabled transitions is extended to aggregates as follows: $\uparrow (a, t) = \uparrow (a.m, t)$ and $\downarrow (a, t) = \downarrow (a.m, t)$ for each transition t enabled by $a.m$. Moreover, given a transition t' enabled by a, $SCR(a, t')$ computes the maximum time one can remain at a without exceeding the (static) latest firing time of t', and is formally defined by $SCR(a, t') = Max(0, (Min_{t'' \in Enable(a)}(Min(\beta^{m(t',t'')}, \beta^{m(t'',t')}) - (\alpha_{t'}^{m(t',t'')} - \alpha_{t'}))))$.

Definition 6. *Let* $a = \langle m, E, Meet \rangle$ *be an aggregate and let* $\langle t, \alpha_t, \beta_t \rangle \in E$.

Assume that t *is fireable at* a *(following Definition 5). The aggregate* $a' = \langle m', E', Meet' \rangle$ *obtained by firing* t *from* a, *denoted by* $a \overset{t}{\leadsto} a'$, *is obtained as follows:*

1. $m' = m - Pre(t) + Post(t)$
2. $E' = E_1' \cup E_2'$, *where* :
   - $E_1' = \bigcup_{t' \in \uparrow (a,t)} \{ \langle t', t'_{min}, t'_{max} \rangle \}$
   - $E_2' = \bigcup_{t' \in \downarrow (a,t)} \{ \langle t', \alpha_{t'}', \beta_{t'}' \rangle \}$ *where* :
     - $\alpha_{t'}' = \alpha_{t'} - SCR(a, t')$
     - $\beta_{t'}' = Min(\beta_{t'}, (\beta_{t'}^{m(t',t)} - \alpha_t^{m(t,t')})$
   - $\forall (\langle t_1, \alpha_1, \beta_1 \rangle, \langle t_2, \alpha_2, \beta_2 \rangle) \in E' \times E'$

$$Meet'(t_1, t_2) = \begin{cases} [t_{1_{min}}, t_{1_{max}}] & \text{if } t_1 \in \uparrow (a, t) \\ [\alpha_1, \beta_1] & \text{if } t_1 \in \downarrow (a, t) \wedge t_2 \in \uparrow (a, t) \\ Meet(t_1, t_2) & \text{if } t_1 \in \downarrow (a, t) \wedge t_2 \in \downarrow (a, t). \end{cases}$$

The computation of a successor a' of an aggregate a by the firing of a transition t is guided by the following intuition: If $\downarrow (a, t) \ne \emptyset$, then *the more the system can remain at* a, *the less it can remain at* a' *and vice versa*. Otherwise, the time elapsed within a' is independent from the time elapsed within a. Thus, given a transition t' enabled by a', two cases are considered: if t' is newly enabled, then its earliest and latest firing times are statically obtained by t'_{min} and t'_{max} respectively. Otherwise, the more one can remain at a, the less will be the necessary wait time at a' before firing t'. The function SCR (Still Can Remain) allows to compute the maximum remaining time at a under the hypothesis that, since t' became enabled, it remains the maximum time at each encountered aggregate before reaching a (Note that this is different from $\Delta(a)$). Thus $SCR(a, t')$ is obtained by the following reasoning: given a transition t'' that is enabled by a, it is clear that since the last time t' and t'' became both enabled, the maximum elapsed time can not be greater than $Min(\beta^{m(t',t'')}, \beta^{m(t'',t')})$ (because of the

STS semantics which is used in this paper). The maximum time the system can remain at a is then obtained by subtracting from this quantity the time that is already spent during the path leading to a (i.e., $(\alpha_{t'}^{m(t',t'')} - \alpha_{t'})$). By analysing all the transitions enabled by a the function SCR takes the minimum values in order to not violate the STS semantics rule. Similarly, the latest firing time of t' corresponds to the situation where, between the last moment t and t' were both enabled and the current aggregate a, each fired transition is fired as soon as possible. Each time a transition is fired, its earliest firing time is subtracted from the latest firing time of the old transitions. However, if the quantity of time that must be subtracted from the latest firing time of t' has already been subtracted in between, then the latest firing time of t' at a' is the same latest firing time of t' at the aggregate a. Concerning the $Meet$ attribute, given two transitions t_1 and t_2 that are enabled at a', the value of $Meet(t_1, t_2)$ is simply obtained by considering the membership of these transitions to $\uparrow (a, t)$ and to $\downarrow (a, t)$. Finally, by considering that $\infty - \infty = 0$, the previous definition allows to handle transitions having infinity as latest firing time.

Definition 7 (Timed Aggregate Graph). *Let $\mathcal{N} = \langle P, T, Pre, Post, I, m_0 \rangle$ be a TPN. The TAG associated with $\mathcal{N}$ is a tuple $G = \langle \mathcal{A}, T, a_0, \delta \rangle$ where:*

1. *$\mathcal{A}$ is a set of timed aggregates;*
2. *$a_0 = \langle m_0, E_0, Meet_0 \rangle$ is the initial timed aggregate s.t.:*
   (a) m_0 is the initial marking of $\mathcal{N}$.
   (b) $E_0 = \{\langle t, t_{\min}, t_{\max} \rangle \mid t \in Enable(m_0)\}$
   (c) $\forall t, t' \in Enable(a), Meet_0(t, t') = [t_{\min}, t_{\max}]$
3. *$\delta \subseteq \mathcal{A} \times T \times \mathcal{A}$ is the transition relation such that:*
   $\forall a \in \mathcal{A}, \forall t \in T, (a, t, a') \in \delta$ iff $a \xrightarrow{t} a'$

Since each transition having infinity as static latest firing time will always maintain the same latest firing time at each aggregate where it is enabled, one can

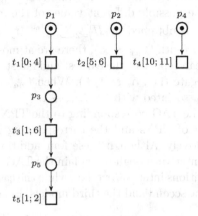

Fig. 1. A TPN example

aggregate	marking	E	Meet
a_0	(p_1,p_2,p_4)	$\{\langle t_1,0,4\rangle,\langle t_2,5,6\rangle,\langle t_4,10,11\rangle\}$	$\begin{pmatrix} - & [0:4] & [0:4] \\ [5:6] & - & [5:6] \\ [10:11] & [10:11] & - \end{pmatrix}$
a_1	(p_2,p_3,p_4)	$\{\langle t_2,1,6\rangle,\langle t_3,1,6\rangle,\langle t_4,6,11\rangle\}$	$\begin{pmatrix} - & [1:6] & [5:6] \\ [1:6] & - & [1:6] \\ [10:11] & [6:11] & - \end{pmatrix}$
a_2	(p_2,p_4,p_5)	$\{\langle t_2,0,5\rangle,\langle t_4,4,10\rangle,\langle t_5,1,2\rangle\}$	$\begin{pmatrix} - & [5:6] & [0:5] \\ [10:11] & - & [4:10] \\ [1:2] & [1:2] & - \end{pmatrix}$
a_3	(p_2,p_4)	$\{\langle t_2,0,4\rangle,\langle t_4,4,9\rangle\}$	$\begin{pmatrix} - & [5:6] \\ [10:11] & - \end{pmatrix}$
a_4	(p_4)	$\{\langle t_4,4,6\rangle\}$	$(-)$
a_5	$(-)$	$\emptyset$	$(-)$
a_6	(p_4,p_5)	$\{\langle t_4,4,6\rangle,\langle t_5,0,2\rangle\}$	$\begin{pmatrix} - & [4:10] \\ [1:2] & - \end{pmatrix}$
a_7	(p_4)	$\{\langle t_4,2,6\rangle\}$	$(-)$
a_8	(p_3,p_4)	$\{\langle t_3,0,5\rangle,\langle t_4,4,6\rangle\}$	$\begin{pmatrix} - & [1:6] \\ [6:11] & - \end{pmatrix}$
a_9	(p_3)	$\{\langle t_3,0,0\rangle\}$	$(-)$
a_{10}	(p_5)	$\{\langle t_5,1,2\rangle\}$	$(-)$
a_{11}	(p_4,p_5)	$\{\langle t_4,0,6\rangle,\langle t_5,1,2\rangle\}$	$\begin{pmatrix} - & [0:6] \\ [1:2] & - \end{pmatrix}$
a_{12}	(p_4)	$\{\langle t_4,0,5\rangle\}$	$(-)$
a_{13}	(p_5)	$\{\langle t_5,0,2\rangle\}$	$(-)$

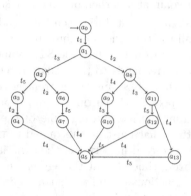

Fig. 2. The TAG associated with the TPN of Fig. 1

prove that the number of aggregates of a TAG is bounded when the corresponding TPN has a finitely many reachable markings. Indeed, given a reachable marking m, the number of different aggregates having m as marking can be bounded by the number of possible values of its attributes. This number is finite because of the following facts: (1) if the number of the transitions that are enabled by m is e, there are $2^{|e|}$ possible subsets of old transitions; (2) for a given subset of old transitions o, the number of possible arrangements of the old transitions regarding the enabling time is at most equal to $|o|!$ (the 2^n elements corresponding to the orderings where two or more old transitions became enabled at the same time are not considered); (3) given an arrangement $t_1 \leq t_2 \leq \cdots \leq t_{|o|}$, the number of possible values of $\alpha_{t_1}^{m(t_1,t_2)}$ is at most equal to $\sum_{i=0}^{t_{1_{\min}}} (t_{1_{\max}} - i + 1)$. Similarly, the possible values of $\alpha_{t_2}^{m(t_2,t_3)}$ is equal to $\sum_{i=0}^{t_{2_{\min}}} (t_{2_{\max}} - i + 1)$, etc. Thus, the number of the possible different values of the matrix $Meet$, for this particular arrangement, is obtained by $\Pi_{j=2}^{|o|} \sum_{i=0}^{t_{j-1_{\min}}} (t_{j-1_{\max}} - i + 1)$; (4) for each enabled transition t (with $t_{max} \neq \infty$), there are at most $\sum_{i=0}^{t_{\min}} (t_{\max} - i + 1)$ different intervals that can represent the earliest and latest firing time associated with t in a given aggregate (i.e., α_t and β_t). When $t_{max} = \infty$, the number of possible time intervals associated with t is $t_{min} + 1$.

Figure 2 illustrates the TAG corresponding to the TPN of Fig. 1[1].

Additional examples of TPNs and the corresponding TAGs are illustrated by Figs. 3 and 4 respectively. Although these four additional models are quite simple, they are representative enough to explain the TAG construction. Indeed, in the first one the transitions intervals overlap, while the case of disjoint intervals is considered through the second and the third models. Finally, the fourth model

---

[1] I thank Olivier H. Roux who supplied this TPN example during our discussions on the TAG approach.

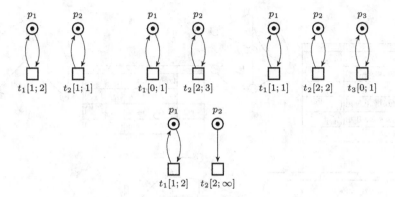

Fig. 3. Four TPN examples

illustrates the case of an infinite latest firing time. In the three first TAGs, the marking associated to aggregates is omitted (the same as the initial one). The second column of the tables gives the dynamic earliest and latest firing time of the enabled transitions (i.e., t_1, t_2 and t_3 respectively) while the third column gives the *Meet* matrix attribute of each aggregate. More significant examples are considered in Sect. 6.

4 Preservation Results

In this section, we establish the analysis power of the TAG-based approach. For the verification of time properties, an abstraction-based approach should allow the computation of the minimum and maximum elapsed time over any path. Moreover, the considered abstraction should preserve the behavior of the underlying timed system according to the desired property so that it can be used in the verification process instead of the original model.

Before we establish the preservation results of the TAG in terms of states and traces with respect to the corresponding TPN, we show in the following how one can compute (using the TAG) the time taken by a given path.

Definition 8. *Let $\mathcal{N}$ be a TPN and let $G = \langle \mathcal{A}, T, a_0, \delta \rangle$ be the corresponding TAG. Let $\pi = a_0 \xrightarrow{t_1} a_1 \longrightarrow \dots \xrightarrow{t_n} a_n$ be a path in G. For each aggregate a_i (for $i = 0 \dots n$), $MinAT_\pi(a_i)$ (resp. $MaxAT_\pi(a_i)$) denotes the minimum (resp. maximum) elapsed time between a_0 and a_i. In particular, $MinAT(a_0) := 0$ and $MaxAT(a_0) := \Delta(a_0)$.*

Proposition 1. *Let $\mathcal{N}$ be a TPN and let $G = \langle \mathcal{A}, T, a_0, \delta \rangle$ be the corresponding TAG. Let $\pi = a_0 \xrightarrow{t_1} a_1 \longrightarrow \dots \xrightarrow{t_n} a_n$ be a path in G. We denote by α_{i_t} (resp. β_{i_t}) the dynamic earliest (resp. latest) firing time of a transition t at aggregate a_i, for $i = 1 \dots n$. Then, $\forall i = 1 \dots n$, the following holds:*

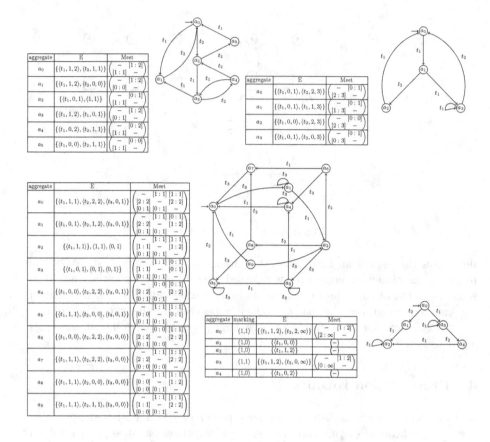

Fig. 4. TAGs associated with TPNs of Fig. 3

- *Minimum and maximum access time*
  - $MinAT_\pi(a_i) = MinAT_\pi(a_{i-1}) + \alpha_{i-1_{t_i}}$
  - $MaxAT_\pi(a_i) = MaxAT_\pi(a_{i-1}) + Min_{t \in Enable(a_i)}SCR(a_i, t)$
- *Minimum and maximum firing time*
  - $MinFT_\pi(t_i) = MinAT_\pi(a_i) + \alpha_{i_{t_i}}$
  - $MaxFT_\pi(t_i) = MaxAT_\pi(a_i)$

In the following, we establish the main result of our approach: for each path in the TPN (resp. in the corresponding TAG) it is possible to find a path in the TAG (resp. TPN) involving the same sequence of transitions and where the time elapsed within a given state is between the minimum and the maximum stay time of the corresponding aggregate.

Theorem 1. *Let $\mathcal{N}$ be a TPN and let $G = \langle \mathcal{A}, T, a_0, \delta \rangle$ be the TAG associated with $\mathcal{N}$. Then $\forall \overline{\pi} = m_0 \xrightarrow{(d_1, t_1)} m_1 \xrightarrow{(d_2, t_2)} \dots \xrightarrow{(d_n, t_n)} m_n \xrightarrow{d_{n+1}}$, with $d_i \in \mathbb{R}_{\geq 0}$, for $i = 1 \dots n+1$, $\exists \pi = a_0 \xrightarrow{t_1} a_1 \longrightarrow \dots \xrightarrow{t_n} a_n$ s.t. $\forall i = 0 \dots n$, $d_{i+1} \leq \Delta(a_i)$, $m_i = a_i.m$ and $\forall i = 1 \dots n$, $d_i \geq \alpha_{i-1_{t_i}}$.*

Proof. Let $\overline{\pi} = m_0 \xrightarrow{(d_1,t_1)} m_1 \xrightarrow{(d_2,t_2)} \dots \xrightarrow{(d_n,t_n)} m_n \xrightarrow{d_{n+1}}$ be a path of $\mathcal{N}$, with $d_i \in \mathbb{R}_{\geq 0}$, for $i = 1 \dots n+1$. Given a path $a_0 \longrightarrow a_1 \dots$, we denote by α_{i_t} (res. β_{i_t}), for $i = 0 \dots$, the dynamic earliest firing time (resp. latest firing time) of a transition t enabled by an aggregate a_i.

Let us prove by induction on the length of $\overline{\pi}$ the existence of a path π in the TAG satisfyingthe conditions of Theorem 1.

- $\mid \overline{\pi} \mid = 0$: Obvious since $m_0 = a_0.m$ (by construction) and since d_1 is less or equal to $\min_{t \in Enable(m_0)} t_{max}$ which is exactly the value of $\Delta(a_0)$.

- $\mid \overline{\pi} \mid = 1$ i.e., $\overline{\pi} = m_0 \xrightarrow{(d_1,t_1)} m_1 \xrightarrow{d_2}$. It is clear that $\alpha_{0_{t_1}} \leq d_1 \leq \Delta(a_0)$. The fact that t_1 is fireable at m_0 implies that it is at a_0 ($\forall t \in Enable(m_0)$, $t_{1_{min}} \leq t_{max}$) and its firing leads to the aggregate a_1 satisfying $a_1.m = m_1$. Let us assume that $d_2 > \Delta(a_1)$ and let t_m be the transition that is enabled at a_1 and which has the smallest latest firing time i.e., $\beta_{1_{t_m}} = \Delta(a_1)$. If t_m is newly enabled at a_1 then d_2 should clearly be greater or equal to $\Delta(a_1)$. If $t_m \in\downarrow (a_0, t_1)$ then $\beta_{1_{t_m}} = t_{m_{max}} - t_{1_{min}}$. Since $d_1 \geq t_{1_{min}}$, then $t_{m_{max}} - t_{1_{min}} \geq t_{m_{max}} - d_1$. The fact that $d_2 > \beta_{1_{t_m}}$ would imply that $d_1 + d_2 > t_{m_{max}}$ which is contradictory with the STS semantics. Thus $d_2 \leq \Delta(a_1)$.

- Assume that for any path $\overline{\pi}$ s.t. $\mid \overline{\pi} \mid \leq n$, there exists a path in the TAG with the same trace and satisfying the above conditions. Let $\overline{\pi} = m_0 \xrightarrow{(d_1,t_1)} m_1 \xrightarrow{(d_2,t_2)} \dots \xrightarrow{(d_n,t_n)} m_n \xrightarrow{(d_{n+1},t_{n+1})} m_{n+1} \xrightarrow{d_{n+2}}$ be a path of length $n+1$. Let $\pi = a_0 \xrightarrow{t_1} a_1 \xrightarrow{t_2} \dots \xrightarrow{t_n} a_n$ be the path in the TAG associated with the n-length prefix of $\overline{\pi}$ (by the induction hypothesis). Then $d_{n+1} \leq \Delta(a_n)$. Let us demonstrate that $d_{n+1} \geq \alpha_{n_{t_{n+1}}}$: It is clear that this is the case when $t_{n+1} \in\uparrow (a_n, t_{n+1})$. If $t_{n+1} \in\downarrow (a_n, t_{n+1})$, let $LastNew_i(t)$ be the function that returns the greatest integer, smaller than (or equal to) i, such that $t \in\uparrow (a_{l-1}, t_l)$. If such a value does not exist, then t became enabled, for the last time, at the initial aggregate a_0 and the function returns 0. Let $k = LastNew_i(t_{n+1})$, then $\alpha_{n_{t_{n+1}}} = t_{n+1_{min}} - \sum_{i=k}^{n-1} SCR(a_i, t_{n+1})$. The STS semantics implies that $\sum_{i=k}^{n-1} SCR(a_i, t_{n+1}) \geq \sum_{i=k}^{n-1} d_{i+1}$ Thus $t_{n+1_{min}} - \sum_{i=k}^{n-1} SCR(a_i, t_{n+1}) \geq t_{n+1_{min}} - \sum_{i=k}^{n-1} d_{i+1}$, and $d_{n+1} > \alpha_{n_{t_{n+1}}}$ would means that $\sum_{i=k}^{n} d_{i+1} < t_{n+1_{min}}$ which would prevent the firing of t_{n+1} at m_n. Thus, $d_{n+1} \leq \alpha_{n_{t_{n+1}}}$. Let us show now that t_{n+1} is fireable at a_n. Assume the opposite, this would imply that there exists a transition t enabled by a_n such that $\alpha^{m(t_{n+1},t)} > \beta^{m(t,t_{n+1})}$. Let $LastNew_n(t_{n+1}) = l$, $LastNew_n(t) = k$, and let us consider the three following cases:
1. $l = k$, then $\beta^{m(t,t_{n+1})} = t_{max}$ and $\alpha^{m(t_{n+1},t)} = t_{n_{min}}$ and the fact that $t_{n_{min}} > t_{max}$ would prevent t_{n+1} from being fireable at m_n which is not the case. Thus, t_{n+1} is fireable at a_n as well.
2. $l < k$. In this case, $\alpha^{m(t_{n+1},t)} = t_{n+1_{min}} - \sum_{j=l}^{k-1} SCR(a_j, t_{n+1})$ and $\beta^{m(t,t_{n+1})} = t_{max}$. Again, the STS semantics implies that $\sum_{i=l}^{k-1} SCR(a_i, t_{n+1}) \geq \sum_{i=l}^{k-1} d_{i+1}$. Thus $t_{n+1_{min}} - \sum_{i=l}^{k-1} SCR(a_i, t_{n+1}) \leq t_{n+1_{min}} - \sum_{i=l}^{k-1} d_{i+1}$, and $\alpha^{m(t_{n+1},t)} > t_{max}$ would means that $\sum_{i=l}^{k} d_{i+1} < t_{n+1_{min}}$ which would prevent the firing of t_{n+1} at m_n. Thus, $\alpha^{m(t_{n+1},t)} \leq \beta^{m(t,t_{n+1})}$ and t_{n+1} is necessarily fireable at a_n.

3. $l > k$. In this case, $\alpha^{m(t_{n+1}, t)} = t_{n+1_{min}}$ and $\beta^{m(t, t_{n+1})} = t_{max} - \sum_{i=k}^{l-1} Max(0, (\alpha^{m(t_{i+1}, t)} - (\beta^{m(t, t_{i+1})} - \beta_{i_t}))$. Since $\sum_{i=k}^{l-1} Max(0, (\alpha^{m(t_{i+1}, t)} - (\beta^{m(t, t_{i+1})} - \beta_{i_t})) \leq \sum_{i=k}^{l-1} d_{i+1}$ (otherwise, the time spent between k and some $i \leq l$ is smaller than $\alpha^{m(t_i, t)}$, which is contradictory with the recurrence hypothesis), $t_{max} - \sum_{i=k}^{l-1} Max(0, (\alpha^{m(t_{i+1}, t)} - (\beta^{m(t, t_{i+1})} - \beta_{i_t})) \geq t_{max} - \sum_{i=k}^{l-1} d_{i+1}$. Thus, if $t_{n+1_{min}} > \beta^{m(t, t_{n+1})}$ then $t_{n+1_{min}} > t_{max} - \sum_{i=k}^{l-1} d_{i+1}$ which prevent the firing of t_{n+1} at m_n (before firing t) which is not true. Thus, t_{n+1} is fireable at a_n.

Let us now demonstrate that $d_{n+2} \leq \Delta(a_{n+1})$. Assume the opposite, and let t_m be the transition enabled by a_{n+1} which has the smallest latest firing time i.e. $\beta_{n+1_{t_m}} = \Delta(a_{n+1})$. It is clear that if $t_m \in \uparrow (a_n, t_{n+1})$ then $d_{n+2} \leq \Delta(a_{n+1})$. Otherwise, if $t_m \in \downarrow (a_n, t_{n+1})$ and $k = LastNew_{n+1}(t_m)$ then $\beta_{n+1_{t_m}} = t_{m_{max}} - \sum_{i=k}^{n} Max(0, (\alpha^{m(t_{i+1}, t_m)}$ Again, since $\sum_{i=k}^{n} d_{i+1} \geq \sum_{i=k}^{n} Max(0, (\alpha^{m(t_{i+1}, t_m)}$, then $\beta_{n+1_{t_m}} \leq t_{m_{max}} - \sum_{i=k}^{n} d_{i+1}$, and the fact that $d_{n+1} > \beta_{n+1_{t_m}}$ would imply that $d_{n+2} + \sum_{i=k}^{n} d_{i+1} > t_{m_{max}}$ which is not allowed by the STS semantics. Thus, $d_{n+2} \leq \Delta(a_{n+1})$.

Since the TAG is supposed to be used to check time properties, it is important to be able to extract a concrete path (involving markings, transitions and the corresponding firing times) from an abstract one found in the TAG. One can imagine that such a path represents a counterexample illustrating the violation of some timed property. To the best of our knowledge, the existing approaches only give sequence of transitions enabled by the initial marking without specifying the time at which transition is fired, in which case the designer has to find such (non trivial) information by himself. Algorithm 1 illustrates how to extract such a concrete path. The intuition of the above algorithm is to build a concrete path $\overline{\pi}$ guided by the abstract path π. $\overline{\pi}$ is built by traversing π by backtracking. Initially (lines 1–3), the stay time at each marking is set to the minimum i.e., as soon as the desired transition is fireable. Then, starting from the last aggregate, each time a transition t_{i+1} is fired from an aggregate a_i (for $i = 1 \ldots n$), the fireability conditions are ensured by (possibly) changing the time that is elapsed before reaching a_i. Roughly speaking, two conditions must be satisfied in order to make the transition t_{i+1} fireable from a_i (i.e., $a_i.m$): (1) The first condition is that the elapsed time, since t_{i+1} became enabled for the last time, belongs to the interval $[t_{i+1_{min}}, t_{i+1_{max}}]$ while the second condition (2), is that there is no transition t enabled by a_i that prevents the firing of t_{i+1}. The only way for the last condition to be satisfied is that t has been enabled (for the last time) before t_{i+1} and the elapsed time between the moment t became enabled and t_{i+1} became enabled is strictly greater than $t_{max} - t_{i+1_{min}}$. The first condition is treated at lines 6–15: If the elapsed time since t_{i+1} has been enabled for the last time and the current state $(a_i.m)$ is strictly smaller than $t_{i+1_{min}}$ (lines 6–10) then it must be increased without exceeding $t_{i+1_{max}}$. This is ensured by the fact that, by construction of the TAG, $\sum_{j=k}^{i-1}(\alpha_{j_{t_{i+1}}} - \alpha_{j+1_{t_{i+1}}}) = T_{i+1_{min}}$ and $\sum_{j=k}^{i-1}(\alpha_{j_t} - \alpha_{j+1_t}) \leq t_{i+1_{max}}$ for any transition $t \in \downarrow (a_{i-1}, t_i)$. Now, the elapsed time since the last time t_{i+1} became enabled can exceed $t_{i+1_{max}}$. This can occur if, in order to ensure the firing

---

Algorithm 1. Construct concrete path

Require: an abstract path $\pi = a_0 \xrightarrow{t_1} a_1 \longrightarrow \dots \xrightarrow{t_n} a_n$

Ensure: a concrete path $\overline{\pi} = m_0 \xrightarrow{(d_1, t_1)} m_1 \longrightarrow \dots \xrightarrow{(d_n, t_n)} m_n$

1: **for all** $i = 1 \dots n$ **do**
2:     $d_i \leftarrow \alpha_{i-1_{t_i}}$
3: **end for**
4: **for all** $i = n - 1 \dots 1$ **do**
5:     $k = LastNew_i(t_{i+1})$
6:     **if** $(\sum_{j=k}^{i-1} d_{j+1} < t_{i+1_{min}})$ **then**
7:         **for all** $k \leq j < i$ **do**
8:             $d_{j+1} = Max(d_{j+1}, \alpha_{j_{t_{i+1}}} - \alpha_{j+1_{t_{i+1}}})$
9:         **end for**
10:     **end if**
11:     **if** $(\sum_{j=k}^{i-1} d_{j+1} > t_{i+1_{max}})$ **then**
12:         **for all** $k \leq j < i$ **do**
13:             $d_{j+1} = Min(d_{j+1}, \alpha_{j_{t_{i+1}}} - \alpha_{j+1_{t_{i+1}}})$
14:         **end for**
15:     **end if**
16:     **for all** $t \in Enable(a_i.m)$ **do**
17:         $l = LastNew_i(t)$
18:         **if** $((k > l) \wedge (t_{max} - \sum_{j=l}^{k-1} d_{j+1} < t_{i+1_{min}}))$ **then**
19:             **for all** $l \leq j < k$ **do**
20:                 $d_{j+1} = Min(d_{j+1}, \alpha_{j_t} - \alpha_{j+1_t})$
21:             **end for**
22:         **end if**
23:     **end for**
24: **end for**

---

of some transition t_j (for $j > i+1$) this time has been increased by the algorithm (lines 6–10). Thus, one has to decrease this time while maintaining the fireability of the transition t_j. This is ensured by lines 11–15. The last condition that could prevent t_{i+1} from being fireable at a_i. is that condition (2) is violated: the time elapsed between the moment some transition t, enabled before, t_{i+1}, and the moment t_{i+1} became enabled is bigger than $t_{max} - t_{i+1_{min}}$. This can happen when the firing of some transition t_j, with $j > i+1$, involved the increase of this quantity of time. This case is treated at lines 16–23, by fixing this problem while maintaining the future fireability of t_j.

In order to illustrate Algorithm 1, let us consider the TPN of Fig. 1 (the corresponding TAG is given in Fig. 2), and the firing sequence $t_1.t_2.t_4$. This sequence traverses the aggregates a_0, a_1, a_8 and a_9 respectively. The corresponding explicit sequence, denoted by $m_0 \xrightarrow{(d_1, t_1)} m_1 \xrightarrow{(d_2, t_2)} m_2 \xrightarrow{(d_3, t_4)} m_3$, is built as follows: Lines 1–3 initialize the values of d_1, d_2 and d_3 with 0, 1 and 4 respectively. Then, since $d_1 + d_2 < t_{4_{min}}$ (1<10), lines 7–9 updates d_1 and d_2 with values 4 and 2 respectively. These values are final and allows to represent the elapsed time within each state of the explicit path.

Theorem 2. *Let $\mathcal{N}$ be a TPN and let $G = \langle \mathcal{A}, T, a_0, \delta \rangle$ be the TAG associated with $\mathcal{N}$. Then, for any path $\pi = a_0 \xrightarrow{t_1} a_1 \longrightarrow \ldots \xrightarrow{t_n} a_n$ in the TAG, there exists a run $\overline{\pi} = m_0 \xrightarrow{(d_1,t_1)} m_1 \longrightarrow \ldots \xrightarrow{(d_n,t_n)} m_n$ in $\mathcal{N}$, s.t. $\forall i = 0 \ldots n$, $m_i = a_i.m$, $\forall i = 1 \ldots n$, $\alpha_{i-1_{t_i}} \leq d_i \leq \Delta(a_{i-1})$, and $\forall d \in \mathbb{R}_{\geq 0}$, $m_n \xrightarrow{d} \Leftrightarrow d \leq \Delta(a_n)$.*

Proof. Let $\pi = a_0 \xrightarrow{t_1} a_1 \longrightarrow \ldots \xrightarrow{t_n} a_n$. We denote by α_{i_t} (res. β_{i_t}) the dynamic earliest firing time (resp. the dynamic latest firing time) of a transition t at aggregate a_i, for $i \in \{0, \ldots, n-1\}$. We propose to proceed by construction and built a path $\overline{\pi}$ satisfying the Theorem 2. Let us demonstrate that the path $\overline{\pi} = m_0 \xrightarrow{(d_1,t_1)} m_1 \longrightarrow \ldots \xrightarrow{(d_n,t_n)} m_n$ obtained by Algorithm 1 is a run of the TPN associated with the TAG and that it satisfies the requirement. It is clear that the values of d_i, for $i = 1 \ldots n$, respects the conditions of Theorem 2. Now, Theorem 1 ensures that if $m_n \xrightarrow{d}$, for some $d \in \mathbb{R}_{\geq 0}$, then $d \leq \Delta(a_n)$. Finally, given $d \in \mathbb{R}_{\geq 0}$ s.t., $d \leq \Delta(a_n)$, the algorithm used to build $\overline{\pi}$ implies that the involved markings are reached as soon as possible. By construction of the TAG, $\Delta(a_n)$ is the maximum time the system can stay at m_n.

5   Analysis of a TPN Using TAGs

Our ultimate goal is to be able, by browsing the TAG, to both detect zeno-runs and check timed properties. For instance, we might be interested in checking whether some state-based or event-based property φ is satisfyied within a time interval $[d, D)$, with $d \in \mathbb{N}$ and $D \in (\mathbb{N} \cup \{\infty\})$, starting from the initial marking.

5.1   Detecting Zenoness of a TPN

A fundamental progress requirement of timed systems is that it should be possible for time to *diverge* [23]. This requirement is motivated by the fact that any timed process, no matter how fast, cannot be infinitely fast. This hypothesis implies that only a finite number of events can occur in a certain amount of time. Runs (of a TPN) which violate this property are called *zeno-runs*. In a deadlock-free model, time progress corresponds to the absence of *timelocks*, that is, states from which all possible infinite executions are zeno. Given a TPN and a marking m, we check whether m is a *zeno-marking*, i.e., whether there is an infinite run from m with a finite duration. In this section, we propose an approach to detect zeno-runs of a TPN using its corresponding TAG. Given a TPN $\mathcal{N}$ and the corresponding TAG $\mathcal{G}$, $\mathcal{N}$ is said to be xeon if and only if there exists a path $\pi = a_0 \xrightarrow{t_1} a_1 \longrightarrow \ldots$ in $\mathcal{G}$ such that, starting from some aggregate a_i (for some $i \geq 0$), forall aggregate a_j, for $j \geq i$, the minimum access time of a_j is equal to the minimum access time of a_i. Note that this is equivalent to the fact that the dynamic earliest firing time of any transition t_j (for $j > i$) is equal to zero. The following proposition highlights a necessary and sufficient condition for zenoness of TPN models.

Proposition 2. *Let $\mathcal{N}$ be a TPN and let $\mathcal{G}$ be the corresponding TAG. $\mathcal{N}$ is zeno iff $\mathcal{G}$ admits a run $\pi = a_0 \xrightarrow{t_1} a_1 \longrightarrow \ldots$ satisfying: $\exists i \geq 0$ s.t., $\forall j \geq i$ $MinAT_\pi(a_i) = MinAT_\pi(a_j)$.*

Proof. The proof comes directly from Theorems 1 and 2.

Corollary 1. *Let $\mathcal{N}$ be a TPN and let $\mathcal{G}$ be the corresponding TAG. $\mathcal{N}$ is zeno iff $\mathcal{G}$ admits a run $\pi = a_0 \xrightarrow{t_1} a_1 \longrightarrow \ldots$ satisfying: $\exists i \geq 0$ s.t., $\forall j > i$ $\alpha_{j-1_{t_j}}) = 0$.*

Corollary 2. *Let $\mathcal{N}$ be a TPN and let $\mathcal{G}$ be the corresponding TAG. Let m be a reachable marking of $\mathcal{N}$. Then, m is a timelock marking iff for any aggregate a of $\mathcal{G}$ s.t., $a.m = m$, there is no zeno run starting from a.*

Since the TAG is finite, the detection of zeno runs can be accomplished by a depth-first on-the-fly search algorithm. In fact, such a detection is reduced to analyzing cycles of the TAG: each time a new computed aggregate belongs to the current path, a cycle is found and must be analyzed, according to Proposition 2 (or Corollary 1) to find whether it represents a zeno run or not.

5.2 Checking Event-Based and State-Based Time Properties

Using the results of the previous section, one can use the TAG associated with a TPN in order to analyse both event and state based properties. Indeed, as established in [12], any abstraction which preserves markings and timed traces of a TPN preserves also the $TCTL_{TPN}$ properties. $TCTL_{TPN}$ is a subclass of TCTL and is defined as follows:

$$TCTL_{TPN} ::= \exists(p_1 U_I p_2) \mid \forall(p_1 U_I p_2) \mid p_1 \mapsto_I p_2 \mid \exists \Diamond_I p_1 \mid \forall \Diamond_I p_1 \mid \exists \Box_I p_1 \mid \forall \Box_I p_1$$
$$\mid p_1 \rightsquigarrow_{I_r} p_2$$

Here, p_1 and p_2 are atomic proposition that can be on markings (for state-based formulae) or on transitions of the TPN (for event-based formulae). Indexes I and I_r represent time intervals (I_r starts from 0). We refer the reader to [12] for the detailed semantics of $TCTL_{TPN}$ formulae.

Using $TCTL_{TPN}$, one can check, for instance, whether a given marking (resp. transition) is reachable (resp. is fireable) before (or after) some time. As event-based formula one can be interested in checking whether the firing of some transition t_1 will be be eventually followed, within some time interval $[d, D)$, by the firing of an other transition t_2. Using Proposition 1, one can browse the TAG graph and compute the minimum and maximum bounds of the elapsed time of the current path on-the-fly. Even if the considered time corresponds to an absolute time (starting from the initial aggregate), we can deduce the relative minimum and maximum time regarding to a particular aggregate through the path. This allows to handle nested formulae where sub formulae are timed as well. If a path of the TAG is considered as a counterexample for some timed property, one can use Algorithm 1 in order to build a concrete counterexample.

To the best of our knowledge, the last two capabilities are not available in the existing analyzing tools for TPNs.

Here, we focus on some usual properties and we give the intuition of the corresponding verification algorithm. Given a state-based or event-based formula φ, we consider the four following usual properties:

1. $\exists\Diamond_{[d;D]}\varphi$: There exists a path starting from the initial state, which takes between d and D time units before reaching a state that satisfies φ.
2. $\forall\Box_{[d;D]}\varphi$: For all paths starting from the initial state, all the states, that are reached after d and before D time units, satisfy φ.
3. $\forall\Diamond_{[d;D]}\varphi$: For all paths starting from the initial state, there exists a state in the path, reached after d and before D time units that satisfies φ.
4. $\exists\Box_{[d;D]}\varphi$: There exists a path from the initial state where all the states, that are reached after d and before D time units, satisfy φ.

Note that the second (resp. fourth) formulae can be deduced from the first (resp. third) one. Thus, in the following, we sketch the verification algorithms of the first and the third formulae only.

The TAG is represented as a tree which is partitioned into three regions (see Fig. 5). The first region ($Region_1$) contains the aggregates that are reachable strictly before d time units. The second region ($Region_2$) contains the aggregates that are reachable between d and D time units and the last region contains the aggregates that are reachable strictly after D time units. In case $D = \infty$ $Region_3$ is empty and $Region_2$ could contain an infinite number of aggregates. Thus, since the TAG is finite, the exploration of $Region_2$ can be cut as soon as reached aggregate has been already treated and belongs to $Region_2$.

Kais Klai

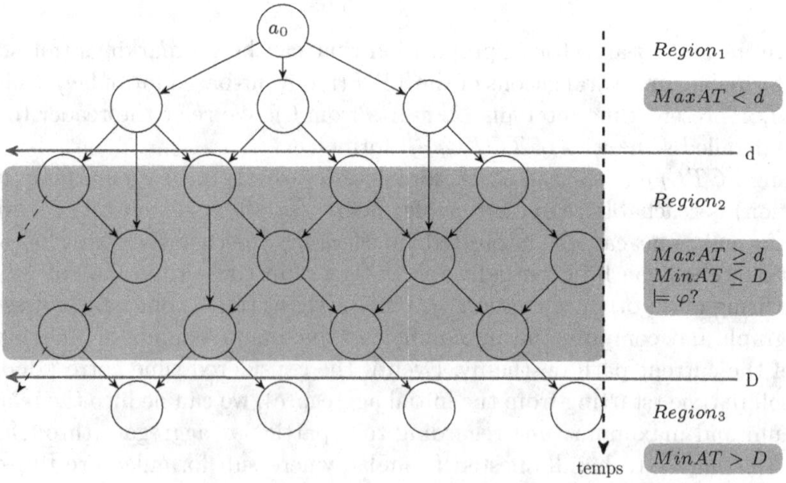

Fig. 5. Reachability analysis on the TAG

Based on this partition of the aggregates of the TAG into these three regions, the verification algorithms behave as follows: only aggregates belonging to $Region_2$ are analyzed with respect to φ. $Region_1$ must be explored in order to compute the maximal and minimum access time of the traversed aggregates, but $Region_3$ is never explored. In fact, as soon as an aggregate is proved to belong to $Region_3$ the exploration of the current path is stopped.

For instance, checking the formula number 1 is reduced to the search of an aggregate a in $Region_2$ that satisfies φ. As soon as such an aggregate is reached the checking algorithm stops the exploration and returns *true*. When, all the aggregates of $Region_2$ are explored (none satisfies φ) the checking algorithm returns *false*. Checking formulae number 3 is slightly more complicated. In fact, it is to check if, along any path in $Region_2$, there exists at least one aggregate satisfying φ. As soon as a path in $Region_2$ is completely explored without encountering an aggregate satisfying φ, the exploration is stopped and the checking algorithm returns *false*. Otherwise, it returns *true*.

6   Experimental Results

The efficiency of the verification of timed reachability properties is closely linked with the size of the explored structure to achieve this verification. Thus, it was important to first check that the TAG is a suitable/reduced abstraction before performing verification on it. Our approach for building TAG-TPN was implemented in a prototype tool (written in C++), and used for experiments in order to validate the size of the graphs generated by the approach (note that the prototype was not optimized for time efficiency yet, therefore no timing figures are given in this section). All results reported in this section have been obtained on a Mac-os with 2 gigahertz Intel with 8 gigabytes of RAM. The implemented prototype allowed us to have first comparison with existing approaches with respect to the size of obtained graphs. This section is dedicated to report, compare and discuss the experimental results obtained with three approaches: The State Class Graphs (SCG) [3], The Zone-Based Graphs (ZBG) [10] and the TAG. A SCG is a finite abstraction of the (possibly) infinite reachability state space of a TPN where nodes, called state classes, are symbolic representation of some infinite set of states sharing the same marking. A state class is then represented by the pair (m, F) where m is the common marking of states agglomerated in the state class, and F is a formula which characterize the union of the firing domains of these states. Each enabled transition in m is represented in F with a variable having the same name and representing its firing time. The ZBG approach is based on the notion of zones, i.e., a convex set of clocks valuation (a particular form of polyhedra) representing a conjunction of atomic constraints.

For our experimentation, we used the TINA tool ([5]) to build SCGs and ROMEO tool ([9]) to build ZBGs. Since TINA do not allow to preserve timed properties, and since ZBG do not supply the size of the built abstraction during the checking of a timed formula, we compare the TAG approach with the SCG and the ZBG versions that preserve(untimed) Linear Temporal Logic (LTL)

Table 1. Experimentation results

Parameters	SCG (with Tina) (nodes/arcs)	ZBG (with Romeo) (nodes/arcs)	TAG-TPN (nodes/arcs)
Nb. prod/cons	TPN model of producer/consumer		
1	34/56	34/56	34/56
2	748/2460	593/1 922	740/2438
3	4604/21891	3240/15200	4553/21443
4	14086/83375	9504/56038	13878/80646
5	31657/217423	20877/145037	30990/207024
6	61162/471254	39306/311304	60425/449523
7	107236/907 708	67224/594795	106101/856050
Nb. processes	Fischer protocol		
1	4/4	4/4	4/4
2	18/29	19/32	20/32
3	65/146	66/153	74/165
4	220/623	221/652	248/712
5	727/2536	728/2615	802/2825
6	2378/9154	2379/10098	2564/10728
7	7737/24744	7738/37961	8178/39697
8	25080/102242	25081/139768	26096/144304
Nb. processes	Train crossing		
1	11/1 4	11/14	11/14
2	123/218	114/200	123/218
3	3101/7754	2817/6944	2879/7280
4	134501/436896	122290/391244	105360/354270

properties. We tested our approach on several TPN models and we report here the obtained results for three well known examples of parametric TPN models. The considered models are a TPN representing a of producer/consumer model [12], the Fischer's protocol for mutual exclusion (adapted from [18]) and the train crossing example [4]. Table 1 reports the results obtained with the SCG, the ZBG and the TAG-TPN approaches, in terms of graph size number of nodes/number of edges). The obtained preliminary results show that the size of the TAG is comparable to the size of the graphs obtained with the ZBG and the SCG approaches. The TAG achieves better performances than both SCG and ZBG for the train crossing example, while it is slightly worse for the Fischer's protocol and performs similarly to SCG but worse than ZBG for the producer/consumer example. This is an encouraging result because of the following reasons: The TAG allows for checking *timed* properties while the SCG approach do not. Also, it can be used for the verification of event-based timed properties while the ZBG approach do not. An other difference consists in the fact that the verification of timed properties can be achieved directly on the TAG, without any synchronisation with an additional automaton (representing the formula to be checked), nor any prior step of translation to timed automata. Moreover, and in the prospect of using the TAG in order to check timed properties, our approach allows to exhibit a concrete run using Algorithm 1. Finally, we claim that the TAG is a suitable abstraction for further reductions, especially the partial order reduction which is based on the exploitation of the independency between the TPN transitions (the third TPN of Fig. 4 is a typical illustration).

7 Conclusion

We proposed a new symbolic graph for the abstraction of the TPN state space. The proposed graph, called TAG, produces a finite representation of the bounded TPN behavior and allows for analyzing of timed state-based and event-based properties. Unlike, the existing approaches, our abstraction can be directly useful to check both *timed* logic properties and zenoness requirement. We think that our approach is more understandable than the SCG and the ZBG approaches (the two main approaches for TPNs analysis since three decades) and easily implementable. Another particularity of our approach is that each path of the TAG can be matched with a concrete timed path of the TPN model.

Several issues have to be explored in the future: A short term perspective is to improve our implementation so that time consumption criterium can be taken into account in the comparaison of the TAG with existing tools. We should also, carry out additional experimentations (using more significant use cases) to better understand the limits of our approach and to better compare the TAG technique to the existing approaches. At mean and long terms, we plan to further reduce the size of the TAG by using reduction techniques such as BDDs or partial order. Moreover, we plan to implement TAG-based algorithms to check timed properties. In particular properties expressed with timed linear time temporal logic (MTL) since the TAG preserves timed traces of the corresponding TPN. Finally, it would be interesting to extend our construction algorithm in order to preserve branching time properties.

References

1. Alur, R., Dill, D.L.: A theory of timed automata. Theor. Comput. Sci. **126**(2), 183–235 (1994)
2. Berthomieu, B., Diaz, M.: Modeling and verification of time dependent systems using time petri nets. IEEE Trans. Softw. Eng. **17**(3), 259–273 (1991)
3. Berthomieu, B., Menasche, M.: An enumerative approach for analyzing time petri nets. In: IFIP Congress, pp. 41–46 (1983)
4. Berthomieu, B., Vernadat, F.: State class constructions for branching analysis of time petri nets. In: Garavel, H., Hatcliff, J. (eds.) TACAS 2003. LNCS, vol. 2619, pp. 442–457. Springer, Heidelberg (2003)
5. Berthomieu, B., Vernadat, F.: Time petri nets analysis with TINA. In: QEST, pp. 123–124 (2006)

6. Boucheneb, H., Gardey, G., Roux, O.H.: TCTL model checking of time petri nets. J. Log. Comput. **19**(6), 1509–1540 (2009)
7. Cassez, F., Roux, O.H.: Structural translation from time petri nets to timed automata. Electr. Notes Theor. Comput. Sci. **128**(6), 145–160 (2005)
8. Cassez, F., Roux, O.H.: Structural translation from time petri nets to timed automata. J. Syst. Softw. **79**(10), 1456–1468 (2006)
9. Gardey, G., Lime, D., Magnin, M., Roux, O.H.: Romeo: a tool for analyzing time petri nets. In: Etessami, K., Rajamani, S.K. (eds.) CAV 2005. LNCS, vol. 3576, pp. 418–423. Springer, Heidelberg (2005)
10. Gardey, G., Roux, O.H., Roux, O.F.: Using zone graph method for computing the state space of a time petri net. In: Niebert, P., Larsen, K.G. (eds.) FORMATS 2003. LNCS, vol. 2791, pp. 246–259. Springer, Heidelberg (2004)
11. Hadjidj, R., Boucheneb, H.: Improving state class constructions for CTL* model checking of time petri nets. STTT **10**(2), 167–184 (2008)
12. Hadjidj, R., Boucheneb, H.: On-the-fly TCTL model checking for time petri nets. Theor. Comput. Sci. **410**(42), 4241–4261 (2009)
13. Henzinger, T.A., Nicollin, X., Sifakis, J., Yovine, S.: Symbolic model checking for real-time systems. Inf. Comput. **111**(2), 193–244 (1994)
14. Klai, K.: On-the-fly model checking of timed properties on time petri nets. In: Proceedings of the International Workshop on Petri Nets and Software Engineering, pp. 35–53 (2014)
15. Larsen, K.G., Pettersson, P., Yi, W.: Model-checking for real-time systems. In: Reichel, H. (ed.) FCT 1995. LNCS, vol. 965, pp. 62–88. Springer, Heidelberg (1995)
16. Lime, D., Roux, O.H.: Model checking of time petri nets using the state class timed automaton. Discrete Event Dyn. Syst. **16**(2), 179–205 (2006)
17. Merlin, P.M., Farber, D.J.: Recoverability of modular systems. Oper. Syst. Rev. **9**(3), 51–56 (1975)
18. Penczek, W., Pólrola, A., Zbrzezny, A.: SAT-based (parametric) reachability for a class of distributed time petri nets. Trans. Petri Nets Other Models Concurrency **4**, 72–97 (2010)
19. Petri, C.A.: Concepts of net theory. In: MFCS 1973. Mathematical Institute of the Slovak Academy of Sciences (1973)
20. Pezzè, M., Young, M.: Time petri nets: a primer introduction. In: Tutorial at the Multi-workshop on Formal Methods in Performance Evaluation and Applications (1999)
21. Ramchandani, C.: Analysis of asynchronous concurrent systems by timed petri nets. Technical report, Cambridge, MA, USA (1974)
22. Toussaint, J., Simonot-Lion, F., Thomesse, J.: Time constraints verification methods based on time petri nets. In: Proceedings of the 6th IEEE Workshop on Future Trends of Distributed Computer Systems (FTDCS 1997), Tunis, Tunisia, 29–31 October 1997, pp. 262–269 (1997)
23. Tripakis, S.: Verifying progress in timed systems. In: Katoen, J.-P. (ed.) AMAST-ARTS 1999, ARTS 1999, and AMAST-WS 1999. LNCS, vol. 1601, pp. 299–314. Springer, Heidelberg (1999)
24. Yoneda, T., Ryuba, H.: CTL model checking of time petri nets using geometric regions (1998)

SMT-Based Abstract Parametric Temporal Planning

Artur Niewiadomski[1] and Wojciech Penczek[1,2]([⊠])

[1] ICS, Siedlce University, 3-Maja 54, 08-110 Siedlce, Poland
artur.niewiadomski@uph.edu.pl

[2] ICS, Polish Academy of Sciences, Jana Kazimierza 5, 01-248 Warsaw, Poland
penczek@ipipan.waw.pl

Abstract. PlanICS is a tool for solving the web service composition problem. It uses a uniform semantic description of the services and the service types as a part of the *ontology* which contains also the objects processed by the services. The user query is expressed in a fully declarative language defined over terms from the ontology by describing two object sets, called the *initial* and the *expected world*. The task of PlanICS consists in finding a sequence of services transforming the initial world into a superset of the expected one using service types available in the ontology and matching them later with real-world services. An abstract planning is the first phase of the task in which PlanICS composes service types. The paper extends this phase with a theory and a module for parametric temporal planning, by extending the user query with object variables and a *PLTLX* formula specifying temporal aspects of world transformations in a plan. Our solution comes together with an example, an implementation, and experimental results.

Keywords: Web service composition · SMT · Abstract temporal planning · LTL

1 Introduction

Web service composition within Service-Oriented Architecture (SOA) [2] is attracting a lot of interest, being a subject of many theoretical and practical approaches. The main idea consists in dealing with independent (software) components available via well-defined interfaces. As a simple web service does not typically satisfy the user objective, a composition is investigated in order to make the user fully satisfied. An automatic composition of Web services aims at relieving the user from a manual preparation of detailed execution plans, matching services to each other, and choosing optimal providers for all the components. The problem of finding such a satisfactory composition is NP-hard and well known in the literature as the Web Service Composition Problem (WSCP)

This work has been partially supported by the National Science Centre under the grant No. 2011/01/B/ST6/01477.

© Springer-Verlag Berlin Heidelberg 2015
M. Koutny et al. (Eds.): ToPNoC X, LNCS 9410, pp. 55–83, 2015.
DOI: 10.1007/978-3-662-48650-4_4

[1,2,23]. There are various approaches to solve WSCP [14,16], some of them are discussed in the next section.

In this paper, we follow the approach of the system PlanICS [8,9], which has been inspired by [1]. The main assumption is that all the web services in the domain of interest as well as the objects which are processed by the services, can be strictly classified in a hierarchy of *classes*, organised in an *ontology*. Another key idea consists in dividing planning into several stages. The first phase, called the *abstract planning*, deals with *classes of services*, where each class represents a set of real-world services. This phase has been implemented in PlanICS using three approaches: the first one based on a translation to an entry of an SMT-solver [17], the second one exploiting genetic algorithms [24], and the third one based on hybrid algorithms combining SMT with GA [19]. The second phase, called the *concrete planning*, deals with *concrete services*, i.e., services equipped in all values of their object attributes. Thus, while the first phase produces an *abstract plan*, it becomes a *concrete plan* in the second phase. Such an approach enables to reduce the number of concrete services to be considered dramatically as they are already eliminated in the abstract planning phase. This paper focuses on the abstract planning problem, but extends it to a so called parametric temporal planning. This extension together with the experimental results is the main contribution of the paper. The main idea behind our approach consists in providing the user with a possibility to specify not only the first and the expected state of a plan in request, but also to specify temporal aspects of state transformations in a plan. Moreover, both the specification parts can be given in a parametric way. To this aim we introduce two general types of atomic properties for writing a temporal formula, namely *propositions* and *level constraints*. The propositions are used to describe (intermediate) states of a plan in terms of existence (or non-existence) of objects and abstract values of object attributes. The level constraints, built over a special set of objects, are used for influencing a service ordering within solutions. However, in order to express such restrictions, the user has to rely on some knowledge about the planning domain. In order to get this knowledge, the planner can be first run without temporal constraints, and then these restrictions can be added after a non-temporal planning results have been obtained. The parametric extension allows us to use object variables for specifying a set of initial states as well as for using integer variables for specifying restrictions on the range of the temporal operators.

We propose a novel approach based on applying SMT-solvers. Contrary to a number of other approaches, we focus not only on searching for a single plan, but we attempt to find all *significantly different* plans. We start with defining the abstract planning problem (APP, for short). Then, we present our original approach to APP based on a compact representation of abstract plans by multisets of service types. We introduce the language of $PLTL^{\alpha}_{-X}$ for specifying parametric temporal aspects of the user query. This approach is combined with a reduction to a task for an SMT-solver. The encoding of blocking formulas allows for pruning the search space with many sequences which use the same multiset of service types in some plan already generated. Moreover, we give details of our algorithms and their implementations that are followed by experimental results. To the best of our knowledge, the above approach is novel, and as our experiments show it is also very promising.

The rest of the paper is organized as follows. Related work is discussed in Sect. 2. Section 3 deals with the abstract planning problem. In Sect. 4 the temporal planning is presented. Section 5 discusses the implementation and the experimental results of our planning system. The last section summarizes this paper and discusses a further work.

2   Related Work

The existing solutions to WSCP can be divided into several groups. A classification matrix aimed at the influence on the effort of Web service composition is presented in [14]. According to [14], situation calculus [6], Petri nets [11], theorem proving [22], and model checking [26] among others belongs to AI planning. A composition method closest to ours based on SMT is presented in [16], where the authors reduce WSCP to a reachability problem of a state-transition system. The problem is encoded by a propositional formula and tested for satisfiability using a SAT-solver. This approach makes use of an ontology describing a hierarchy of types and deals with an inheritance relation. However, we consider also the states of the objects, while [16] deals with their types only. Moreover, among other differences, we use a multiset-based SMT encoding instead of SAT.

Most of the applications of SMT in the domain of WSCP is related to the automatic verification and testing. For example, a message race detection problem is investigated in [10], the paper [4] takes advantage of symbolic testing and execution techniques in order to check behavioural conformance of WS-BPEL specifications, while [15] exploits SMT to verification of WS-BPEL specifications against business rules.

Recently, there have also appeared papers dealing with temporal logics in the context of WSCP. Bersani et al. in [5] present a formal verification technique for an extension of LTL that allows the users to include constraints on integer variables in formulas. This technique is applied to the substitutability problem for conversational services. The paper [13] deals with the problem of automatic service discovery and composition. The authors characterize the behaviour of a service in terms of a finite state machine, specify the user's requirement by an LTL formula, and provide a translation of the problem defined to SAT. However, the paper does not specify precisely experimental results and such important details as, e.g., the number of services under consideration. An efficient application of the authors method is reported for plans of length up to 10 only. The authors of [3] address the issue of verifying whether a composite Web services design meets some desirable properties in terms of deadlock freedom, safety, and reachability. The authors report on automatic translation procedures from the automata-based design models to the input language of the NuSMV verification tool. The properties to be verified can be expressed as LTL or CTL formulae.

Searching for plans meeting temporal restrictions is also a topic of interest of a broad planning community. The PDDL language [12] has been also extended with LTL-like modal operators, but for planning automata-based methods are used instead of SMT-based symbolic ones.

To the best of our knowledge there are no approaches to parametric temporal planning.

3   Abstract Planning

This section introduces APP as the first stage of WSCP in the PlanICS framework. First, the PlanICS ontology is presented. Next, we provide some basic definitions and explain the main goals of APP.

3.1   PlanICS Ontology

The OWL language [21] is used as the PlanICS ontology format. The concepts are organized in an inheritance tree of *classes*, all derived from the base class - *Thing*. There are 3 children of *Thing*: *Artifact*, *Stamp*, and *Service* (Fig. 1).

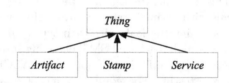

Fig. 1. The base classes in PlanICS ontology

The branch of classes rooted at *Artifact* is composed of the types of the objects, which the services operate on. Each object consists of a number of attributes, whereas an attribute consists of a name and a type. Note that the types of the attributes are irrelevant in the abstract planning phase since they are not used by the planner. The values of the attributes of an object determine its state, but in the abstract planning it is enough to know only whether an attribute has some value (i.e., is set), or it does not have one (i.e., it is null). The *Stamp* class and its descendants define special-purpose objects, often useful in constructing a user query, and in the planning process. A stamp is a specific type aimed at a confirmation of the service execution. The specialized descendants of the *Service* class can produce the *stamp* being an instance of any subtype of *Stamp* and describing additional execution features. Note that each service produces exactly one confirmation object. The classes derived from *Artifact* and *Stamp* are called the *object types*.

Each class derived from *Service*, called a *service type*, stands for a description of a set of real-world services. It contains a formalized information about their activities. A service type affects a set of objects and transforms them into a new set of objects. The detailed information about this transformation is contained in the attributes of a service type: the sets *in, inout,* and *out,* and the Boolean formulas *pre* and *post*. These sets enumerate the objects, which are processed by the service. The objects of the *in* set are read-only, i.e., they are passed unchanged to the next world. Each object of *inout* can be modified - the service can change some values of its attributes. The objects of *out* are produced by the service.

3.2 Basic Definitions

Let $\mathbb{I}$ denote the set of all *identifiers* used as the type names, the objects, and the attributes. In APP we deal with abstract values only, the types of the attributes are irrelevant, and we identify the attributes with their names. Moreover, we denote the set of all attributes by A, where $A \subset \mathbb{I}$. An *object type* is a pair $(t, Attr)$, where $t \in \mathbb{I}$, and $Attr \subseteq A$. That is, an object type consists of the type name and a set of the attributes. By $\mathbb{P}$ we mean a set of all object types.

Example 1. Consider the following exemplary ontology containing in addition to *Thing* also the classes *Artifact* and *Stamp*. The class *Artifact* corresponds to the object type $(Artifact, \{id\})$ (the only attribute is an identifier) while the class *Stamp* corresponds to the object type $(Stamp, \{serviceClass, serviceId, level\})$, introducing the attributes describing the service generating the stamp, and the position of this service in an execution sequence we consider. □

We define also a transitive, irreflexive, and antisymmetric *inheritance* relation $Ext \subseteq \mathbb{P} \times \mathbb{P}$, such that $((t_1, A_1), (t_2, A_2)) \in Ext$ iff $t_1 \neq t_2$ and $A_1 \subseteq A_2$. That is, a subtype contains all the attributes of a base type and optionally introduces more attributes.

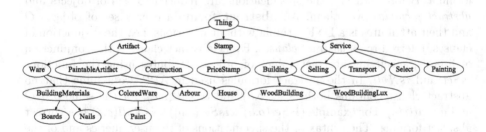

Fig. 2. Example ontology

Example 2. Consider the ontology depicted in Fig. 2. In the *Artifact* branch one can see several types of objects such as *Arbour* (the main point of interest of this example), which is a subclass of *Ware*, *PaintableArtifact*, and *Construction*. At the right hand side the *Service* branch and its subclasses are located. The service *Select* (*St*) is able to search any *Ware*, *Selling* (*Sg*) allows to purchase it, while *Transport* (*T*) can be used to change its location. The *Painting* (*P*) service is able to change colour of any *PaintableArtifact*, but it needs to use some *Paint*. The *Building* (*B*) service can be used to obtain some *Construction*,

but it needs *BuildingMaterials*. Finally, two subclasses of *Building* are specialized in production of wooden constructions using the supplied boards and nails.
The services *WoodBuilding* (*Wb*) and *WoodBuildingLux* (*Wbx*) are similar,
but the latter also paints the product to the chosen colour using their own paint,
however for a higher price. Consider the following object types:

- (*Ware*, {*id*, *owner*, *location*}),
- (*Boards*, {*id*, *owner*, *location*, *woodKind*, *thickness*, *volume*}),
- (*Nails*, {*id*, *owner*, *location*, *size*, *weight*}),
- (*Arbour*, {*id*, *owner*, *location*, *colour*}),
- (*PriceStamp*, {*serviceType*, *serviceId*, *level*, *price*}).

We have $(Artifact, Ware) \in Ext$ (i.e., *Ware* is a subclass of *Artifact*),
as the set of attributes of *Artifact* is included in that of *Ware*. Similarly,
$\{(Ware, Boards), (Ware, Nails), (Ware, Arbour), (Stamp, PriceStamp)\} \subseteq$
Ext. From transitivity of Ext also $\{Artifact\} \times \{Boards, Nails, Arbour\} \subseteq$
Ext. □

An *object* o is a pair $o = (id, type)$, where $id \in \mathbb{I}$ and $type \in \mathbb{P}$. By $type(o)$
we denote the type of o. The set of all objects is denoted by $\mathbb{O}$. Amongst all the
objects we distinguish between the *artifacts* (the instances of the *Artifact* type)
and the *stamps* (the instances of the *Stamp* type). The set of all the stamps is
denoted by $\mathbb{ST}$, where $\mathbb{ST} \subseteq \mathbb{O}$. Moreover, we define the function $attr : \mathbb{O} \longmapsto 2^A$
returning the set of all attributes for each object of $\mathbb{O}$.

Service Types and User Queries. The service types available for composition are
defined in the ontology by *service type specifications*. The user goal is provided
in a form of a *user query specification*, which is then extended by a temporal
formula. Before APP, all the specifications are reduced to sets of objects and
abstract formulas over them. An **abstract formula** over a set of objects O
and their attributes is a DNF formula without negations, i.e., the disjunction of
clauses, referred to as *abstract clauses*. Every abstract clause is the conjunction
of literals, specifying abstract values of object attributes using the functions
isSet and *isNull*. In the abstract formulas used in APP, we assume that no
abstract clause contains both $isSet(o.a)$ and $isNull(o.a)$, for the same $o \in O$
and $a \in attr(o)$. For example $(isSet(o.a) \wedge isSet(o.b)) \vee isNull(o.a)$ is a correct
abstract formula. The syntax of the specifications of the user queries and of the
service types is the same and it is defined below.

Definition 1. *A* **specification** *is a 5-tuple* (in, inout, out, pre, post), *where in,
inout, out are pairwise disjoint sets of objects, and* pre *is an abstract formula
defined over objects from* in $\cup$ inout, *while* post *is an abstract formula defined
over objects from* in $\cup$ inout $\cup$ out.

In what follows we use user query specifications q and service type specifications
s, typically denoting them by $spec_x = (in_x, inout_x, out_x, pre_x, post_x)$, where $x \in$
$\{q, s\}$, resp. This reflects the idea that a user query specification and a service
type specification are of the same type, which, intuitively, means that each user
query specifies a service type.

Example 3. Consider the ontology of Example 2. Assume the user wants to get a wooden arbour painted in blue. The query is asked as follows: $in = inout = \emptyset$, $pre = true$, $out = \{Arbour\ a\}$, $post = (a.colour = blue \wedge a.owner = Me \wedge a.location = MyAddress)$. The *post* formula is translated to its abstract form, that is $(isSet(a.colour) \wedge isSet(a.owner) \wedge isSet(a.location))$.   □

In order to formally define the *user queries* and the *service types*, which are interpretations of their specifications, we need to define the notions of *valuation functions* and *worlds*.

Definition 2. *Let* $\varphi = \bigvee_{i=1..n} \alpha_i$ *be an abstract formula. A* **valuation of the attributes** *over* α_i *is the partial function* $v_{\alpha_i} : \bigcup_{o \in \mathbb{O}} \{o\} \times attr(o) \longmapsto \{true, false\}$, *where:*

- $v_{\alpha_i}(o, a) = true$ *if* $isSet(o.a)$ *is a literal of* α_i, *and*
- $v_{\alpha_i}(o, a) = false$ *if* $isNull(o.a)$ *is a literal of* α_i, *and*
- $v_{\alpha_i}(o, a)$ *is undefined, otherwise.*

We define the restriction of a valuation function v_{α_i} to a set of objects $O \subset \mathbb{O}$ as $v_{\alpha_i}(O) = v_{\alpha_i}\big|_{\bigcup_{o \in O} \{o\} \times attr(o)}$. The undefined values appear when the interpreted abstract formula does not specify abstract values of some attributes, which is a typical case in the WSC domain. The undefined values are used also for representing families of total valuation functions. Next, for a partial valuation function f, by $total(f)$ we denote the family of the total valuation functions on the same domain, which are consistent with f, i.e., agree on the values defined of f. Moreover, we define a *family of the total valuation functions* $\mathcal{V}_\varphi$ over the abstract formula φ as the union of the sets of the consistent valuation functions over every abstract clause α_i, i.e., $\mathcal{V}_\varphi = \bigcup_{i=1}^{n} total(v_{\alpha_i})$. The restriction of the family of functions $\mathcal{V}_\varphi$ to a set of objects O and their attributes is defined as $\mathcal{V}_\varphi(O) = \bigcup_{i=1}^{n} total(v_{\alpha_i}(O))$.

Example 4. Consider the singleton $O = \{a\}$, where a is an instance of the *Arbour* type. Let $\varphi = (isSet(a.colour) \wedge isSet(a.owner) \wedge isNull(a.location))$ be an abstract formula, consisting of a single abstract clause. Let us recall that besides the three attributes *colour*, *owner*, and *location* mentioned in the formula φ, the objects of the *Arbour* type have also the attribute *id*. Thus, the valuation function v_φ is defined as follows: $v_\varphi(a, colour) = v_\varphi(a, owner) = true$, $v_\varphi(a, location) = false$, and $v_\varphi(a, id)$ *is undefined*. Moreover, there exist two total valuation functions consistent with v_φ: the first assigns *true* to $a.id$ while the second assigns *false*. Formally, $\mathcal{V}_\varphi = \mathcal{V}_\varphi(O) = \{t_1, t_2\}$, where:

$$t_1(a, colour) = true \qquad t_2(a, colour) = true$$
$$t_1(a, owner) = true \qquad t_2(a, owner) = true$$
$$t_1(a, location) = false \qquad t_2(a, location) = false$$
$$t_1(a, id) = true \qquad t_2(a, id) = false.$$ □

Definition 3. *A* **world** w *is a pair* (O_w, v_w), *where* $O_w \subseteq \mathbb{O}$ *and* $v_w = v(O_w)$ *is a total valuation function equal to some valuation function* v *restricted to* O_w. *The* size *of* w, *denoted by* $|w|$ *is equal to* $|O_w|$.

That is, a world represents a state of a set of objects, where each attribute is either set or null. By a *sub-world* of w we mean a world built from a subset of O_w and v_w restricted to the objects from the chosen subset. Moreover, a pair consisting of a set of objects and a family of total valuation functions defines a *set of worlds*. That is, if $\mathcal{V} = \{v_1, \dots, v_n\}$ is a family of total valuation functions and $O \subseteq \mathbb{O}$ is a set of objects, then $(O, \mathcal{V}(O))$ means the set $\{(O, v_i(O)) \mid 1 \le i \le n\}$, for $n \in \mathbb{N}$. Finally, the set of all worlds is denoted by $\mathbb{W}$.

Now, we are in a position to define a *service type* and a (basic) *user query* as an interpretation of its specification. In the next section the user query is extended to a temporal version.

Definition 4. *Let* $spec_x = (\text{in}_x, \text{inout}_x, \text{out}_x, \text{pre}_x, \text{post}_x)$ *be a user query or a service type specification, where* $x \in \{q, s\}$, *resp. An interpretation of* $spec_x$ *is a pair of world sets* $x = (W^x_{pre}, W^x_{post})$, *where:*

- $W^x_{pre} = (\text{in}_x \cup \text{inout}_x, \mathcal{V}^x_{pre})$, *where* $\mathcal{V}^x_{pre}$ *is the family of the valuation functions over* pre_x,
- $W^x_{post} = (\text{in}_x \cup \text{inout}_x \cup \text{out}_x, \mathcal{V}^x_{post})$, *where* $\mathcal{V}^x_{post}$ *is the family of the valuation functions over* post_x.

An interpretation of a user query (service type) specification is called simply a user query *(service type, resp.).*

For a service type (W^s_{pre}, W^s_{post}), W^s_{pre} is called the *input world set*, while W^s_{post} - the *output world set*. The set of all the service types defined in the ontology is denoted by $\mathbb{S}$. For a user query (W^q_{pre}, W^q_{post}), W^q_{pre} is called the *initial world set*, while W^q_{post} - the *expected world set*, and denoted by W^q_{init} and W^q_{exp}, respectively.

Abstract Planning Overview. The main goal of APP is to find a composition of service types satisfying a user query, which specifies some initial and some expected worlds as well as some temporal aspects of world transformations. Intuitively, an initial world contains the objects owned by the user, whereas an expected world consists of the objects required to be the result of the service composition.

To formalize the notion of an abstract plan, we need several auxiliary concepts. Let $o, o' \in \mathbb{O}$ and v and v' be valuation functions. We say that $v'(o')$ is compatible with $v(o)$, denoted by $v'(o') \succ^{obj} v(o)$, iff the types of both objects are the same, or the type of o' is a subtype of type of o, i.e., $type(o) = type(o')$ or $(type(o'), type(o)) \in Ext$, and for all attributes of o, we have that v' agrees with v, i.e., $\forall_{a \in attr(o)} v'(o', a) = v(o, a)$. Intuitively, an object of a richer type (o') is compatible with the one of the base type (o), provided that the valuations of all common attributes are equal.

Let $w = (O, v)$, $w' = (O', v')$ be worlds. We say that the world w' is compatible with the world w, denoted by $w' \succ^{wrl} w$, iff there exists a one-to-one mapping

$map : O \longmapsto O'$ such that $\forall_{o \in O} v'(map(o)) \succ^{obj} v(o)$. Intuitively, w' is compatible with w if both of them contain the same number of objects and for each object from w there exists a compatible object in w'. The world w' is called *sub-compatible* with the world w, denoted by $w' \succ^{swrl} w$ iff there exists a sub-world of w' compatible with w.

World Transformations. One of the fundamental concepts in our approach concerns a world transformation. A world w, called a *world before*, can be transformed by a service type s, having specification $spec_s$, if w is sub-compatible with some input world of s. The result of such a transformation is a world w', called a *world after*, in which the objects of out_s appear, and, as well as the objects of $inout_s$, they are in the states consistent with some output world of s. The other objects of w do not change their states. In a general case, there may exist a number of worlds possible to obtain after a transformation of a given world by a given service type, because more than one sub-world of w can be compatible with an input world of s. Therefore, we introduce a *context function*, which provides a strict mapping between objects from the worlds before and after, and the objects from the input and output worlds of a service type s.

Definition 5. *A **context function** $ctx_O^s : in_s \cup inout_s \cup out_s \longmapsto O$ is an injection, which for a given service type s and a set of objects O assigns an object from O to each object from in_s, $inout_s$, and out_s.*

Now, we can define a world transformation.

Definition 6. *Let $w, w' \in \mathbb{W}$ be worlds, called a* world before *and a* world after, *respectively, and $s = (W_{pre}^s, W_{post}^s)$ be a service type. Assume that $w = (O, v)$, $w' = (O', v')$, where $O \subseteq O' \subseteq \mathbb{O}$, and v, v' are valuation functions. Let $ctx_{O'}^s$ be a context function, and the sets IN, IO, OU be the $ctx_{O'}^s$ images of the sets in_s, $inout_s$, and out_s, respect., i.e., $IN = ctx_{O'}^s(in_s)$, $IO = ctx_{O'}^s(inout_s)$, and $OU = ctx_{O'}^s(out_s)$. Moreover, let $IN, IO \subseteq (O \cap O')$ and $OU = (O' \setminus O)$.*

We say that a service type s transforms the world w into w' in the context $ctx_{O'}^s$, denoted by $w \overset{s, ctx_{O'}^s}{\rightarrow} w'$, if for some $v_{pre}^s \in V_{pre}^s$ and $v_{post}^s \in V_{post}^s$, all the following conditions hold:

1. $(IN, v(IN)) \succ^{wrl}(in_s, v_{pre}^s(in_s))$,
2. $(IO, v(IO)) \succ^{wrl}(inout_s, v_{pre}^s(inout_s))$,
3. $(IO, v'(IO)) \succ^{wrl}(inout_s, v_{post}^s(inout_s))$,
4. $(OU, v'(OU)) \succ^{wrl}(out_s, v_{post}^s(out_s))$,
5. $\forall_{o \in (O \setminus IO)} \forall_{a \in attr(o)} v(o, a) = v'(o, a)$.

Intuitively, (1) the *world before* contains a sub-world built over IN, which is compatible with a sub-world of some input world of the service type s, built over the objects from in_s. (2) The *world before* contains a sub-world built over IO, which is compatible with a sub-world of the input world of the service type s, built over the objects from $inout_s$. (3) After the transformation the state of objects from IO is consistent with $post_s$. (4) The objects produced during the transformation (OU) are in a state consistent with $post_s$. (5) The objects from IN and the objects not involved in the transformation do not change their states.

In the standard way we extend a world transformation to a sequence of world transformations seq. We say that a world w_0 *is transformed by the sequence seq into a world* w_n, denoted by $w_0 \overset{seq}{\rightsquigarrow} w_n$, iff there exists a sequence of worlds $\rho = (w_0, w_1, \ldots, w_n)$ such that $\forall_{1 \le i \le n} \ w_{i-1} \overset{s_i, ctx^{s_i}_{O_i}}{\rightarrow} w_i = (O_i, v_i)$ for some v_i. Then, the sequence $seq = (s_1, \ldots, s_n)$ is called a *transformation sequence* and ρ is called a *world sequence*.

Having the transformation sequences defined, we introduce the concept of *user query solutions* or simply *solutions*, in order to define a plan.

Definition 7. *Let* seq *be a transformation sequence,* $q = (W^q_{init}, W^q_{exp})$ *be a user query. We say that* seq *is a solution of q, if for* $w \in W^q_{init}$ *and some world* w' *such that* $w \overset{seq}{\rightsquigarrow} w'$, *we have* $w' \succ^{swrl} w^q_{exp}$, *for some* $w^q_{exp} \in W^q_{exp}$. *The world sequence corresponding to* seq *is called a* world solution. *The set of all the (world) solutions of the user query q is denoted by* $QS(q)$ *(*$WS(q)$, resp.*).*

Intuitively, by a solution of q we mean any transformation sequence transforming some initial world of q to a world sub-compatible to some expected world of q.

Plans. Based on the definition of a solution to the user query q, we can now define the concept of an (abstract) plan, by which we mean a non-empty set of solutions of q. Given a user query solution $seq = (s_1, \ldots, s_n)$ and a service type s. Let $\#_s(seq) = |\{i \mid s_i = s \land 1 \le i \le n\}|$, i.e., $\#_s(seq)$ is the number of the ocurrences of s in seq.

We define a plan as an equivalence class of the solutions, which do not differ in the service types used. The idea is that we do not want to distinguish between solutions composed of the same service types, which differ only in the ordering of their occurrences or in their contexts. So we group them into the same class. There are clearly two motivations behind that. First, the user is typically not interested in obtaining many very similar solutions. Second, from the efficiency point of view, the number of equivalence classes can be exponentially smaller than the number of the solutions.

Thus, two user query solutions seq and seq' are equivalent if they consist of the same number of the same service types, regardless of their contexts, i.e., formally, $\#_s(seq) = \#_s(seq')$, for each service type s.

Definition 8. *Let* seq $\in QS(q)$ *be a solution of some user query q. An abstract plan is a set of all the solutions equivalent to* seq, *denoted by* $[seq]_\sim$.

It is important to notice that all the solutions within an abstract plan are built over the same *multiset* of service types, so a plan is denoted using a multiset notation, e.g., the plan $[2S + 4T + 3R]$ consists of 2 services S, 4 services T, and 3 services R.

Example 5. Consider our working example and the query of Example 3. The shortest plans are $[St + Sg]$ and $[St + Sg + T]$. The former satisfies the user query only if the *Selling* service is located in a close proximity of the user's address.

Assume that during the next planning steps (i.e., the offer collecting and the concrete planning) those plans turn out to have no realization acceptable by the user. Perhaps, there are no blue arbours in nearby shops or they are too expensive. Then, the alternative plan is to buy and transport an arbour in any colour, as well as some blue paint, and then use the *Painting* service: $[2St + 2Sg + 2T + P]$, where one triple of services (St, Sg, T) provides the arbour, and the other a blue paint.

However, it could be the case that, e.g., the transport price of such a big object like an arbour exceeds the budget. If so, the possible solution is to buy boards, nails, and paint, transport them to the destination address, then to assembly the components with an appropriate building service, and paint, finally. This scenario is covered, for example, by the following plan: $[3St + 3Sg + 3T + Wb + P]$, where the triples of services (St, Sg, T) provide and transport boards, nails, and the paint.

Although, there are over eight hundred abstract plans of length from 2 to 11 satisfying the above user query, including these with multiple transportations of the arbour, or painting it several times. In order to restrict the plans to more specific ones, the user can refine the query demanding of specific types of services to be present in the plan using stamps. Thus, for example, by adding the following set of stamps to *out*: $\{Stamp\ t_1, Stamp\ t_2, Stamp\ t_3\}$ and extending *post* by: $\bigwedge_{i=1..3}(t_i.serviceClass\ instanceOf\ Transport)$, the number of possible abstract plans (of length from 2 to 11) can be reduced below two hundred. Then, if instead of buying a final product the user wants to buy and transport the components, in order to build and paint the arbour, he can add two more stamps and conditions to the query. That is, by adding to *out* the set $\{Stamp\ b, Stamp\ p\}$, and by extending *post* by the expression $(\wedge\ b.serviceClass\ instanceOf\ Building\ \wedge\ p.serviceClass\ instanceOf\ Painting)$, one can reduce the number of resulting plans to 2 only: $[3St + 3Sg + 3T + Wb + P]$ and $[3St + 3Sg + 3T + Wbx + P]$.

However, even 2 abstract plans only can be realized in a number of different ways, due to possible many transformation contexts, and the number of different partial orders represented by a single abstract plan. If the user wants to further reduce the number of possible plan realizations by interfering with an order of services, he should specify some temporal restrictions, considered in the next section.

3.3   Parametric User Queries

If there is no plan for a given user query, then the user may want to modify the query specification $spec_q = (in_q, inout_q, out_q, pre_q, post_q)$, by extending the sets in_q and $inout_q$ by some extra objects. Since, the user can hardly predict which objects are necessary for a plan to exist, we allow him to use object variables to this aim, and shift the task of valuating these variables to the planner, so to find required objects.

Formally, let OV be a finite set of *object variables*. By a parametric query specification we mean $spec_q^p = ((in_q, OV_1), (inout_q, OV_2), out_q, pre_q, post_q)$, where $OV_1, OV_2 \subseteq OV$. This parametric specification defines the set of (standard) user query specifications, where each object variable is replaced with some object. Formally, let $v : OV \longrightarrow \mathbb{O}$ be an object valuation function and OVF be the set of all the object valuation functions. The set of standard user query specifications is defined as $\{(in_q \cup v(OV_1), inout_q \cup v(OV_2), out_q, pre_q, post_q) \mid v \in OVF\}$. If there is a plan for the user query corresponding to some user query specification defined by $spec_q^p$, then the planner returns a valuation of each object variable in OV_1 and OV_2.

Example 6. Consider the plans discussed in the last two paragraphs of Example 5. If the maximal length of a plan is restricted to, e.g., 9, then no solutions exist, unless an object variable is added to the $inout_q$ set. In this case, an SMT-solver assigns an object variable a type and such a valuation of the attributes, that it becomes one of the objects necessary to realise the plan. According to the running example, this object would be an instance of the class *Nails*, *Boards*, or *Paint*.   □

In order to give the user a possibility to specify not only the initial and expected states of a solution, we extend the user query with a $PLTL_{-X}^\alpha$ formula φ specifying temporal aspects of world transformations in a solution. Then, the temporal solutions are these solutions for which the world sequences satisfy φ. This way we can can give tighter constraints and reduce the number of possible plans. Formal definitions are introduced in the next section.

4   Parametric Temporal Abstract Planning

In this section we extend the user query by a $PLTL_{-X}^\alpha$ parametric temporal formula and a solution to a temporal solution by requiring the formula to be satisfied. The choice of linear time temporal logic is quite natural since our user query solutions are defined as sequences of worlds. In this version of the logic we do not define the operator X. However, if the user wants to introduce the order on two consequtive service types, then he can use formulas involving level constraints. On the other hand our language and the temporal planning method can be easily extended with the operator X.

We start with defining the set of propositional variables, the level constraints, and then the syntax and the semantics of $PLTL_{-X}^\alpha$.

4.1   Propositional Variables

Let $o \in \mathbb{O}$ be an object and $a \in attr(o)$ its attribute. The set of propositional variables (propositions) $PV = \{\mathbf{pEx}(o), \mathbf{pSet}(o.a), \mathbf{pNull}(o.a) \mid o \in \mathbb{O}, a \in attr(o)\}$. Intuitively, $\mathbf{pEx}(o)$ holds in each world where the object o exists, $\mathbf{pSet}(o.a)$ holds in each world, where the object o exists and the attribute a

is set, and **pNull**($o.a$) holds in each world, where the object o exists and the attribute a is null.

In addition to PV we use also the set of *level constraints* **LC** over the stamps $\mathbb{ST}$ defined by the following grammar:

$$\mathbf{lc} ::= \mathbf{lexp} \sim \mathbf{lexp}$$
$$\mathbf{lexp} ::= c \mid s.level \mid \mathbf{lexp} \oplus \mathbf{lexp} \tag{1}$$

where $s \in \mathbb{ST}$, $c \in \mathbb{Z}$, $\oplus \in \{+, -, \cdot, /, \%\}$, $\sim \in \{\leq, <, =, >, \geq\}$, and $/, \%$ stand for integer division and modulus, respectively.

Intuitively, $s.level < c$ holds in each world, where the stamp s exists and the value of its level is smaller than c.

4.2   Syntax of $PLTL^{\alpha}_{-X}$

Let PV be the set of propositional variables and Var be the set of the integer variables. The $PLTL^{\alpha}_{-X}$ formulae are defined by the following grammar:

$$\varphi ::= p \mid \neg p \mid \mathbf{lc} \mid \neg\mathbf{lc} \mid \varphi \wedge \varphi \mid \varphi \vee \varphi \mid \varphi U_{<\alpha}\varphi \mid \varphi R_{<\alpha}\varphi.$$

where $p \in PV$, $\mathbf{lc} \in \mathbf{LC}$, $\alpha \in \mathbb{N} \cup \text{Var}$.

Observe that we assume that the $PLTL^{\alpha}_{-X}$ formulae are given in the *negation normal form* (NNF), in which the negation can be only applied to the propositional variables and the level constraints. The parametric modalities $U_{<\alpha}$ and $R_{<\alpha}$ are named as usual α-restricted *until* and *release*, respectively. Intuitively, $\varphi U_{<\alpha}\psi$ means that eventually, but in less than α steps, ψ holds and always earlier φ holds. The formula $\varphi R_{<\alpha}\psi$ expresses that either for the next $\alpha - 1$ states ψ holds or in less than α steps, φ holds and always earlier ψ holds.

The derived basic temporal modalities are defined as follows: $F_{<\alpha}\varphi \overset{def}{=} trueU_{<\alpha}\varphi$ and $G_{<\alpha}\varphi \overset{def}{=} falseR_{<\alpha}\varphi$.

4.3   Semantics of $PLTL^{\alpha}_{-X}$

We start with defining models over the world solutions, which are finite sequences of worlds.

Definition 9. *A* model *is a pair* $M = (\rho, V_\rho)$, *where* $\rho = (w_0, w_1, \ldots, w_n)$ *is a world solution with* $w_i = (O_i, v_i)$ *for* $0 \leq i \leq n$, *and* $V_\rho : \bigcup_{i=0}^{n}\{w_i\} \times \mathbb{ST} \longrightarrow \mathbb{N} \cup \{\infty\}$ *is the function over the worlds of* ρ *valuating the expressions of the form stamp.level, defined as follows:*

- $V_\rho(w_i, s.level) = \infty$ *if* $s \notin O_i$,
- $V_\rho(w_i, s.level) = 0$ *if* $s \in O_0$,
- $V_\rho(w_i, s.level) = j$ *if* $s \in O_j$ *and* $s \notin O_{j-1}$, *for some* $1 \leq j \leq i$.

The intuition behind the definition of V_ρ is as follows. If a stamp s is not an element of a world w, then the value of $s.level$ in w does not exist, and this is denoted by ∞. If a stamp s is an element of the world w_0, then the value of $s.level$ is 0 in all the worlds. If w_j is the world, where s appears for the first time, then the value of $s.level$ is equal to j in w_j as well as in all further worlds.

Before defining the semantics of $PLTL^\alpha_{-X}$ we extend the stamp.level valuation function V_ρ from $\mathbb{ST}$ to the level expressions as follows:

- $V_\rho(w_i, c) = c$,
- $V_\rho(w_i, \mathbf{lexp} \oplus \mathbf{lexp'}) = V_\rho(w_i, \mathbf{lexp}) \oplus V_\rho(w_i, \mathbf{lexp'})$ if $V_\rho(w_i, \mathbf{lexp}) \neq \infty \neq V_\rho(w_i, \mathbf{lexp'})$,
- $V_\rho(w_i, \mathbf{lexp} \oplus \mathbf{lexp'}) = \infty$ if $V_\rho(w_i, \mathbf{lexp}) = \infty$ or $V_\rho(w_i, \mathbf{lexp'}) = \infty$,
  Thus, strict evaluation.

Let $v : \mathrm{Var} \to \mathbb{N}$ be a valuation of Var. It is convenient to overload v by assuming that $v(k) = k$, for $k \in \mathbb{N}$. We say that a $PLTL^\alpha_{-X}$ formula φ is true in $M = (\rho, V_\rho)$ under the valuation v (in symbols $M \models_v \varphi$) iff $w_0 \models_v \varphi$, where for $0 \leq m \leq n$ we have,

- $w_m \models_v \mathbf{pEx}(o)$ iff $o \in O_m$,
- $w_m \models_v \mathbf{pSet}(o.a)$ iff $o \in O_m$ and $v_m(o, a) = true$,
- $w_m \models_v \mathbf{pNull}(o.a)$ iff $o \in O_m$ and $v_m(o, a) = false$,
- $w_m \models_v \neg p$ iff $w_m \not\models p$, for $p \in PV$,
- $w_m \models_v (\mathbf{lexp} \sim \mathbf{lexp'})$ iff $V_\rho(w_m, \mathbf{lexp}) \sim V_\rho(w_m, \mathbf{lexp'})$ and $V_\rho(w_m, \mathbf{lexp}) \neq \infty \neq V_\rho(w_m, \mathbf{lexp'})$,
- $w_m \models_v \neg lc$ iff $w_m \not\models_v lc$, for $lc \in \mathbf{LC}$,
- $w_m \models_v \varphi \wedge \psi$ iff $w_m \models_v \varphi$ and $w_m \models \psi$,
- $w_m \models_v \varphi \vee \psi$ iff $w_m \models_v \varphi$ or $w_m \models_v \psi$,
- $w_m \models_v \varphi U_{<\alpha} \psi$ iff $(\exists_{min(m+v(\alpha)-1, n) \geq l \geq m})(w_l \models_v \psi$ and $(\forall_{m \leq j < l})w_j \models_v \varphi)$,
- $w_m \models_v \varphi R_{<\alpha} \psi$ iff $(\forall_{min(m+v(\alpha)-1, n) \geq l \geq m}) w_l \models_v \psi)$ or $(\exists_{min(m+v(\alpha)-1, n) \geq l \geq m})(w_l \models_v \varphi$ and $(\forall_{m \leq j \leq l})w_j \models_v \psi)$.

The semantics of the propositions follows their definitions, for the level constraints the semantics is based on the valuation function V_ρ, whereas for the temporal operators the semantics is quite standard. Note that we interpret our language over finite sequences as the solutions we are dealing with are finite.

Let $spec_q = (in_q, inout_q, out_q, pre_q, post_q)$ be the user query specification of a query q (as defined in the former section). Now, by a *(parametric) temporal query* we mean a query q extended with a $PLTL^\alpha_{-X}$ formula φ such that φ is defined over propositions and stamps that refer to objects from the set $\mathbb{O}_q = in_q \cup inout_q \cup out_q$. Clearly, we have $\mathbb{O}_q \subseteq \mathbb{O}$.

If the parametric temporal query does not use integer variables, then the *temporal solutions* are these solutions for which the world sequences satisfy φ and a *temporal plan* is an equivalence class of the temporal solutions, defined over the same multiset of services.

However, if the parametric temporal query contains integer variables, then in addition to the temporal solutions we get also functions v for which these temporal solutions exist.

Example 7. We continue our working example in order to show examples of temporal queries and parametric temporal queries. Assume that the user wants to ensure that all the transports are executed before the building starts, he can express it as a formula:

$$\varphi_1 = \mathrm{F}\big((b.level > t_1.level) \wedge (b.level > t_2.level) \wedge (b.level > t_3.level)\big)$$

Moreover, if the intention of the user is to proceed with some service directly after another one, for example, to start building just after the third transport, one can express such a constraint as:

$$\varphi_2 = \mathrm{F}(b.level = t_3.level + 1)$$

Moreover, using a temporal query the user can prevent some services from occurring in the plan. For example, using the following formula:

$$\varphi_3 = \neg\mathbf{pEx}(a) \ \mathrm{U} \ \mathbf{pNull}(a.colour),$$

which means that just after the arbour has been produced, its colour is not set, the user excludes the $WoodBuildingLux$ service (which builds and paints the arbour).

The other possibility of extending the user query by a temporal component includes using the k-restricted versions of modal operators. For example, consider the following formula:

$$\varphi_4 = \mathrm{F}_{<10}(\mathbf{pEx}(t_1) \wedge \mathbf{pEx}(t_2) \wedge \mathbf{pEx}(t_3)),$$

which states that three transportations should be executed in the first nine steps of the plan.

If we replace 10 with a variable α, then we get the following parametric formula:

$$\varphi_5 = \mathrm{F}_{<\alpha}(\mathbf{pEx}(t_1) \wedge \mathbf{pEx}(t_2) \wedge \mathbf{pEx}(t_3)),$$

which could be used for asking for the minimal value of α such that three transportations are executed in the first α-steps of the plan.

Another example involving a parametric temporal extension of PlanICS is shown in the following formula:

$$\varphi_6 = \mathrm{F}_{<\alpha}(\mathbf{pEx}(t_1) \wedge \mathbf{pEx}(t_2) \wedge \mathbf{pEx}(t_3) \wedge \mathrm{F}_{<\beta}(\mathbf{pEx}(a))),$$

which could be used to find the earliest position in a plan, where all the three transportations were executed and then the arbour was built. Note that this time we ask for the minimal sum of the values of the parameters α and β. $\qquad\square$

5   Implementation and Experimental Results

In this section we briefly introduce the architecture of PlanICS- our web service composition toolset, in order to embed the implementation details in a broader context. Next, we sketch the implementation (of selected formulas) and then evaluate its efficiency using several scalable benchmarks.

5.1   Implementation

The PlanICS architecture is presented in Fig. 3. As mentioned in Sect. 1, this paper deals with the abstract planning phase of the web service composition problem. So far, we have implemented three abstract planners: the first one based on SMT [17], the second one based on Genetic Algorithms (GA) [25], and the third one based on hybrid algorithms combining SMT with GA [19]. We work also on a translation of the abstract planning to a task for tools dealing with Petri nets, like LoLA [20].

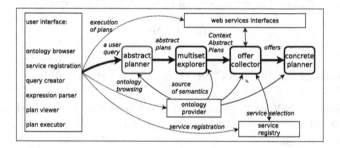

Fig. 3. PlanICS architecture

The current version of the tool contains the SMT-based planner that has been modified in order to support temporal and parametric extensions. In general, our SMT-based planning method consists in encoding the abstract planning problem by a formula which is satisfiable iff there is an abstract solution. This formula encodes the user query and all possible world transformations of a given length. In order to deal with temporal extensions we consider the conjunction of the formula encoding the abstract planning problem with the formula encoding a (parametric) temporal formula. In what follows we recall several encoding details of the non-temporal planning from [18].

The implementation of the propositions and the level constraints exploits our symbolic representation of world sequences. The objects and the worlds are represented by sets of *variables*, which are first allocated in the memory of an SMT-solver, and then used to build formulas mentioned in Sect. 4. The representation of an object is called a *symbolic object*. It consists of an integer variable representing the type of an object, called a *type variable*, and a number of Boolean variables to represent the object attributes, called the *attribute variables*. In order to represent all types and identifiers as numbers, we introduce a function $num : \mathbb{A} \cup \mathbb{P} \cup \mathbb{S} \cup \mathbb{O} \longmapsto \mathbb{N}$, which with every attribute, object type, service type, and object assigns a natural number.

A *symbolic world* consists of a number of symbolic objects. Each symbolic world is indexed by a natural number from 0 to n. Formally, the i-th symbolic object from the j-th symbolic world is a tuple: $\mathbf{o}_{i,j} = (\mathbf{t}_{i,j}, \mathbf{a}_{i,0,j}, ..., \mathbf{a}_{i,max_{at}-1,j})$, where $\mathbf{t}_{i,j}$ is the type variable, $\mathbf{a}_{i,x,j}$ is the attribute variable for $0 \leq x < max_{at}$, where max_{at} is the maximal number of the attribute variables needed to represent the object.

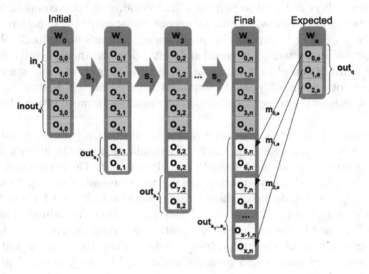

Fig. 4. Symbolic worlds of a transformation sequence

Note that actually a symbolic world represents *a set of worlds*, and only a *valuation* of its variables makes it a single world. The j-th symbolic world is denoted by $\mathbf{w}_j$, while the number of the symbolic objects in $\mathbf{w}_j$ - by $|\mathbf{w}_j|$. Note that the set of the initial worlds of the query q (W_{init}^q) is represented by a symbolic world $\mathbf{w}_0$. Figure 4 shows subsequent symbolic worlds of a transformation sequence.

One of the important features of our encoding is that for a given index of a symbolic object i we are able to determine the step of a solution, in which the object was produced. This is done by the function $lev_q : \mathbb{N} \mapsto \mathbb{N}$, such that for a given query q:

$$lev_q(i) = \begin{cases} 0 \text{ for } i < |\mathbf{w}_0| \\ \lfloor \frac{(i-|\mathbf{w}_0|)}{max_{out}} \rfloor + 1 \text{ for } i \geq |\mathbf{w}_0| \end{cases} \tag{2}$$

where max_{out} is the maximal number of the objects produced by a single service.

Another important feature of our encoding is that the objects of out_q need to be identified among the objects of the symbolic world $\mathbf{w}_n$ (of indices greater than $|\mathbf{w}_0|$). In other words, we do not know in advance which steps of the solution produce the objects in request and we do know their indexes. Thus, we have to encode all the possible mappings. To this aim, we allocate a new symbolic world $\mathbf{w}_e$ (with $e = n + 1$), containing all the objects from out_q (see Fig. 4. Note that the world $\mathbf{w}_e$ is not a part of a world solution, but it provides a set of additional, helper variables. Finally, we need a mapping between the objects from a final world $\mathbf{w}_n$ produced during the subsequent transformations and the objects from $\mathbf{w}_e$. To this aim we allocate p additional *mapping variables* in the symbolic world $\mathbf{w}_e$, where $p = |out_q|$. These variables, denoted by $\mathbf{m}_{0,e}, \ldots, \mathbf{m}_{p-1,e}$, are intended to store the indices of the objects from a final world, which are compatible with the objects encoded over $\mathbf{w}_e$. Thus, we encode the state of the expected worlds of the query q (W_{exp}^q), imposed by $post_q$, using two sets of symbolic objects. The objects of $in_q \cup inout_q$ are encoded directly over the (final) symbolic world $\mathbf{w}_n$. The state of the objects from out_q are encoded over $\mathbf{w}_e$, and since their indices are not known, all possible mappings between objects from $\mathbf{w}_e$ and $\mathbf{w}_n$ are considered, by encoding a disjunction of equalities between objects from $\mathbf{w}_e$ and $\mathbf{w}_n$.

Summarizing, if ont is a PlanICS ontology and q is a (non-temporal) user query, then by $[\psi_{ont}^q]_n$ we denote the SMT formula encoding the query q and all the transformation sequences of length n built over ont. The correctness of the encoding $[\psi_{ont}^q]_n$ and many encoding details were presented in [18]. Thus, the formula $[\psi_{ont}^q]_n$ is satisfiable iff there exists a world solution sol for q of length n built over ont. The world solution sol is extracted from the valuation of SMT variables returned by the solver. This valuation is further referred to as V_{SMT}.

The translation of the propositions defined over the objects and their attributes of a user query q in a symbolic world $\mathbf{w}_m$ ($0 \leq m \leq n$) is as follows:

$$[\mathbf{pEx}(o)]^m = \begin{cases} true, & \text{for } o \in in_q \cup inout_q, \\ false, & \text{for } o \in out_q, m = 0, \\ lev_q(\mathbf{m}_{num(o),e}) \leq m, & \text{for } o \in out_q, m > 0. \end{cases} \tag{3}$$

That is, the objects from the initial world exist in all the subsequent worlds, the objects from the out set do not exist in the world $\mathbf{w}_0$, and they appear in some subsequent world. Then, since the index of the object o is stored as the value of corresponding mapping variable $\mathbf{m}_{num(o),e}$, we can determine if it exists in the world $\mathbf{w}_m$ using the lev_q function.

The proposition $\mathbf{pSet}(o.a)$ is encoded over the symbolic world $\mathbf{w}_m$ as:

$$[\mathbf{pSet}(o.a)]^m = [\mathbf{pEx}(o)]^m \wedge \begin{cases} \mathbf{a}_{j,x,m}, & \text{for } o \in in_q \cup out_q, \\ \bigvee_{i=|\mathbf{w}_0|}^{|\mathbf{w}_m|-1}(\mathbf{m}_{j,e} = i \wedge \mathbf{a}_{i,x,m}), & \text{for } o \in out_q \end{cases} \tag{4}$$

where $j = num(o)$ and $x = num(a)$.

It follows from our symbolic representation that the indices of objects from an initial world are known, and we can get the value of the appropriate attribute variable directly. However, in the case of objects from out_q we have to consider all possible mappings between objects from $\mathbf{w}_e$ and $\mathbf{w}_m$. Note that the encoding of the proposition $\mathbf{pNull}(o.a)$ over the symbolic world $\mathbf{w}_m$ (i.e., $[\mathbf{pNull}(o.a)]^m$) is very similar. The only change is the negation of $\mathbf{a}_{i,x,m}$ in the above formula.

In order to encode the level constraints, we introduce a set of the special *level variables*. That is, for every stamp s used in some level constraint we introduce to the world $\mathbf{w}_e$ an additional integer variable $\mathbf{l}_{i,e}$, where $i = num(s)$ is intended to store the level value of the stamp s. The level value is assigned to $\mathbf{l}_{i,e}$ using the following formula:

$$[bind(i)] := (\mathbf{l}_{i,e} = lev_q(\mathbf{m}_{i,e})) \tag{5}$$

for $i = num(s)$, where q is a user query. Then, for every stamp s used in a level constraint we add the corresponding $[bind(num(s))]$ formula as an SMT assertion. Thus, the encoding of the level constraints is as follows:

$$[\mathbf{lexp}] = \begin{cases} c \text{ for } \mathbf{lexp} = c \\ \mathbf{l}_{i,e}, \text{ for } \mathbf{lexp} = s.level, i = num(s) \\ [\mathbf{lexp}'] \oplus [\mathbf{lexp}''] \text{ for } \mathbf{lexp} = \mathbf{lexp}' \oplus \mathbf{lexp}'' \end{cases} \tag{6}$$

The encoding of arithmetic operators is straightforward, since they are supported by theories built in SMT-solvers, like, e.g., Linear Integer Arithmetic or Bitvector theory. In what follows, $[\varphi]_n^m$ denotes the translation of the formula φ at the state w_m of the world sequence of length $n + 1$.

Definition 10 (Translation of the $PLTL_{-X}^\alpha$ formulae to SMT). *Let φ be a $PLTL_{-X}^\alpha$ formula, $(\mathbf{w}_0, \ldots, \mathbf{w}_n)$ be a sequence of symbolic worlds, and $0 \le m \le n$, $k \in \mathbb{N}$, and $\alpha \in \text{Var}$.*

- $[p]_n^m := [p]^m$, *for* $p \in PV$,
- $[\neg p]_n^m := \neg [p]^m$, *for* $p \in PV$,
- $[\mathbf{lexp}' \sim \mathbf{lexp}'']_n^m := [\mathbf{lexp}'] \sim [\mathbf{lexp}''] \bigwedge_{s \in st(\mathbf{lexp}')} [\mathbf{pEx}(s)]^m$
  $\bigwedge_{s \in st(\mathbf{lexp}'')} [\mathbf{pEx}(s)]^m$,
- $[\neg \mathbf{lc}]_n^m := \neg [\mathbf{lc}]_n^m$, *for* $\mathbf{lc} \in \mathbf{LC}$,
- $[\varphi \wedge \psi]_n^m := [\varphi]_n^m \wedge [\psi]_n^m$,
- $[\varphi \vee \psi]_n^m := [\varphi]_n^m \vee [\psi]_n^m$,
- $[\varphi U_{<\alpha} \psi]_n^m := \bigvee_{v_\alpha=1}^n (\alpha = v_\alpha \wedge (\bigvee_{i=m}^{min(m+v_\alpha-1,n)} ([\psi]_n^i \wedge \bigwedge_{j=m}^{i-1} [\varphi]_n^j)))$,
- $[\varphi U_{<k} \psi]_n^m := \bigvee_{i=m}^{min(m+k-1,n)} ([\psi]_n^i \wedge \bigwedge_{j=m}^{i-1} [\varphi]_n^j)$,
- $[\varphi R_{<\alpha} \psi]_n^m := \bigvee_{v_\alpha=1}^n (\alpha = v_\alpha \wedge (\bigwedge_{i=m}^{min(m+v_\alpha-1,n)} [\psi]_n^i \vee$
  $\bigvee_{i=m}^{min(m+v_\alpha-1,n)} ([\varphi]_n^i \wedge \bigwedge_{j=m}^{i} [\psi]_n^j)))$,
- $[\varphi R_{<k} \psi]_n^m := \bigwedge_{i=m}^{min(m+k-1,n)} [\psi]_n^i \vee \bigvee_{i=m}^{min(m+k-1,n)} ([\varphi]_n^i \wedge \bigwedge_{j=m}^{i} [\psi]_n^j)$,

where $st(\mathbf{lexp})$ returns the set of the stamps over which the expression $\mathbf{lexp}$ is built.

Let $[\psi^q_{ont}]_n$ be the SMT formula encoding a user query q and all the transformation sequences of length n built over the PlanICS ontology ont (see page 18).

Theorem 1 (Correctness of the $PLTL^{\alpha}_{-X}$ Encoding). *The encoding of a parametric temporal query φ is correct, i.e., $[\psi^q_{ont}]_n \wedge [\varphi]^0_n$ is satisfiable iff there exist a valuation v and a world solution sol of q of length n built over ont, such that $M \models_v \varphi$, where M is the model over sol.*   □

Proof. We show that $[\psi^q_{ont}]_n \wedge [\varphi]^0_n \iff \exists M \wedge \exists v : \ M \models_v \varphi$. Notice that v is only necessary for interpreting the formulas including parametric modalities, therefore we ignore v in the first part of the proof, where we deal with the non-parametric formulas. The proof is by induction on the length of φ.

From [18] we have that $[\psi^q_{ont}]_n$ is satisfiable iff there exists a world solution *sol* of q. Thus, we assume that we have the model M over *sol* obtained from an SMT valuation V_{SMT}, such that $V_{SMT}([\psi^q_{ont}]_n) = true$. Next, we focus only on the part of the proof involving the encoding of a (parametric) temporal formula. To fix the notations, let $M = (sol, V_{sol})$, where $sol = (w_0, w_1, \dots, w_n)$ for some $w_m = (O_m, v_m)$ with $0 \leq m \leq n$. Morevoer, let PV_q be the set of the propositional variables referring to objects from $\mathbb{O}_q$ only, and $\mathbb{ST}_q = \mathbb{ST} \cap \mathbb{O}_q$. We start with showing that the encoding of the propositional variables is correct, i.e., $V_{SMT}([p]^m) = true \iff w_m \models_v p$, where $p \in PV_q$.

Propositional Variables. ($\Longrightarrow$) First, we show that $V_{SMT}([p]^m) = true \Longrightarrow w_m \models_v p$, where $p \in PV_q$. Let $p = \mathbf{pEx}(o)$ be a proposition expressing the existence of an object $o \in \mathbb{O}_q$ in a world. According to our semantics, $w_m \models_v \mathbf{pEx}(o)$ iff $o \in O_m$. So, we have to show that $V_{SMT}([\mathbf{pEx}(o)]^m) = true \Longrightarrow o \in O_m$. We consider the three cases displayed in Formula 3. The first and the second one follow easily from the PlanICS semantics, while the third case exploits features of the symbolic representation of the transformation sequences.

Case 1. We have $[\mathbf{pEx}(o)]^m = true$, for $o \in in_q \cup inout_q$. So, $V_{SMT}([\mathbf{pEx}(o)]^m) = true$, for any valuation V_{SMT} and m. This case deals with the situations when the object o is given by the user query q as a member of the initial worlds, i.e., o belongs to in_q or $inout_q$. Thus, $o \in O_0$. It follows from the PlanICS semantics that the objects cannot be removed from the worlds. Therefore, since the object $o \in O_0$, we have $o \in O_m$ for each $m > 0$.

The second and the third case concern the objects specified as members of the set out_q.

Case 2. We have $[\mathbf{pEx}(o)]^m = false$, for $o \in out_q$ and $m = 0$. So, $V_{SMT}([\mathbf{pEx}(o)]^m) = false$, for any valuation V_{SMT}. Thus, the implication $V_{SMT}([\mathbf{pEx}(o)]^m) = true \Longrightarrow o \in O_0$ holds trivially.

Case 3. We have $[\mathbf{pEx}(o)]^m = (lev_q(\mathbf{m}_{num(o),e}) \leq m)$, for $o \in out_q$ and $m > 0$.

So, this case concerns presence of the object o from out_q in all worlds of *sol* except for the initial one. In all these situations the valuation of $[\mathbf{pEx}(o)]^m$ depends on the function lev_q, which, for the given index of o, assigns the index of the state of *sol* where this object appears for the first time.

The encoding of the lev_q function (see Formula 2) corresponds faithfully to its definition. For a given query q the size of the initial world ($|w_0|$) is known, and it is equal to the number of objects belonging to $in_q \cup inout_q$. The parameter max_{out} is also known, since it depends on the ontology ont, and corresponds to the maximal number of the objects produced by a single service. The encoding of the subsequent worlds of the world solution consists in adding max_{out} new symbolic objects in each step. If a service produces less than max_{out} objects, then some of them remain empty by setting the types of the unused objects to $null$. Thus, the indexes of the objects produced in the i-th step of the plan belong to the interval $\big[(|w_0| + (i-1) \cdot max_{out}), (|w_0| + i \cdot max_{out} - 1)\big]$, where $i > 0$. Moreover, the object indexes remain constant, that is, the same object has the same index in the next and all the subsequent worlds up to the final one. Therefore, knowing the object index, one can find out in which step of the plan it was created. Thus, assuming $V_{SMT}([\mathbf{pEx}(o)]^m) = true$, the index of o equals to $V_{SMT}(\mathbf{m}_{num(o),e})$. Moreover, we have $lev_q(V_{SMT}(\mathbf{m}_{num(o),e})) \leq m$, so the object o has been produced in the m-th step or earlier. Consequently, we have $o \in O_m$, for $o \in out_q$ and $0 < m \leq n$, which ends the proof of this case.

Assume now that $p = \mathbf{pSet}(o.a)$ for $o \in \mathbb{O}_q$ and $a \in attr(o)$. From the semantics: $w_m \models_v \mathbf{pSet}(o.a)$ iff $o \in O_m$ and $v_m(o, a) = true$. So, we have to show that $V_{SMT}([\mathbf{pSet}(o.a)]^m) = true \implies (o \in O_m \wedge (v_m(o, a) = true)$. By definition, we have $[\mathbf{pSet}(o.a)]^m = [\mathbf{pEx}(o)]^m \wedge [attr(o, a)]^m$, where $[attr(o, a)]^m$ is the two-case formula encoding the abstract value of the attribute $o.a$ (see Formula 4). Because we proved that $V_{SMT}([\mathbf{pEx}(o)]^m) = true \implies o \in O_m$, it is sufficient to show that $V_{SMT}([attr(o, a)]^m) = true \implies (v_m(o, a) = true)$.

Consider the first case where $o \in in_q \cup inout_q$. Then, the index of o is known, the encoding is straightforward, and the proof is trivial.

In the second case, where $o \in out_q$, we have to consider all possible mappings between the objects produced in all the steps of the solution and the objects from the expected world. This is encoded as the disjunction of the expressions $(\mathbf{m}_{j,e} = i \wedge \mathbf{a}_{i,x,m})$, where i ranges over the indexes of all objects produced until the m-th step of the plan. Because of $V_{SMT}([\mathbf{pEx}(o)]^m) = true$ and $o \in out_q$, there exists an appropriate mapping, and $V_{SMT}(\mathbf{m}_{j,e}) = i$ for some $i \geq 0$. If so, $V_{SMT}([\mathbf{pSet}(o.a)]^m)$ is equal to the valuation of the attribute variable $V_{SMT}(\mathbf{a}_{i,x,m})$, where $i = V_{SMT}(\mathbf{m}_{j,e})$. Therefore, we have $v_m(o, a) = true$.

For $p = \mathbf{pNull}(o.a)$ the proof is similar.

Propositional Variables. ($\Longleftarrow$) Now, we show that $(w_m \models_v p) \implies \exists V_{SMT}:$ $V_{SMT}([p]^m) = true$, where $p \in PV_q$. Let $p = \mathbf{pEx}(o)$.

Case 1: $o \in in_q \cup inout_q$.

If $w_m \models_v \mathbf{pEx}(o)$, then the proof is trivial, because $[\mathbf{pEx}(o)]^m = true$ for any valuation.

Case 2: $m = 0, o \in out_q$.

In this case the proof is also trivial, because $w_0 \not\models_v \mathbf{pEx}(o)$ for $o \in out_q$, since the initial world does not contain objects from out_q.

Case 3: $0 < m \leq n, o \in out_q$.

This case concerns presence of the objects from out_q in other states than the initial one. Assume that $w_m \models_v \mathbf{pEx}(o)$. Thus, according to the PlanICS semantics, o has been produced in some k-th step of the solution, where $0 < k \leq m$. Following the encoding (given in [18], and recalled briefly in this section), every object is represented by a symbolic object. If so, o is represented by some i-th symbolic object, where $lev_q(i) = k$. Therefore, $V_{SMT}([\mathbf{pEx}(o)]^m) = true$ for any SMT valuation V_{SMT} such that $V_{SMT}(\mathbf{m}_{num(o),e}) = i$.

Consider now $p = \mathbf{pSet}(o.a)$ for $o \in \mathbb{O}_q$ and $a \in attr(o)$. We have to show that $o \in O_m \wedge (v_m(o,a) = true) \implies \exists V_{SMT} : V_{SMT}([\mathbf{pSet}(o.a)]^m) = true$, that is $o \in O_m \wedge (v_m(o,a) = true) \implies \exists V_{SMT} : V_{SMT}([\mathbf{pEx}(o)]^m \wedge [attr(o,a)]^m) = true$. We have to consider two cases, but in both of them the value of $[attr(o,a)]^m$ depends on the boolean variable $\mathbf{a}_{j,x,m}$, where j is the index of o (see Formula 4). In the first case, where $o \in in_q \cup inout_q$, we have already showed that $[\mathbf{pEx}(o)]^m$ is true for any valuation. Since j is known and constant, $V_{SMT}([attr(o,a)]^m) = true$ for any SMT valuation V_{SMT} which assigns $true$ to $\mathbf{a}_{j,x,m}$. In the second case, where $o \in out_q$, if we have $o \in O_m$, then the index of o equals $V_{SMT}(\mathbf{m}_{num(o),e})$ (see the previous paragraph). Thus, $V_{SMT}([\mathbf{pSet}(o.a)]^m) = true$ for a valuation V_{SMT} satisfying $V_{SMT}(\mathbf{m}_{num(o),e}) = j$ and $V_{SMT}(\mathbf{a}_{j,x,m}) = true$.

For $p = \mathbf{pNull}(o.a)$ the proof is similar.

Let us now proceed with the level constraints. The encoding of the level expressions is quite straightforward, but it relies on the encoding of the propositions $\mathbf{pEx}(o.a)$, which has been already proved correct.

Level Constraints LC Over the Stamps $\mathbb{ST}_q$. According to the semantics, we have: $w_m \models_v (\mathbf{lexp} \sim \mathbf{lexp'})$ iff $V_{sol}(w_m, \mathbf{lexp}) \sim V_{sol}(w_m, \mathbf{lexp'})$ and $V_{sol}(w_m, \mathbf{lexp}) \neq \infty \neq V_{sol}(w_m, \mathbf{lexp'})$. Thus, the level constraints are predicates over level expressions.

$(\implies)$

We have to show that $V_{SMT}([\mathbf{lexp} \sim \mathbf{lexp'}]_n^m) = true \implies V_{sol}(w_m, \mathbf{lexp}) \sim V_{sol}(w_m, \mathbf{lexp'}) \wedge V_{sol}(w_m, \mathbf{lexp}) \neq \infty \neq V_{sol}(w_m, \mathbf{lexp'})$.

In the simplest case a level expression is an (integer) constant, so its encoding is straightforward and the proof is trivial.

Another possible form of a level expression is a *stamp.level* expression, for $stamp \in st(\mathbf{lexp}) \cup st(\mathbf{lexp'}) \subseteq \mathbb{ST}_q$. In this case, the encoding involves an integer variable $\mathbf{l}_{i,e}$ bounded with the value equal to the step of the solution in which a given stamp has been created, computed by lev_q function (see Formulae 5, 6). Once created, the stamp has a constant value of its *level* attribute in all subsequent worlds. Therefore, it is sufficient to introduce only one variable $\mathbf{l}_{i,e}$, where $i = num(stamp)$, for each stamp used to construct the level constraints. Thus, if $V_{SMT}([\mathbf{lexp} \sim \mathbf{lexp'}]_n^m) = true$, then also $V_{SMT}([\mathbf{pEx}(stamp)]^m) = true$. Then, the valuation V_{SMT} assigns an integer value to each variable $\mathbf{l}_{i,e}$, which gives us $V_{SMT}(\mathbf{l}_{i,e}) = V_{sol}(w_m, stamp.level) = c_i$, where $c_i \in \mathbb{N}$, and $c_i \leq m$.

Therefore, for such V_{SMT} the level expression $\mathbf{lexp} \sim \mathbf{lexp'}$ becomes a simple predicate over integers, and we have also $V_{sol}(w_m, \mathbf{lexp}) \neq \infty \neq V_{sol}(w_m, \mathbf{lexp'})$ satisfied.

$(\Longleftarrow)$

If we assume that $V_{sol}(w_m, \textbf{lexp}) \sim V_{sol}(w_m, \textbf{lexp}') \wedge V_{sol}(w_m, \textbf{lexp}) \neq \infty \neq V_{sol}(w_m, \textbf{lexp}')$, then from Definition 9 we have that $V_{sol}(w_m, \textbf{lexp}) = c$, where $c \in \mathbb{N}$. Consequently, if $\textbf{lexp}$ is of form $stamp.level$, we have that $stamp \in O_m$, thus also $w_m \models_v \textbf{pEx}(stamp)$. Since we have already showed that $w_m \models_v \textbf{pEx}(stamp)$ iff $[\textbf{pEx}(stamp)]^m$ is satisfiable, and the encoding of $[\textbf{lexp}] \sim [\textbf{lexp}']$ is straightforward, then there is such an SMT valuation V_{SMT} that $V_{SMT}([\textbf{lexp} \sim \textbf{lexp}']_n^m) = true$.

Arithmetic Over Level Expressions. We use arithmetic operators built in SMT-solver theories (like, e.g. Linear Integer Arithmetic), and we just rewrite the composite level expressions to the syntax accepted by the SMT-solver making use of simple level expressions, discussed above. We do the same while building the level constraint predicates. To this aim we exploit the standard comparison operators also built in SMT-solver theories.

Thus, since the encoding of simple level expressions has been already proved correct, we have also the correctness of the encoding of arithmetic over level expressions.

Next, having the propositions and level constraints proved to be correctly encoded, we discuss the encoding of the $PLTL_{-X}^{\alpha}$ modalities.

Formulae of $PLTL_{-X}^{\alpha}$. The cases of the negations of the propositions and of the level constraints are straightforward. Similarly, the conjunction and disjunction of $PLTL_{-X}^{\alpha}$ formulae are just the conjunction and disjunction, respectively, of their encoded counterparts.

However, a bit more attention is needed in the case of the $U_{<k}$ and $R_{<k}$ modalities. One can see that the universal and existential quantifiers used in the semantics correspond directly to the disjunctions and the conjunctions, respectively, in the encoding. The encoding of their parametric extensions $U_{<\alpha}$ and $R_{<\alpha}$ result in adding one more level of the disjunction, which is used to deal with all the possible values of the parameter α in order to find a value for $v(\alpha)$. $\square$

5.2 Finding Minimal Values of the Parameters in a Parametric Query

The above translation allows for returning some values of the parameters α in a formula φ, provided there is a model in which φ holds. However, while formulating a parametric query the user may be interested in receiving the minimal values of the parameters. Unfortunately, if the parametric query contains two or more different parameters, then each of them cannot be minimized separately. To see this, consider the formula $F_{<\alpha_1}(\phi_1 \wedge F_{<\alpha_2}(\phi_2))$ and a model M of more than 2 worlds such that ϕ_1 holds in all the worlds while ϕ_2 holds in the last two worlds only. Then, the minimal value for α_1 and α_2 is 1, since $M \models F_{<1}(\phi_1 \wedge F_{<n}(\phi_2))$ and $M \models F_{<n}(\phi_1 \wedge F_{<1}(\phi_2))$ but, clearly, $M \not\models F_{<1}(\phi_1 \wedge F_{<1}(\phi_2))$.

Therefore, we offer a method for returning values of the parameters such that their sum is minimal. In the above example this would mean that $\alpha_1 + \alpha_2$ is minimized. It is easy to see that the minimal value for $\alpha_1 + \alpha_2$ is n.

Assume that φ contains K parameters: $\alpha_1, \ldots, \alpha_K$. In order to find the minimal value of the sum of these parameters, the encoding is extended iteratively by the following formula:

- $\alpha_1 + \cdots + \alpha_K < FW$,

where FW is the value of $\alpha_1 + \cdots + \alpha_K$ returned in the former call to the SMT-solver. The SMT-solver is run as long as the encoding is satisfiable. When it becomes unsatisfiable, then the value of FW becomes the minimal value of $\alpha_1 + \cdots + \alpha_K$. Note that for the first time the solver is run without this additional constraint, but if the instance is satisfiable, then the initial value of FW is read from the returned model.

5.3   Parametric User Queries

Parametric user queries are another parametric extension of PlanICS. They allow to introduce object variables to the sets *in* and *inout* of a query. The implementation of object variables is quite simple. While encoding the initial states of the object variables we just omit the clauses setting their types. Then, the SMT-solver is free to set such types and (abstract) attribute valuations of them, which can play a useful role in finding a plan. Obviously, the attributes of the object variables cannot be used in *pre* and *post* of the query as one does not know in advance what types are set for them by the solver.

5.4   Experimental Results

In order to evaluate the efficiency of our approach we performed several experiments using standard PC with 2 GHz CPU and 8 GB RAM, and Z3 [7] version 4.3 as an SMT-solver. The results are summarized in Table 1. Using our Ontology Generator (OG) we generated 15 ontologies, each of them consisting of 150 object types and from 64 to 256 service types (the column named **n** of Table 1). For each ontology a query has been generated in such a way that it is satisfied by exactly 10 plans of length from 6 to 18 (the parameter **k**). The queries demand at least two objects to be produced, and impose restrictions on (abstract) values of some of their attributes. A generated query example is as follows: $in = \{Rjlbp\ rjlbp1\}$, $inout = \{Bozwd\ bozwd1\}$, $out = \{Opufo\ opufo1, Ehxjb\ ehxjb2\}$, $pre = isSet(bozwd1.avg) \wedge isSet(rjlbp1.ppw)$, $post = isSet(opufo1.epv) \wedge isNull(bozwd1.dyn) \wedge isSet(ehxjb2.zdv) \wedge isNull(ehxjb2.rxz) \wedge isSet(bozwd1.fsl)$.

First, we ran our planner for each ontology and each query instance without a temporal query (column ψ_1), in order to collect statistics concerning the time needed to find the first plan ($\mathbf{P}_1$), all 10 plans ($\mathbf{P}_{10}$), as well as the total time (column **T**) and the memory consumed (**M**) by the SMT-solver in order to find all the plans and checking that no more plans of length k exist. We imposed the time limit of $1000\,$s for the SMT-solver. Each time-out is reported in the table by TO. It is easy to observe that during these experiments as many as 9 instances ran out of time.

Table 1. Experimental results

n	k	$\psi_1 = true$				ψ_3				ψ_4				ψ_5			
		P_1	P_{10}	T	M	P_1	P_{10}	T	M	P_1	P_{10}	T	M	P_1	P_{10}	T	M
		[s]	[s]	[s]	[MB]	[s]	[s]	[s]	[MB]	[s]	[s]	[s]	[MB]	[s]	[s]	[s]	[MB]
	6	7.23	9.73	19.5	19.7	2.34	7.17	8.49	14.1	2.19	4.14	4.21	11.6	3.51	4.7	6.48	10.8
	9	23.5	53.1	177	173	20.1	34.5	47.0	38.3	15.9	18.8	19.2	22.3	14.8	40.1	44.7	36.0
64	12	165	479	TO	-	101	216	354	117	60.5	85.2	87.6	59.3	95.1	122	127	68.1
	15	305	TO	TO	-	329	762	TO	-	119	216	241	105	195	345	351	129
	18	TO	TO	TO	-	TO	TO	TO	-	461	TO	TO	-	604	TO	TO	-
	6	16.0	28.1	55.7	42.7	9.75	19.8	22.6	21.3	7.68	10.1	10.2	16.8	10.9	12.7	15.1	16.3
	9	53.1	94.9	270	250	55.5	98.2	104	44.7	21.8	34.0	34.2	31.0	38.1	54.7	62.6	44.9
128	12	136	677	TO	-	134	428	474	96.3	76.8	99.9	102	61.9	93.1	114	117	47.9
	15	TO	TO	TO	-	456	780	TO	-	116	199	202	86	183	258	263	79.8
	18	TO	TO	TO	-	TO	TO	TO	-	381	556	573	143	383	708	714	130
	6	16.1	30.6	41.5	35.4	20.3	25.7	30.0	26.1	11.1	13.9	14.1	21.7	14.9	18.3	21	21.6
	9	84.4	137	374	466	63.7	99.3	131	53.4	26.2	38.4	39.1	37.5	88.5	119	156	74.9
256	12	267	TO	TO	-	242	584	692	112	114	181	183	80.6	250	315	321	73.4
	15	685	TO	TO	-	562	TO	TO	-	198	304	309	86.8	472	582	592	120
	18	TO	TO	TO	-	TO	TO	TO	-	574	919	937	137	942	TO	TO	-

The next experiments involve temporal queries using level constraints. To this aim we extended the *out* set of the generated queries by the appropriate stamp set. Moreover, the *post* formulas of the queries have been also extended with the expression: $\bigwedge_{i=1}^{\lfloor \frac{k}{2} \rfloor}(s_i.serviceClass\ instanceOf\ C_i)$, where $s_i \in \mathbb{ST}$, while $C_i \in \mathbb{S}$ are service types occurring in the solutions generated by OG.

Our second group of experiments involved the temporal formula ψ_2:

$$\psi_2 = \mathrm{F}(\bigwedge_{i=1}^{\lfloor \frac{k}{2} \rfloor -1} s_i.level < s_{i+1}.level),$$

which expresses that about a half of the stamps being effects of the solution execution, should be produced in the given order. We do not present detailed results, because they are in general comparable with the performance in the former experiments. Similarly, there are 9 time-outs, but the time and the memory consumption varies a bit - for some cases the results are slightly better, while for others are a little worse.

In the third group of the experiments we imposed stronger restrictions on the possible service orders of the solutions using the following formula:

$$\psi_3 = F(\bigwedge_{i=1}^{\lfloor \frac{k}{2} \rfloor} s_i.level < i + 2).$$

This formula still leaves a certain degree of freedom in a service ordering, however its encoding as an SMT-instance is more compact, since the constant values are introduced in place of some level variables. Thus, probably, it is also easier to solve. The results are summarized in the column ψ_3 in Table 1. It is easy to observe that the time and the memory consumption is significantly lower. Moreover, the number of time-outs dropped to 6. Thus, this is an example showing an improvement in the planning efficiency using a temporal query.

Our next experiment involves the formula ψ_4 specifying the strict ordering of several services in a solution using stamp-based level constraints:

$$\psi_4 = F(\bigwedge_{i=1}^{\lfloor \frac{k}{2} \rfloor} s_i.level = i).$$

The analysis of the results (given in the column ψ_4 of Table 1) indicates a dramatic improvement of our planner efficiency, in terms of time and memory consumption by the SMT-solver. Moreover, in this experiments group the planner has been able to terminate its computations in the given time limit for all but one instances.

Finally, we want to confront the planner behaviour with other types of temporal formulae. Using the *Until* modality, we demand that one of the objects from out_q has to be produced no later than in the middle of the solution. Moreover, knowing the structure of the generated queries, we impose that after the object appears one of its attributes should already be set. This is expressed by the following formula:

$$\psi_5 = \neg\mathbf{pEx}(o) \; U_{< \lceil \frac{k}{2} \rceil} \; \mathbf{pSet}(o.a)$$

where $o \in out_q$, $a \in attr(o)$, and the expression $isSet(o.a)$ is not contradictory with $post_q$. The results have been summarised in the column ψ_5 of Table 1. It is easy to observe that also this time the plans have been found faster and using less memory than in the case when no temporal formula is involved.

In order to test the efficiency of finding the minimal values for temporal parameters, we introduce a parameter α into the formula ψ_5 obtaining our next benchmark:

$$\psi_6 = \neg\mathbf{pEx}(o) \; U_{< \alpha} \; \mathbf{pSet}(o.a)$$

The results are displayed in the column ψ_6 of Table 2. The subsequent values (from the left to the right) denote the time needed to find: the first plan (P_1), the minimal value of α for the first plan (m_1), all the ten plans (P_{10}), and the minimal value of α for all the ten plans (m_{10}). Next, we give the minimal value

Table 2. Experimental results involving parametric extensions

		ψ_6							one object variable						two object variables					
n	k	P_1	m_1	P_{10}	m_{10}	α	T	M	m_k	Pl.	P_1	P_{all}	T	M	m_k	Pl.	P_1	P_{all}	T	M
		[s]	[s]	[s]	[s]		[s]	[MB]			[s]	[s]	[s]	[MB]			[s]	[s]	[s]	[MB]
	6	3.30	4.45	10.9	11.9	3	19.2	20	4	2	1.20	1.78	2.35	7.66	4	20	1.48	4.45	5.20	12.4
	9	36.9	40.7	71.7	72.7	4	215	192	5	10	2.98	5.85	8.73	18.0	2	3	0.09	0.10	0.17	4.60
64	12	186	187	580	662	6	TO	-	7	4	20.8	104	148	53.2	3	3	1.12	1.19	1.75	7.35
	15	584	749	TO	TO	8	TO	-	9	14*	75.8	941*	TO	-	3	5	0.50	1.57	2.04	7.69
	18	TO	TO	TO	TO	-	TO	-	10	2*	618	716*	TO	-	3	5	0.54	0.99	2.60	8.78
	6	21.5	21.5	39.8	40.2	3	53.9	31	4	2	6.24	6.43	7.46	11.7	4	20	4.80	10.5	12.8	20.7
	9	74.5	92.3	172	173	4	414	240	5	10	14.0	25.4	29.0	26.1	2	3	0.13	0.27	0.30	5.90
128	12	222	229	756	810	6	TO	-	7	10	14.0	25.4	29.0	26.2	3	4	1.13	1.22	2.13	8.42
	15	695	773	TO	TO	8	TO	-	9	9*	124	910*	TO	-	3	5	0.74	1.75	2.45	8.67
	18	TO	TO	TO	TO	-	TO	-	10	1*	491	491*	TO	-	3	5	1.26	2.32	3.12	9.35
	6	31.3	33.0	54.2	54.3	3	76.0	36	4	2	11.7	11.8	17.6	16.7	4	20	10.1	15.7	21.6	26.8
	9	128	142	212	238	4	686	468	5	10	18.9	40.4	49.4	32.3	2	3	0.23	0.25	0.85	8.22
256	12	412	427	TO	TO	6	TO	-	7	4	102	247	414	52.7	3	4	2.24	3.91	5.63	14.3
	15	TO	TO	TO	TO	-	TO	-	9	4*	292	730*	TO	-	3	5	1.21	3.71	5.50	13.1
	18	TO	TO	TO	TO	-	TO	-	10	1*	676	676*	TO	-	3	5	1.53	2.43	5.04	14.9

of the α parameter $(alpha)$, the total time (T), and the memory (M) consumed by the SMT-solver.

It is not surprising that the results are worst than in the case of testing ψ_5. First of all, in order to find the minimal value of α an SMT-solver has to be run several times. Secondly, while searching for the minimal value of α, all the potential values of the α parameter have to be encoded. Thus, the formula ψ_6 is not such a strong restriction for the solver as ψ_5, and therefore it does not reduce the search space so significantly.

Concerning parametric user queries, we conducted two series of experiments also summarized in Table 2. The first series introduced a single object variable, while the second one added two object variables to the *inout* set of the user query. Thus, the SMT-solver assigned them such object valuations that allowed to obtain significantly shorter plans. The subsequent columns of Table 2 display the length of the shortest plans found (m_k), the number of the different plans of length m_k $(Pl.)$, the amount of time consumed by the SMT solver in order to find the first plan (P_1) and all the (shortest) plans (P_{all}), and finally, the total time and the memory consumed by the SMT-solver. The stars denote that neither the number of the plans nor the computation time are exhaustive, i.e., the cases when the planning process has been aborted by the timeout. It is obvious that a reduction of the plan lengths results in a better planning efficiency. Thus, adding object variables to the user query could be a way to decompose a single hard planning problem (i.e., demanding a calculation of a long abstract plan), into several easier tasks. In this case, the subsequent planning steps should be focused on producing the objects found as valuations of the object variables.

6 Conclusions

In this paper we have applied the logic $PLTL^{\alpha}_{-X}$ to specifying parametric temporal queries for temporal planning within the tool PlanICS. This is a quite natural extension of our web service composition system, in which the user gets an opportunity to specify more requirements on plans. These requirements are not declarative any more.

The overall conclusion is that the more restrictive temporal query, the more efficient planning, given the same ontology. Assuming that the more restrictive temporal queries, the longer formulas expressing them, the above conclusion shows a difference with model checking, where the complexity depends exponentially on the length of an LTL formula.

Our parametric temporal planner is the first step towards giving the user even more freedom by defining a so-called fully parametric approach. We aim at having a planner which in addition to the current capabilities, could also suggest what extensions to the ontology or services should be made in order to get realizable plans. The idea is to get a feedback from the planner about missing objects or missing services modifying object attributes in case there are no realizable plans. This is going to be a subject of our next paper.

References

1. Ambroszkiewicz, S.: Entish: A language for describing data processing in open distributed systems. Fundam. Inform. **60**(1–4), 41–66 (2004)
2. Bell, M.: Introduction to Service-Oriented Modeling. Wiley, Hoboken (2008)
3. Bentahar, J., Yahyaoui, H., Kova, M., Maamar, Z.: Symbolic model checking composite web services using operational and control behaviors. Expert Syst. Appl. **40**(2), 508–522 (2013)
4. Bentakouk, L., Poizat, P., Zaïdi, F.: Checking the behavioral conformance of web services with symbolic testing and an SMT solver. In: Wolff, B., Gogolla, M. (eds.) TAP 2011. LNCS, vol. 6706, pp. 33–50. Springer, Heidelberg (2011)
5. Bersani, M.M., Cavallaro, L., Frigeri, A., Pradella, M., Rossi, M.: SMT-based verification of LTL specification with integer constraints and its application to runtime checking of service substitutability. In: SEFM, pp. 244–254 (2010)
6. Chifu, V., Salomie, I., St. Chifu, E.: Fluent calculus-based web service composition - from OWL-S to fluent calculus. In: Proceedings of the 4th International Conference on Intelligent Computer Communication and Processing, pp. 161–168 (2008)
7. de Moura, L., Bjørner, N.S.: Z3: an efficient SMT solver. In: Ramakrishnan, C.R., Rehof, J. (eds.) TACAS 2008. LNCS, vol. 4963, pp. 337–340. Springer, Heidelberg (2008)
8. Doliwa, D., Horzelski, W., Jarocki, M., Niewiadomski, A., Penczek, W., Półrola, A., Skaruz, J.: HarmonICS - a tool for composing medical services. In: ZEUS, pp. 25–33 (2012)
9. Doliwa, D., Horzelski, W., Jarocki, M., Niewiadomski, A., Penczek, W., Półrola, A., Szreter, M., Zbrzezny, A.: PlanICS - a web service compositon toolset. Fundam. Inform. **112**(1), 47–71 (2011)

10. Elwakil, M., Yang, Z., Wang, L., Chen, Q.: Message race detection for web services by an SMT-based analysis. In: Zhang, D., Sadjadi, S.M., Xie, B., Branke, J., Zhou, X. (eds.) ATC 2010. LNCS, vol. 6407, pp. 182–194. Springer, Heidelberg (2010)
11. Gehlot, V., Edupuganti, K.: Use of colored Petri nets to model, analyze, and evaluate service composition and orchestration. In: System Sciences, HICSS 2009, pp. 1–8, January 2009
12. Gerevini, A.E., Haslum, P., Long, D., Saetti, A., Dimopoulos, Y.: Deterministic planning in the fifth international planning competition: PDDL3 and experimental evaluation of the planners. Artif. Intel. **173**(5–6), 619–668 (2009). Advances in Automated Plan Generation
13. Hao, S., Zhang, L.: Dynamic web services composition based on linear temporal logic. In: 2010 International Conference of Information Science and Management Engineering (ISME), vol. 1, pp. 362–365, August 2010
14. Li, Z., O'Brien, L., Keung, J., Xu, X.: Effort-oriented classification matrix of web service composition. In Proceedings of the Fifth International Conference on Internet and Web Applications and Services, pp. 357–362 (2010)
15. Monakova, G., Kopp, O., Leymann, F., Moser, S., Schäfers, K.: Verifying business rules using an SMT solver for BPEL processes. In: BPSC, pp. 81–94 (2009)
16. Nam, W., Kil, H., Lee, D.: Type-aware web service composition using boolean satisfiability solver. In: Proceedings of the CEC 2008 and EEE 2008, pp. 331–334 (2008)
17. Niewiadomski, A., Penczek, W.: Towards SMT-based abstract planning in PlanICS ontology. In: Proceedings of KEOD 2013 - International Conference on Knowledge Engineering and Ontology Development, pp. 123–131, September 2013
18. Niewiadomski, A., Penczek, W., Półrola, A.: Abstract planning in PlanICS ontology. An SMT-based approach. Technical report 1027, ICS PAS (2012)
19. Niewiadomski, A., Penczek, W., Skaruz, J.: Hybrid approach to abstract planning of web services. In: Service Computation 2015: The Seventh International Conferences on Advanced Service Computing, pp. 35–40 (2015)
20. Niewiadomski, A., Wolf, K.: LoLA as abstract planning engine of PlanICS. In: Proceedings of International Workshop on Petri Nets and Software Engineering, pp. 349–350 (2014)
21. OWL 2 web ontology language document overview (2009). http://www.w3.org/TR/owl2-overwiew/
22. Rao, J., Küngas, P., Matskin, M.: Composition of semantic web services using linear logic theorem proving. Inf. Syst. **31**(4), 340–360 (2006)
23. Rao, J., Su, X.: A survey of automated web service composition methods. In: Cardoso, J., Sheth, A.P. (eds.) SWSWPC 2004. LNCS, vol. 3387, pp. 43–54. Springer, Heidelberg (2005)
24. Skaruz, J., Niewiadomski, A., Penczek, W.: Automated abstract planning with use of genetic algorithms. In: GECCO (Companion), pp. 129–130 (2013)
25. Skaruz, J., Niewiadomski, A., Penczek, W.: Evolutionary algorithms for abstract planning. In: Wyrzykowski, R., Dongarra, J., Karczewski, K., Waśniewski, J. (eds.) PPAM 2013, Part I. LNCS, vol. 8384, pp. 392–401. Springer, Heidelberg (2014)
26. Traverso, P., Pistore, M.: Automated composition of semantic web services into executable processes. In: van Harmelen, F., Plexousakis, D., McIlraith, S.A. (eds.) ISWC 2004. LNCS, vol. 3298, pp. 380–394. Springer, Heidelberg (2004)

Kleene Theorems for Synchronous Products with Matching

Ramchandra Phawade[(✉)] and Kamal Lodaya

The Institute of Mathematical Sciences, CIT Campus, Chennai 600113, India
ramchandra@imsc.res.in

Abstract. In earlier work [LMP11], we showed that a graph-theoretic condition called "structural cyclicity" enables us to extract syntax from a conflict-equivalent product system of automata. In this paper we have a "pairing" property in our syntax which allows us to connect to a broader class of synchronous product systems [Arn94] with a "matching" property, where the conflict-equivalence is not statically fixed. These systems have been related to labelled free choice nets.

1 Introduction

The Kleene and Büchi theorems link finite automata, a model of sequential computation, to regular expressions and monadic second-order logic, both syntactic entities. More than a decade ago [LW00], these ideas were extended to branching automata, a model of bounded fork-join concurrency. It was also observed [LRR03] that on the models side we can have a labelled Petri net representation called SR-systems. The lack of an explicit synchronization mechanism is manifest, and a first work was to solve the Kleene problem for 1-bounded T-systems, going through an intermediate automaton mechanism called T-products. It was observed in this work [LMP11] that the proofs extend to a class of FC-products (conflict-equivalent products of automata, these will be defined below, they are known to be weaker than 1-bounded nets [Zie87, Muk11]), restricted to a graph-theoretic property called "structural cyclicity" which translates in the syntax to disallowing nested Kleene star operators as in regular expressions. But we did not rely on a renaming operator in the syntax, as has been the case with earlier efforts on 1-bounded nets [Gra81, GR92].

In the present paper[1], we make an effort to match the live and 1-bounded free choice nets, a very well-studied subclass [Hac72] with more efficient analysis and algorithms [DE95], but with labelled transitions. It has been claimed that free choice nets can be useful in business process modelling [SH96], but our motivation is more conceptual than dictated by business concerns. We have not studied the logical (Büchi) side of our problem, we note that it has been argued that it suffices to consider free choice nets for the decidability of the monadic second-order theory [TY14].

---

[1] A preliminary version of this paper appeared at the 8th PNSE workshop in Tunis [PL14]. We thank the organizers for all the help provided for the presentation.

© Springer-Verlag Berlin Heidelberg 2015
M. Koutny et al. (Eds.): ToPNoC X, LNCS 9410, pp. 84–108, 2015.
DOI: 10.1007/978-3-662-48650-4_5

As in our earlier paper [LMP11], we rely on an intermediate formalism of products of automata, without any structural cyclicity property. This time the products are equipped with an "FC-matching" condition derived from Zielonka automata [Zie87] (which can describe 1-bounded nets) and Arnold and Nivat's synchronous products [Arn94], but restricted to stay within the labelled free choice nets. On the syntax side we do not place any restriction on the Kleene stars, thus (unlike in our earlier paper) including all regular expressions. We do have global restrictions in the syntax. A "pairing" condition identifies synchronizations which will take place at run-time.

Our products translate easily into labelled free choice nets. The converse from nets to products shown in [Pha14a] requires a distributed choice property to give an FC-matching product. This is a generalization of the property that in a synchronization cluster of a free choice net all the synchronizations are differently labelled (call this "deterministic synchronization"). In brief we can say the intermediate representation in this paper is related to 1-bounded labelled distributed free choice nets.

The problem of syntactically characterizing a natural subclass of 1-bounded labelled free choice nets, those which can be modelled using deterministic synchronization, is not fully solved. Consider a "distributed counter" product system which we denote by the informal expression $fsync((a^2)^*, (a^3)^*)$, for which no "pairing" in our sense exists. There is an intuitively corresponding free choice net which has deterministic synchronization, by pairing three iterations of the loop on the left with two iterations of the loop on the right. Applying our theorems to such an unfolded net produces a product system with matching and then the expression $fsync((a^6)^*, (a^6)^*)$ with obvious pairing, defining the same language. Thus our syntax is expressive but our pairings are deficient: they have to be relaxed to also incorporate distributed counting of this kind. We conjecture this can be done.

This paper is organized as follows. In the next section, we introduce some properties of regular expression using derivatives. In Sect. 3, we give syntax of connected expressions and define some properties in terms of properties of regular expressions defined earlier, and derivatives of connected expressions. In subsequent section, we formally define the subclass of product systems we work with, and discuss its properties. In Sect. 5, we present main results of this paper: two way conversion between connected expressions and product systems defined earlier. In the next section, we outline how combining the results of this paper with those in [Pha14a] gives Kleene theorems for a subclass of free choice net systems.

2   Regular Expressions, Derivatives and States

Let Σ be a finite alphabet and Σ^* be the set of all words over alphabet Σ, including the empty word ε. A language over an alphabet Σ is a subset $L \subseteq \Sigma^*$. The projection of a word $w \in \Sigma^*$ to a set $\Delta \subseteq \Sigma$, denoted as $w\!\downarrow_\Delta$, is defined by:

$$\varepsilon\!\downarrow_\Delta = \varepsilon \text{ and } (a\sigma)\!\downarrow_\Delta = \begin{cases} a(\sigma\!\downarrow_\Delta) & \text{if } a \in \Delta, \\ \sigma\!\downarrow_\Delta & \text{if } a \notin \Delta. \end{cases}$$

Definition 1. *Let Loc denote the set* $\{1, 2, \ldots, k\}$. *A* **distribution** *of* Σ *over Loc is a tuple of nonempty sets* $(\Sigma_1, \Sigma_2, \ldots, \Sigma_k)$ *with* $\Sigma = \bigcup_{1 \leq i \leq k} \Sigma_i$. *For each action* $a \in \Sigma$, *its* **locations** *are the set* $loc(a) = \{i \mid a \in \Sigma_i\}$. *Actions* $a \in \Sigma$ *such that* $|loc(a)| = 1$ *are called* **local**, *otherwise they are called* **global**.

A regular expression over alphabet Σ_i such that constants 0 and 1 are not in Σ_i is given by:

$$s ::= 0 \mid 1 \mid a \in \Sigma_i \mid s_1 \cdot s_2 \mid s_1 + s_2 \mid s_1^*$$

The languages defined are $Lang(0) = \emptyset$, $Lang(1) = \{\varepsilon\}$ and $Lang(a) = \{a\}$. For regular expressions $s_1 + s_2$, $s_1 \cdot s_2$ and s_1^*, the languages are defined inductively as union, concatenation and Kleene star of the component languages respectively.

As a measure of the size of an expression we will use $wd(s)$ for its alphabetic width—the total number of occurrences of letters of Σ in s. We will use syntactic entities associated with regular expressions which are known since the time of Brzozowski [Brz64], Mirkin [Mir66] and Antimirov [Ant96]. For each regular expression s over Σ_i, its initial actions form the set $Init(s) = \{a \mid \exists v \in \Sigma_i^* \text{ and } av \in Lang(s)\}$ which can be defined syntactically. (For a set of expressions D, $Init(D)$ collects the initial actions of members of D.) Similarly, we can syntactically check whether the empty word $\varepsilon \in Lang(s)$. Below we inductively define Antimirov derivatives [Ant96].

Definition 2. *Given regular expression s and symbol a, the set of partial derivatives of s wrt a, written $Der_a(s)$ are defined as follows.*

$$Der_a(0) = \emptyset$$
$$Der_a(1) = \emptyset$$
$$Der_a(b) = \{1\} \text{ if } b = a, \quad \emptyset \text{ otherwise}$$
$$Der_a(s_1 + s_2) = Der_a(s_1) \cup Der_a(s_2)$$
$$Der_a(s_1^*) = Der_a(s_1) \cdot s_1^*$$
$$Der_a(s_1 \cdot s_2) = \begin{cases} Der_a(s_1) \cdot s_2 \cup Der_a(s_2) & \text{if } \varepsilon \in Lang(s_1) \\ Der_a(s_1) \cdot s_2 & \text{otherwise} \end{cases}$$

$$Inductively \, Der_{aw}(s) = Der_w(Der_a(s)).$$

The set of all partial derivatives $Der(s) = \bigcup_{w \in \Sigma_i^*} Der_w(s)$, *where* $Der_\varepsilon(s) = \{s\}$. *A derivative d of s with global $a \in Init(d)$ is called an a-**site** of s. Expression s is said to have* **equal choice** *if for all a, all its a-sites have the same set of initial actions.*

The Antimirov derivatives are $Der_a(ab + ac) = \{b, c\}$ and $Der_a(a(b + c)) = \{b + c\}$, whereas the Brzozowski a-derivative [Brz64] (which is used for constructing deterministic automata, but which we do not use in this paper) for both expressions would be $\{b + c\}$.

Example 1. Consider a regular expression $r = a(b + c)d(b + c)^*$. The set of its derivatives is $Der(r) = \{r, (b + c)d(b + c)^*, d(b + c)^*, (b + c)^*\}$. For derivative

$(b + c)d(b + c)^*$ of r, its set of initial actions is $Init((b + c)d(b + c)^*) = \{b, c\}$. Therefore, derivative $(b+c)d(b+c)^*$ is a b-site and a c-site but it is not an a-site. For b-site $(b + c)^*$ of r, its set of initial actions is $Init((b + c)^*) = \{b, c\}$. Sets of initial actions for all b-sites of r are equal, and this is true for all c-sites and a-sites. Therefore, expression r has equal choice property.

Now consider another regular expression $r' = a(b + c)d(b + e)^*$. The set of its b-sites is $\{(b + c)d(b + e)^*, (b + e)^*\}$. For b-site $(b + c)d(b + e)^*$ of r', its set of initial actions is $Init((b + c)d(b + e)^*) = \{b, c\}$. For b-site $(b + e)^*$ of r', its set of initial actions is $Init((b + e)^*) = \{b, e\}$. Since sets of initial actions are not equal for these two b-sites, expression r' does not have equal choice property.

We wish to club together derivatives which may correspond to the same state in a finite automaton. For this we use partitions of the set of derivatives of expression s. If for every global action a, the partition of a-sites of s consists of a single block, then we say s has **unique sites**. We syntactically determine a partition of the a-sites of s. This kind of idea appears in the work of Lombardy and Sakarovitch [LS05, LS10]. We go on to define a semantic property, which first appeared in the conference version of this paper [PL14]. Later in this paper we will consider coarsenings of this partition.

Definition 3. *We define an equivalence relation $\sim_a$ between a-sites, given by $s_1 \sim_a s_1 + s_2$, $s_2 \sim_a s_1 + s_2$, $s_1 \cdot s_2 \sim_a s_2$ in case $\varepsilon \in Lang(s_1)$, $s_1 \cdot s_1^* \sim_a s_1^*$ and one of the sides is not an a-derivative of the other, and also $s_1^* \cdot s_1^* \sim_a s_1^*$. The partition defined on the a-sites of s is denoted $Part_a(s)$.*

Example 2. For expression aa the partition of a-sites is: $Part_a(aa) = \{\{aa\}, \{a\}\}$. For expression b it is $Part_a(b) = \emptyset$. The a-sites of expression $aa + b$ can be partitioned by this representation: $Part_a(aa + b) = \{\{aa + b\}, \{a\}\}$. The a-sites of expression $(aa + b)^*aa$ are: $Part_a((aa + b)^*aa) = \{\{(aa + b)^*aa\}, \{a(aa + b)^*aa\}, \{a\}\}$. Finally, the a-sites of $a^*(aa + b)^*aa$ are described by the partition: $Part_a(a^*(aa + b)^*aa) = \{\{a^*(aa + b)^*aa\}, \{a(aa + b)^*aa\}, \{(aa + b)^*aa\}, \{a\}\}$. Here we do not have $a^*(aa + b)^*aa \sim_a (aa + b)^*aa$ even though $\varepsilon \in Lang(a^*)$ because the right hand expression is an a-derivative of the left hand one.

Definition 4. *Given a set D of a-sites of regular expression s, an action a and a language L, we define the relativized language $L^D = \{xay \mid xay \in L, \exists d \in Der_x(s) \cap D, \exists d' \in Der_{ay}(d)$ with $\varepsilon \in Lang(d')\}$, and the prefixes $Pref_a^D(L) = \{x \mid xay \in L^D\}$, and the suffixes $Suf_a^D(L) = \{y \mid xay \in L^D\}$. We say that the derivatives in set D a-**bifurcate** L if $L^D = Pref_a^D(L)$ a $Suf_a^D(L)$. (The left to right direction always holds.)*

Example 3. Let $L = Lang((aa)^*) = \{(aa)^k \mid k \geq 0\}$. Then $L^{(aa)^*} = L^{a(aa)^*} = \{(aa)^k \mid k \geq 1\}$. Hence we have, $Pref_a^{a(aa)^*}(L) = \{a^{2k} \mid k \geq 0\} = Suf_a^{(aa)^*}(L)$ and $Suf_a^{a(aa)^*}(L) = \{a^{2k+1} \mid k \geq 0\} = Pref_a^{(aa)^*}(L)$. The derivatives $(aa)^*$ and $a(aa)^*$ both a-bifurcate L, but the set $D = \{(aa)^*, a(aa)^*\}$ does not, as $a^2 \in Pref_a^{a(aa)^*}(L)$, and $a^2 \in Suf_a^{(aa)^*}(L)$, but $a^2aa^2 \notin L^D$.

Proposition 1. *Every block D of the partition $Part_a(s)$ a-bifurcates $Lang(s)$.*

Proof. Let $L = Lang(s), x \in Pref_a^D(L), y \in Suf_a^D(L)$. We have to show that $xay \in L$, for which we use induction on s. The base case $s = a$ is easy as there is only one a-derivative. Below we use $D[s/r]$ to mean the derivatives in D where the expression r is replaced by the expression s.

(Case $s = s_1 + s_2$): In the case that $D[s_1/s_1 + s_2]$ was from $Part_a(s_1)$ or $D[s_2/s_1 + s_2]$ was from $Part_a(s_2)$, then from the induction hypothesis D a-bifurcates $Lang(s_1)$ or $Lang(s_2)$ and hence also $Lang(s_1 + s_2)$. The remaining case is where $s \in D$, but since $s_1 + s_2$ cannot be an a-derivative of itself, this requires that either $s_1 \sim_a s$ or $s_2 \sim_a s$ and we can again apply the induction hypothesis.

(Case $s = s_1 \cdot s_2$): If $D = D_1 \cdot s_2 \in Part_a(s_1) \cdot s_2$, then y factorizes as y_1y_2 with $y_2 \in Lang(s_2)$ and we use the induction hypothesis to show xay_1 in $Lang(s_1)$. If $D \in Part_a(s_2)$ then x factorizes as x_1x_2 with $x_1 \in Lang(s_1)$ and we use the induction hypothesis to show x_2ay in $Lang(s_2)$. With $s_1s_2 \in D$ we can have both the conditions

- $x \in Pref_a^{s_1s_2}(L) \setminus Pref_a^{s_1}(L)$, this implies $x \in Lang(s_1)$, and
- $y \in Suf_a^D(L) \cap Suf_a^{s_2}(Lang(s_2))$, this implies $\varepsilon \in Pref_a^{s_2}(Lang(s_2))$.

Induction hypothesis, applied to the block $D[s_2/s_1s_2]$ of $Part_a(s_2)$ (because under these conditions $s_2 \sim_a s_1s_2$), gives ay in $Lang(s_2)$. Since $\varepsilon \in Lang(s_1)$, ay is in $Lang(s_1s_2)$. So $xay \in L^{s_1s_2} \subseteq L^D$.

(Case $s = s_1^*$): If $D = D_1 \cdot s_1^* \in Part_a(s_1) \cdot s_1^*$, then xay factorizes as $x_1x_2ay_1y_2$ with $x_1, y_2 \in Lang(s_1^*), x_2 \in Pref_a^{D_1}(Lang(s_1)), y_1 \in Suf_a^{D_1}(Lang(s_1))$ and we use the induction hypothesis to show x_2ay_1 is in $Lang(s_1)$. The remaining case is where $x \in Lang(s_1^*)$ and $ay \in Lang(s_1^*)$, we deal with this as in the previous case using the conditions $s_1 \cdot s_1^* \sim_a s_1^*$ and $s_1^* \cdot s_1^* \sim s_1^*$. $\qquad\square$

3   Connected Expressions over a Distribution

We have a simple syntax of **connected expressions**. The component expression s_i can be any regular expression (of any star-height), which is different from our earlier paper [LMP11]. A connected expression is given in the form:

$$e ::= \text{fsync}(s_1, s_2, \ldots, s_k), \quad s_i \text{ defined over } \Sigma_i$$

When $e = \text{fsync}(s_1, s_2, \ldots, s_k)$ and $I \subseteq \Sigma$, let the projection $e{\downarrow}I = \Pi_{i \in I}s_i$.

For the connected expression $e = \text{fsync}(s_1, s_2, \ldots, s_k)$, its language is given by

$$Lang(e) = Lang(s_1) \| Lang(s_2) \| \ldots \| Lang(s_k),$$

where the **synchronized shuffle** $L = L_1 \| \ldots \| L_k$ is defined by

$$w \in L \text{ iff } \text{ for all } i \in \{1, \ldots, k\}, w{\downarrow}_{\Sigma_i} \in L_i.$$

The definitions of derivatives can be easily extended to connected expressions. Given $e = \text{fsync}(s_1, s_2, \ldots, s_k)$, its derivatives are defined using the derivatives of the s_i on action a:

$$Der_a(e) = \{\text{fsync}(r_1, r_2, \ldots, r_k) \mid \forall i \in loc(a),\ r_i \in Der_a(s_i);\ \text{otherwise } r_j = s_j\}.$$

We will use the word **derivative** for expressions such as $d = \text{fsync}(r_1, r_2, \ldots, r_k)$ above (essentially tuples of derivatives of regular expressions), and $d[i]$ for r_i. The number of derivatives can be exponential in k. Define $Init(d)$ to be those actions a such that $Der_a(d)$ is nonempty. If $a \in Init(d)$ we call d an a-site. A connected expression has **unique sites** if each of its component regular expressions has the unique sites property. The reachable derivatives are $Der(e) = \{d \mid d \in Der_x(e), x \in \Sigma^*\}$. For example, $\text{fsync}(ab, ba)$ does not have reachable derivatives other than itself.

3.1 Pairings of Connected Expressions

In our syntax, along with connected expressions we are supplied with "pairings" which specify which part of a component in a connected expression will intersect with which part of another component in the expression. This is done using derivatives, more precisely partitions of derivatives, since being in a state of an automaton corresponds to any one of the blocks in the partition. This machinery is to be set up now.

Definition 5. *Let $e = \text{fsync}(s_1, s_2, \ldots, s_k)$ be a connected expression over Σ. For a global action a and given partitions of derivatives of each s_i, **pairing(a)** is a subset of tuples of $\Pi_{i \in loc(a)} Der(s_i)$ which respects the partitions. (For instance, if the partitions are $Part_a(s_i)$ for Σ_i, pairing(a) is a subset of tuples such that the projection of these tuples includes all the blocks of $Part_a(s_i)$, and if a block of $Part_a(s_j), j \in loc(a)$ appears in one tuple of the pairing, it does not appear in another tuple.) We call pairing(a) **equal choice** if for every tuple in the pairing, the blocks of derivatives in the tuple have equal choice.*

*We extend the definition to connected expressions. A derivative fsync $(r_1, \ldots, r_k)$ is in **pairing(a)** if there is a tuple $D \in$ pairing(a) such that $r_i \in D[i]$ for all $i \in loc(a)$. For convenience we may write a derivative as an element of pairing(a). Expression e is said to have **(equal choice) pairing of actions** if for all global actions a, there exists an (equal choice) pairing(a). Expression e is said to be **consistent with a pairing of actions** if every reachable a-site $d \in Der(e)$ is in pairing(a).*

Example 4. Consider a distribution $\Sigma_1 = \Sigma_2 = \{a\}$ and a connected expression $\text{fsync}(aa, a)$ defined over it. The partition for aa over Σ_1 is $Part_a(aa) = \{\{aa\}, \{a\}\}$ and for the expression a over Σ_2 is $Part_a(a) = \{\{a\}\}$. Since two blocks of $Part_a(aa)$ cannot be paired with one block of $Part_a(a)$, expression $\text{fsync}(aa, a)$ does not have a pairing. Since there are two blocks in the partition $Part_a(aa)$, expression aa does not have unique sites property, neither does $\text{fsync}(aa, a)$.

Example 5. Consider a connected expression $e = fsync(aa, bad + caf)$ over the distribution $(\Sigma_1 = \{a\}, \Sigma_2 = \{a, b, c, d, f\})$. For action a, The partition over Σ_1 is $Part_a(aa) = \{\{aa\}, \{a\}\}$ and the partition over Σ_2 is $Part_a(bad + caf) = \{\{ad\}, \{af\}\}$. The a-sites of expression e are $\{fsync(aa, ad), fsync(aa, af)\}$. There are two possible pairings for action a: one is $\{(\{aa\}, \{af\}), (\{a\}, \{ad\})\}$ and another is $\{(\{aa\}, \{ad\}), (\{a\}, \{af\})\}$. The derivative aa on the left appears in the pairing with two different reachable a-sites of the right hand side, which belong to two different blocks of $Part_a(bad + caf)$. Hence e is not consistent with respect to any of the above pairings.

Example 6. Consider the connected expression $fsync(r_1, r_2, r_3)$ with $r_1 = (ac)^*$, $r_2 = (bc)^*$ and $r_3 = (a(b+c))^*$ over the distribution $(\Sigma_1 = \{a, c\}, \Sigma_2 = \{b, c\}, \Sigma_3 = \{a, b, c\})$. Now we have $r_1' = Der_a(r_1) = c(ac)^*$ and $Init(r_1') = \{c\}$. For r_3 we have, $r_3' = Der_a(r_3) = (b+c)(a(b+c))^*$ and $Init(r_3') = \{b, c\}$. Expressions r_1' and r_3' are c-sites of expressions r_1 and r_3 respectively. With sets of derivatives $D_1 = \{r_1'\}$ and $D_3 = \{r_3'\}$ as the only blocks in the respective partitions of c-sites i.e., $Part_c(r_1) = \{D_1\}$ and $Part_c(r_3) = \{D_3\}$. As $Init(D_1) = Init(r_1') = \{c\}$, $Init(D_3) = Init(r_3') = \{b, c\}$ and $pairing(c) = \{(D_1, D_3)\}$, $pairing(c)$ is not equal choice. Therefore, connected expression e does not have equal choice. However one can see that e has unique sites property.

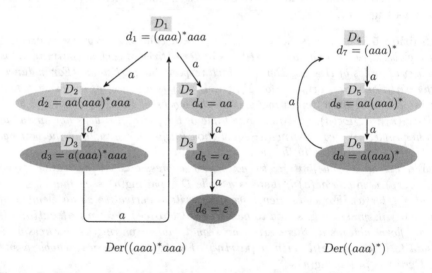

Fig. 1. Derivatives of d_1 and d_7 of expression $e = fsync(d_1, d_7)$ with $pairing(a) = \{(D_1, D_4), (D_2, D_5), (D_3, D_6)\}$.

Example 7. Consider a connected expression $e = fsync((aaa)^*aaa, (aaa)^*)$. The a-derivatives are $Der_a(e) = \{fsync(aa(aaa)^*aaa, aa(aaa)^*), fsync(aa, aa(aaa)^*)\}$. With respect to word aa, $Der_{aa}(e) = \{fsync(a(aaa)^*aaa, a(aaa)^*), fsync(a,$

$a(aaa)^*)$}. With respect to word aaa, $Der_{aaa}(e) = \{fsync((aaa)^*aaa, (aaa)^*),$ $fsync(\varepsilon, (aaa)^*)\}$. The language of connected expression e is $Lang(e) = \{(aaa)^k \mid k \geq 1\}$. See Fig. 1 where derivatives of $d_1 = (aaa)^*aaa$ and $d_7 = (aaa)^*$ are shown. The set of derivatives of $e = fsync(d_1, d_7)$, with respect to all words $w \in \Sigma^*$: $Der(e) = \{(d_1, d_7), (d_2, d_8), (d_4, d_8), (d_3, d_9), (d_5, d_9), (d_6, d_7)\}$ and, its set of a-sites is $\{(d_1, d_7), (d_2, d_8), (d_4, d_8), (d_3, d_9), (d_5, d_9)\}$.

Let D_1, D_2, D_3 be sets of a-sites for expressions d_1 where, $D_1 = \{d_1\}$, $D_2 = \{d_2, d_4\}$, and $D_3 = \{d_3, d_5\}$. And let D_4, D_5, D_6 be sets of a-sites for expressions d_2 where, $D_4 = \{d_7\}$, $D_5 = \{d_8\}$ and $D_6 = \{d_9\}$. For expression d_1, $Part_a(d_1) = \{D_1, D_2, D_3\}$ and for d_2, $Part_a(d_2) = \{D_4, D_5, D_6\}$. For action a, we have a pairing relation $pairing(a) = \{(D_1, D_4), (D_2, D_5), (D_3, D_6)\}$. We can see that expression has equal choice property and it is consistent with pairing of actions.

Proposition 2. *For a connected expression checking existence of a pairing of actions and checking whether it is equal choice can be done in polynomial time, checking consistency with a pairing of actions is in* PSPACE.

Proof. We have to visit each derivative of all the regular expressions to construct the a-partitions for every a. We can record their initial actions. Maximum number of Antimirov derivatives of any regular expression s is at most $wd(s) + 1$ [Ant96]. If the number of blocks in two a-partitions is not the same, there cannot be a $pairing(a)$, otherwise there always exists a pairing(a). For an equal choice pairing, we have to count blocks whose sets of initial actions are the same, this can be done in cubic time. On the other hand, to check consistency with a pairing of actions, we have to visit each reachable derivative, this can be done in PSPACE. $\square$

4 Product Systems over a Distribution

Fix a distribution $(\Sigma_1, \Sigma_2, \ldots, \Sigma_k)$ of Σ. We now define an automaton over some alphabet Σ_i.

Definition 6. *A* **sequential system** *over a set of actions* Σ_i *is a tuple* $A_i = \langle P_i, \rightarrow_i, G_i, p_i^0 \rangle$ *where* P_i *are called* **places**, $G_i \subseteq P_i$ *are final places,* $p_i^0 \in P_i$ *is the initial place, and* $\rightarrow_i \subseteq P_i \times \Sigma_i \times P_i$ *is a set of* **local moves**.

Let $\rightarrow_a^i$ denote the set of all a-labelled moves in the sequential system A_i.

For a local move $t = \langle p, a, p' \rangle$ of $\rightarrow_i$, p is called pre-place and p' is called post-place of t. A run of the sequential system A_i on word w is a sequence $p_0 a_1 p_1 a_2, \ldots, a_n p_n$, from set $(P_i \times \Sigma_i)^* P_i$, such that $p_0 = p_i^0$ and for each $j \in \{1, \ldots, n\}$, $p_{j-1} \xrightarrow{a_j} p_j$. This run is said to be accepting if $p_n \in G_i$. The sequential system A_i accepts word w, if there is at least one accepting run of A_i on w. The language $L = Lang(A_i)$ of sequential system A_i is defined as $L = \{w \in \Sigma_i^* \mid w \text{ is accepted by } A_i\}$.

Given a place p of A_i, we also define relativized languages and we will extend this definition to product systems: $Pref_a^p(L) = \{x \mid xay \in L, p_0 \xrightarrow{x} p \xrightarrow{ay} G_i\}$, similarly $Suf_a^p(L)$, $L^p = \{xay \mid xay \in L, p_0 \xrightarrow{x} p \xrightarrow{ay} G_i\}$. Say the place p a-**bifurcates** L if $L^p = Pref_a^p(L)$ a $Suf_a^p(L)$.

We now define products of automaton.

Definition 7. *Let* $A_i = \langle P_i, \rightarrow_i, G_i, p_i^0 \rangle$ *be a sequential system over alphabet* Σ_i *for* $1 \leq i \leq k$. *A* **product system** A *over the distribution* $\Sigma = (\Sigma_1, \ldots, \Sigma_k)$ *is a tuple* $\langle A_1, \ldots, A_k \rangle$.

Let $\Pi_{i \in Loc} P_i$ be the set of product states of A. We use $R[i]$ for the projection of a product state R in A_i, and $R{\downarrow}I$ for the projection to $I \subseteq Loc$. The relativizations L^R of a language $L \subseteq \Sigma_i^*$ consider projections to place $R[i]$ in A_i.

The initial product state of A is $R^0 = (p_1^0, \ldots, p_k^0)$, while $G = \Pi_{i \in Loc} G_i$ denotes the final states of A.

Let $\Rightarrow_a = \Pi_{i \in loc(a)} \rightarrow_a^i$. The set of global moves of A is $\Rightarrow = \bigcup_{a \in \Sigma} \Rightarrow_a$. Then for a global move

$$g = \langle \langle p_{l_1}, a, p_{l_1}' \rangle, \langle p_{l_2}, a, p_{l_2}' \rangle, \ldots \langle p_{l_m}, a, p_{l_m}' \rangle \rangle \in \Rightarrow_a, \ loc(a) = \{l_1, l_2, \ldots, l_m\},$$

we write $g[i]$ for $\langle p_i, a, p_i' \rangle$, the projection to A_i, $i \in loc(a)$ and $pre(a)$ for the product states where such a move is enabled.

Please note that the set of product states as well as the global moves are not explicitly provided when a product system is given as input to some algorithm.

4.1 Matchings of Product Systems

Analogously to what we did for expressions, we now set up "matching" relations between places in different components of a product system which correspond to pre-places of a global move. ("Separation" below is a stronger property.) Thus matchings restrict the possible synchronizations in a product, an idea developed for transition systems by Arnold and Nivat [Arn94]. That the restriction involves places is the key to translation into clusters of labelled free choice nets, which is outlined in Sect. 6.

Definition 8. *For global* $a \in \Sigma$, **matching(a)** *is a subset of tuples* $\Pi_{i \in loc(a)} P_i$ *such that for all* i *in* $loc(a)$, *projection of these tuples is the set of all pre-places of* a-*moves in* $\rightarrow_i^a$, *and if a place* $p \in P_i$ *appears in one tuple, it does not appear in another tuple. We say a product state* R *is in* **matching(a)** *if its projection* $R{\downarrow}loc(a)$ *is in the matching.*

A product system is said to have **matching of labels** *if for all global* $a \in \Sigma$, *there is a suitable matching(a). A product system* A *is said to have* **separation of labels** *if for all* $i \in Loc$, *and for all global actions* a, *if* $\langle p, a, p' \rangle, \langle q, a, q' \rangle \in \rightarrow_i$ *then* $p = q$.

Example 8. Let $\Sigma = \{a, b\}$ be a distributed alphabet with distribution $(\Sigma_1 = \Sigma_2 = \Sigma)$. Consider the product system $A = (A_1, A_2)$ shown in Fig. 2. For global action a, place p_1 is the only place in A_1 having outgoing a-moves and, place p_3 is the only place in A_2 having outgoing a-moves.

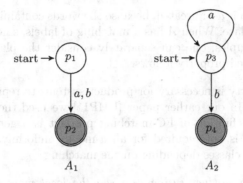

Fig. 2. Product system $A = (A_1, A_2)$ with separation of labels

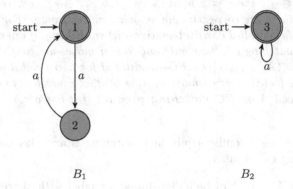

Fig. 3. Product system $B = (B_1, B_2)$ without separation of labels

Similarly these are the only places, in respective sequential systems, which have outgoing local b-moves. Therefore, product system A has separation of labels property.

On the other hand, consider product system $B = (B_1, B_2)$ shown in Fig. 3, and defined over the distributed alphabet $\Sigma' = \{a\}$ having distribution $\Sigma'_1 = \Sigma'_2 = \Sigma'$. Since sequential system B_1 has more than one place having outgoing a-moves, product system B does not have the separation of labels property.

Proposition 3. *Let $A = \langle A_1, \ldots, A_k \rangle$ be a product system over distribution $\Sigma = (\Sigma_1, \ldots, \Sigma_k)$. If A has separation of labels, then for every i and every global action a, $L_i = \text{Lang}(A_i)$ is a-bifurcated. If A has matching of labels, then for every i and every global action a,*

$$L_i \cap \Sigma_i^* a \Sigma_i^* = \bigcup_{R \downarrow loc(a) \in matching(a)} \text{Pref}_a^{R[i]}(L_i)\, a\, \text{Suf}_a^{R[i]}(L_i).$$

Proof. Let A be a product system as above with separation of labels. Let $L(q)$ be the set of words accepted starting from any place q in A_i. If $\text{Pref}_a(L(q))$ is nonempty then $L(q)$ is a-bifurcated, because the words containing a have to pass through a unique place. When A has a matching of labels, since the places $R[i]$ appear in unique tuples, one can separately consider the places a-bifurcating $L(q)$ and the required property follows.   □

The next property is necessary for product systems to represent free choice in equivalent nets. In our earlier paper [LMP11] we used the definition of an FC-product. The definition of FC-matching product is a generalization since conflict-equivalence is not required for all a-moves uniformly but refined into smaller equivalence classes depending on the matching.

Definition 9. *In a product system, we say the local move $\langle p, a, q_1 \rangle \in \rightarrow_i$ is* **conflict-equivalent** *to the local move $\langle p', a, q'_1 \rangle \in \rightarrow_j$, if for every other local move $\langle p, b, q_2 \rangle \in \rightarrow_i$, there is a local move $\langle p', b, q'_2 \rangle \in \rightarrow_j$ and, conversely, for moves from p' there are corresponding outgoing moves from p. For global action a, its $matching(a)$ is called* **conflict-equivalent matching**, *if whenever p, p' are related by the $matching(a)$, their outgoing local a-moves are conflict-equivalent.*

We call $A = \langle A_1, \ldots, A_k \rangle$ an **FC-product** *if for every global action $a \in \Sigma$, and for all $i, j \in loc(a)$, every a-move in A_i is conflict-equivalent to every a-move in A_j and we call A an* **FC-matching product** *if it has a conflict-equivalent $matching(a)$.*

A system having a conflict-equivalent matching is a weaker condition than the system being FC-product.

Example 9. Let $\Sigma = \{a, b, c\}$ be a distributed alphabet with distribution ($\Sigma_1 = \Sigma_2 = \Sigma$). Consider the product system $A = (A_1, A_2)$ shown in Fig. 4. The matching relations are: $matching(b) = \{(1, 4)\}$, $matching(a) = \{(2, 5), (1, 4)\}$ and $matching(c) = \{(2, 5)\}$.

The local move $\langle p_1, a, p_2 \rangle \in \rightarrow_1$ in A_1 is conflict-equivalent with local move $\langle p_4, a, p_5 \rangle \in \rightarrow_2$, but it is not conflict-equivalent with local move $\langle p_5, a, p_7 \rangle \in \rightarrow_2$.

For global action a, consider places p_1 and p_4 which appear in a tuple of $matching(a)$, they have all their outgoing moves conflict-equivalent with each other. This is true for places p_2 and p_5 as well. Hence, $matching(a)$ is conflict-equivalent. In fact, $matching(b)$ and $matching(c)$ are also conflict-equivalent.

Since local move $\langle p_1, a, p_2 \rangle \in \rightarrow_1$ is not conflict equivalent with local move $\langle p_5, a, p_7 \rangle \in \rightarrow_2$, for global action a, not all local a-moves are conflict-equivalent to each other. Therefore, product system A is not an FC-product.

Proposition 4. *For product system A, checking if it has separation of labels, and if it has matching of labels, can be done in* PTIME.

Proof. To check if A has separation of labels, we visit all local moves of each A_i once for all i in $\{1, \ldots, k\}$, to make sure that for each global action a, all a-moves of $\rightarrow_i$ have same pre-place. This takes time linear in the size of A.

For a global action $a \in \Sigma$, to check if $matching(a)$ exists, we need to visit each place p of A_i, for all i in $loc(a)$, to count how many places have outgoing

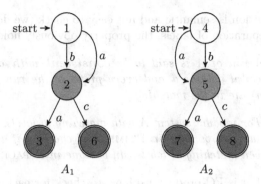

Fig. 4. Product system with matching of labels

a-moves. If this count is same for each i in $loc(a)$, then a $matching(a)$ exists. We repeat above step for each global a. So we need to visit each place of A at most $|\Sigma|$ times. Therefore, the total time needed to check if matching of labels exist for product system A is $O(|\Sigma||A|)$.

Proposition 5. *Let A be an FC-matching product system. For any i, if there exist local moves $\langle p, a, p' \rangle, \langle p, b, p'' \rangle$ in $\rightarrow_i$, then $loc(a) = loc(b)$.*

Proof. Since p has an outgoing a-move, p belongs to some tuple of $matching(a)$. If $j \in loc(a)$, then in this tuple there exists a place $q \in P_j$, which has an outgoing a-move. Since A is an FC-matching product, $matching(a)$ is conflict-equivalent. And, as places p and q appear in a tuple of $matching(a)$, a-moves outgoing from p and q are conflict-equivalent. Therefore there exists a local move $(q, b, q') \in \rightarrow_j$. This implies that $j \in loc(b)$. $\qquad\square$

4.2 Language of a Product System

Now we describe runs of A over some word w by associating product states with prefixes of w: the empty word is assigned initial product state R^0, and for every prefix va of w, if R is the product state reached after v and Q is reached after va where, for all $j \in loc(a), \langle R[j], a, Q[j] \rangle \in \rightarrow_j$ and for all $j \notin loc(a), R[j] = Q[j]$. Let $pre(a) = \{R \mid \exists Q, R \xrightarrow{a} Q\}$.

A run is said to be accepting if the product state reached after w is in G. We define the language $Lang(A)$ of product system A, as the words on which the product system has an accepting run.

We use the following characterization of direct product languages, which appears in [MR02,Muk11].

Proposition 6. *$L = Lang(A)$ is the language of product system $A = \langle A_1, \dots, A_k \rangle$ defined over distributed alphabet Σ iff*

$$L = \{w \in \Sigma^* \mid \forall i \in \{1, \dots, k\}, \exists u_i \in L \text{ such that } w{\downarrow}_{\Sigma_i} = u_i{\downarrow}_{\Sigma_i}\}.$$

Further $L = Lang(A_1) \| \dots \| Lang(A_k)$.

The next definition is semantic and not easy to check (we do it in PSPACE). If a system has separation of labels, the property obviously holds.

Definition 10. *A* run *of A is said to be* **consistent with a matching of labels** *if for all global actions a and every prefix of the run* $R^0 \overset{v}{\Rightarrow} R \overset{a}{\Rightarrow} Q$, *the pre-places* $R \downarrow loc(a)$ *are in the matching.*

Proposition 7. *For product system A with matching of labels, checking if A is FC-matching product can be done in* PTIME, *and checking if all runs of A are consistent with given matching of labels can be done in* PSPACE.

Proof. To check if A is FC-product we have to check for each global action a, whether $matching(a)$ is conflict-equivalent. Let $(p_1, p_2, \ldots, p_m)$ be a tuple in $matching(a)$. For any two places p_i and p_j of this tuple, we have to check if their sets of labels of outgoing local moves are same. This comparison between two sets takes $O(k|\Sigma|)$ time. We need to carry out this step for all tuples in $matching(a)$. This can be done by visiting all local moves of A_i, for all i in $loc(a)$ at most once. Therefore, for each global action a in Σ, we need to visit all local moves of A at most $|\Sigma|$ times. Hence, the total time required is polynomial in the size of Σ and A.

To check if all runs of A are consistent with given matching of labels we need to visit each reachable global state of A at most once, which can be done in PSPACE.

5   Connected Expressions and Product Systems

In this section we prove two main theorems of the paper. To place them in context of our earlier paper [LMP11], there we used a "structural cyclicity" condition which allowed a run to be split into finite parts from the initial product state to itself, since it was guaranteed to be repeated. The new idea in this paper is that runs are split up using matchings which correspond to synchronizations; what happens in between is not relevant for the connections across sequential systems. Hence extending our syntax to allow full regular expressions for the sequential systems does not affect the synchronization properties which are the main issue we are addressing. In Sect. 6 we outline the connections to labelled free choice nets.

5.1   Synthesis of Systems from Expressions

We begin by constructing products of automata for our syntactic entities. For regular expressions, this is well known. We follow the construction of Antimirov, which in polynomial time gives us a finite automaton of size $O(wd(s))$, using partial derivatives as states. Now for connected expressions we need to construct a product of automata.

Lemma 1. *Let e be a connected expression with partitions which give unique sites (for every global action). Then there exists a product system A with separation of labels accepting Lang(e) as its language. If e had equal choice, then A is FC-product.*

Proof. Let $e = \text{fsync}(s_1, s_2, \ldots, s_k)$. Then for each s_i, which is a regular expression defined over some alphabet Σ_i, we produce a sequential system A_i over Σ_i, using Antimirov's derivatives, such that $Lang(s_i) = Lang(A_i)$, $\forall\, i \in \{1, \ldots, k\}$. Next we trim it—remove places not reachable from the initial place p_i^0 and places from where a final place is not reachable. Now, for each global action a, we quotient A_i by merging all derivatives d such that $a \in Init(d)$ into a single place.

Call the resulting automaton A_i'. Let p be the merged place in A_i' which is now the source of all a-moves. Clearly $Lang(A_i) \subseteq Lang(A_i')$ since no paths are removed, we show next that the inclusion in the other direction also holds, using the unique sites condition.

Let a be a global action. Consider a word $w = x_1 a x_2 \ldots a x_n$ in $Lang(A_i')$, where the factors $x_1, x_2, \ldots, x_n$ do not contain the letter a. We wish to find derivatives $d_0, d_1, \ldots, d_n$ of A_i such that d_n is a final place and for every j there is a run $d_j \xrightarrow{ax_{j+1}} \ldots \xrightarrow{ax_n} d_n$ of A_i when $j > 0$, and $d_0 \xrightarrow{x_1} \xrightarrow{ax_2} \ldots \xrightarrow{ax_n} d_n$ when $j = 0$, which will show the desired inclusion.

We proceed from n downwards. For any place d_n in G there is a run from d_n on $\varepsilon \in Lang(d_n)$ in A_i. Inductively assume we have d_j such that there is a run $d_j \xrightarrow{ax_{j+1}} \ldots \xrightarrow{ax_n} d_n$ of A_i, so $x_{j+1} a x_{j+2} \ldots a x_n$ is in $Suf_a(Lang(s_i))$ since d_j is reachable from the initial place. Since there is a run $p \xrightarrow{ax_j} p$ in A_i' there are derivatives d_{j-1}, c_j of s_j, such that there is a run $d_{j-1} \xrightarrow{ax_j} c_j$ in A_i (when $j = 1$ we get $d_0 \xrightarrow{x_1} c_1$ by this argument). Since c_j quotients to p, it has an a-derivative c such that c is in $Der_{ax_j a}(d_{j-1})$ ($Der_{x_0 a}(d_0)$ when $j = 1$). Because d_{j-1} is reachable from the initial place by some v and because some final place is reachable from c, $v x_j \in Pref_a(Lang(s_i))$ which is nonempty. By the unique sites condition and Proposition 1, since $x_{j+1} \ldots a x_n$ is in $Suf_a(Lang(s_i))$, $v a x_j a x_{j+1} \ldots a x_n$ is in $Lang(s_i)$ and so $x_j a x_{j+1} \ldots a x_n$ is in $Suf_a(Lang(s_i))$. This means that there is a run from some d_{j-1} on $ax_j a x_{j+1} \ldots a x_n$ ending in a final place d_n of A_i. So we have the induction hypothesis restored. If $j = 1$ we get d_0 which quotients to p_0 and has a run on w to d_n in G.

So we get a product system $A' = \langle A_1', A_2', \ldots, A_k' \rangle$ defined over Σ. Because of the quotienting A' has separation of labels. That means for a global action a, for i, j in $loc(a)$, sequential machines A_i', A_j' has only one place which has outgoing local a-moves. Let p_i^a be that place in A_i' and let p_j^a be that place in A_j'. On the other hand, since e had unique sites, for a global action a and for i, j in $loc(a)$, expression s_i has only one block D_i in the partition of a-sites of s_i and expression s_j has only one block D_j in the partition of a-sites of s_j. Therefore, all a-sites of s_i are in this block D_i, and all a-sites of s_j are in block D_j. Therefore $pairing(a)$ has only one tuple which have D_i and D_j appearing in it. Since e has equal choice property, we have $Init(D_i) = Init(D_j)$. Because of quotienting construction, block D_i corresponds to the place p_i^a in A_i' and block

D_j corresponds to the place p_j^a in A'_j. So each outgoing local a-move of p_i^a is conflict-equivalent to each outgoing local a-move of place p_j^a.

Now we prove language equivalence of expression e and product system A' constructed from it.

$$w \in Lang(e) \text{ iff } \forall i, w{\downarrow}_{\Sigma_i} \in Lang(s_i), \text{ by definition of synchronized shuffle}$$
$$\text{iff } \forall i, w{\downarrow}_{\Sigma_i} \in Lang(A'_i)$$
$$\text{iff } w \in Lang(A'), \text{ by Proposition 6.} \qquad \square$$

Theorem 1. *Let $e = fsync(s_1, \ldots, s_k)$ be a connected expression over a distribution Σ with a pairing of actions. Then there exists an FC-matching product system A over Σ, accepting $Lang(e)$. If the pairing was equal choice, the matching is conflict-equivalent. If the expression is consistent with the pairing, all runs of A will be consistent with the matching.*

Proof. We first rewrite e to another expression e', construct an automaton A' for $Lang(e')$, and then change it to recover an automaton for $Lang(e)$.

Consider global action a and tuple of blocks $D = \Pi_{i \in loc(a)} D_i$ in $pairing(a)$. By Proposition 1 D_i a-bifurcates $Lang(s_i)$. We rename for all i in $loc(a)$, the occurrences of a in s_i which correspond to an a in $Init(D_i)$, by the new letter a^{D_i}. This is done for all global actions to obtain from e a new expression $e' = fsync(s'_1, \ldots, s'_k)$ over a distribution Σ', where every s'_i now has the unique sites property. For any word $w \in Lang(e)$, there is a well-defined word $w' \in Lang(e')$.

By Lemma 1 we obtain a product system A' with separation of labels for $Lang(e')$. Say $pre(a^D)$ is the pre-place for action a^D in A'_i. We change all the $\langle pre(a^D), a^D, q \rangle$ moves to $\langle pre(a^D), a, q \rangle$ in all the A'_i to obtain a product system A over the alphabet Σ. As $w' \in Lang(e') = Lang(A')$ is well-defined from w and, as the renaming of labels of moves does not remove any paths, w is in $Lang(A)$. Conversely, for every run on w accepted by A, because of the separation of labels property, there is a well-defined run on w' with the label of a move appropriately renamed depending on the source state, which is accepted by A', hence w' is in $Lang(e')$. So renaming w' to w gives a word in $Lang(e)$.

Now we refer to the pairing of actions in e. This defines for each global action a and tuple of blocks of a-sites D, a relation between pre-places of a^D-moves in different components in the product A'. By the separation of labels property of A', the tuples in the relation are disjoint, that is, the relation is functional. So for pre-places of a-moves in the product A we have a matching. If the pairing was equal choice, the matching is conflict-equivalent.

If the expression e is consistent with the pairing, all reachable a-sites are in the pairing, so we can partition $Lang(e) \cap \Sigma^* a \Sigma^*$ using the partitions in $Part_a(e)$. Letting D range over blocks of connected expressions, each block D contributes a global action a^D in the renaming, so we get an expression e' such that for every global action a^D, we have the unique a-sites property. Applying Lemma 1, we have the product system A' with separation of labels. By Proposition 3, every $Lang(A'_i)$ is a^D-bifurcated, and using the characterization of Proposition 6, $Lang(A') \cap (\Sigma')^* a^D (\Sigma')^* = Pref_{a^D}(Lang(A')) a^D Suf_{a^D}(Lang(A'))$.

Since several actions a^D are renamed to a and the corresponding tuples of pre-places are recorded in the matching, by Propositions 3 and 6:

$$\bigcup_{R \in matching(a)} Pref_a^R(Lang(A)) \; a \; Suf_a^R(Lang(A)) \subseteq Lang(A) \cap \Sigma^* a \Sigma^*.$$

But this means that all runs of A are consistent with the matching. $\qquad\square$

As an illustration of constructing product system with matching from expression with pairing, using Theorem 1 which employs Lemma 1 in its proof, consider the expression in Example 7, for which we produce a product system as was shown in Example 10.

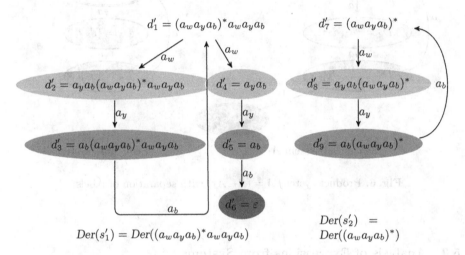

Der(s_1') = Der($(a_w a_y a_b)^* a_w a_y a_b$)

Der(s_2') =
Der($(a_w a_y a_b)^*$)

Fig. 5. Derivatives of s_1' and s_2' of $e' = fsync(s_1', s_2')$ with unique sites property

Example 10. As we have seen in Example 7, the pairing relation for expression $e = fsync((aaa)^* aaa, (aaa)^*))$, $pairing(a) = \{(D_1, D_4), (D_2, D_5), (D_3, D_6)\}$. Let $w = (D_1, D_4), y = (D_2, D_5)$ and $b = (D_3, D_6)$.

Then using these tuples, we get a new alphabet $\Sigma' = \{a_w, a_y, a_b\}$ with distribution $\Sigma_1' = \{a_w, a_y, a_b\}$ and $\Sigma_2' = \{a_w, a_y, a_b\}$. Each a in s_i belong to only one block in $Part_a(s_i)$ and that block belong to only one tuple in the $pairing(a)$. Therefore, by renaming each a in s_i by its corresponding tuple in $pairing(a)$, we get $s_1' = (a_w a_y a_b)^* a_w a_y a_b$ and $s_2' = (a_w a_y a_b)^* a_w a_r a_b$ over alphabet Σ_1' and Σ_2' respectively. Hence, we have a connected expression e' over Σ' as, $e' = fsync((a_w a_y a_b)^* a_w a_y a_b, (a_w a_y a_b)^*)$.

Expressions s_1' and s_2' have unique sites property. In Fig. 5, derivatives of s_1' and s_2' are shown. The blocks in the partitions of their respective a_x-sites, where $x \in \{w, y, b\}$ are: $D_1' = \{d_1'\}, D_2' = \{d_2', d_4'\}, D_3' = \{d_3', d_5'\}, D_4' = \{d_7'\}$,

$D'_5 = \{d'_5\}$, $D'_6 = \{d'_6\}$. Now by Lemma 1 we can fuse derivatives in the respective blocks to get product system $A' = (A'_1, A'_2)$, having separation of labels property, and which is language equivalent to expression e'. The set of places of sequential system A'_1, is $\{D'_1, D'_2, D'_3, d'_6\}$, and of sequential system A'_2, is $\{D'_4, D'_5, D'_6\}$. In each A'_i we have only one place which has outgoing a_x-moves. So each a_x contributes only one tuple of places in $matching(a)$. Therefore, $matching(a) = \{(D_1, D_4), (D_2, D_5), (D_3, D_6)\}$. The final product system over Σ is shown in Fig. 6.

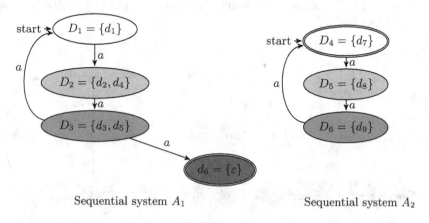

Sequential system A_1 　　　　　　　　　　Sequential system A_2

Fig. 6. Product system $A = (A_1, A_2)$ with separation of labels

5.2 Analysis of Expressions from Systems

Lemma 2. *Let A be a conflict-equivalent product system with separation of labels. Then we can compute a connected expression for the language of A with partitions of the regular expressions which have unique sites and specified pairings which have equal choice.*

Proof. Let $A = \langle A_1, \dots, A_k \rangle$ be a product system with separation of labels, where A_i is a sequential system of A with places P, initial place p_0 and final places G. Kleene's theorem gives us expressions for the words which have runs from a given state to another using a specified set of states [MY60] and these are put together. Let us suppose that all the states which do not have any global actions enabled are dealt with first. After that we add the states with global actions, we do an induction on the number of these states.

Now we consider a global action a. By separation of labels there is a single place p in A_i enabling a. Let Q be the states which have already been dealt with and $R = Q \cup \{P\}$. Let T be the set of moves outgoing from p and which are not a-moves. Depending on whether we have an a-move $p \xrightarrow{a} p$, or a-moves

$p \xrightarrow{a} p_j$, $p_j \neq p$, or a combination of these two types, we obtain the expression below (where the expressions on the right hand side have already been computed):

$$e_{p_0,f}^R = e_{p_0,f}^Q + e_{p_0,p}^Q (e_{p,p}^Q)^* e_{p,f}^Q,$$

where the expression $e_{p,p}^Q$ is given by one of the following refinements, for the three cases considered above respectively:

$$(a + e_{p,p}^T), \text{ or } ((\sum_j a e_{p_j,p}^T) + e_{p,p}^T), \text{ or } (a + (\sum_j a e_{p_j,p}^T) + e_{p,p}^T).$$

The superscripts Q and T indicates that these expressions are derived, as in the McNaughton-Yamada construction [MY60], for runs which only use the places Q and, respectively, runs which only use the places Q and moves T (these expressions have already been computed). Whichever be the case, we note that we have an expression with $D^a(e_{p_0,f}^R) = \{(e_{p,p}^Q)^* e_{p,f}^Q\}$ as its singleton set of a-sites. Therefore, expression $e_{p_0,f}^R$ has the unique a-sites property. Since the product system was conflict-equivalent, this argument extends if there are other global actions enabled at state p, and the expression obtained is equal choice.

Now consider a global action c enabled at a state q in Q. The c-sites are obtained from several parts of the expression:

$$D^c(e_{p_0,f}^R) = D^c(e_{p_0,f}^Q) \cup D^c(e_{p_0,p}^Q) \cdot (e_{p,p}^Q)^* \cdot e_{p,f}^Q \cup D^c(e_{p,p}^T) \cdot (e_{p,p}^Q)^* \cdot e_{p,f}^Q \cup D^c(e_{p,f}^Q).$$

By induction the right hand expressions had the unique c-sites property, the c-partition collapses all the derivatives above into a single block. We claim the derivatives in this four-way union c-bifurcate the language $Lang(e_{p_0,f}^R)$. If the state q was visited in only one of the four cases there is nothing to prove. The interesting case is when there is a path from p to q as well as from q to p, and separate paths from p_0 to p and from p_0 to q. In this case the second and the third components of the union will both be nonempty. Suppose $w_1 = x_1 c y_1$ with $x_1 \in Lang(e_{p_0,q}^Q)$ and $cy_1 \in Lang(e_{q,p}^T (e_{p,p}^Q)^* e_{p,f}^Q)$, and $w_2 = x_2 c y_2$ with $x_2 \in Lang(e_{p_0,p}^Q e_{p,q}^T)$ and $cy_2 \in Lang(e_{q,p}^T (e_{p,p}^Q)^* e_{p,f}^Q)$. But then $x_1 c y_2$ is in $Lang(e_{p_0,q}^Q e_{q,p}^T (e_{p,p}^Q)^* e_{p,f}^Q)$ and hence in $Lang(e_{p_0,f}^R)$. Similarly $x_2 c y_1$ is in $Lang(e_{p_0,p}^Q e_{p,q}^T e_{q,p}^T (e_{p,p}^Q)^* e_{p,f}^Q)$ and also in $Lang(e_{p_0,f}^R)$. In both cases the same derivatives, giving the language for the expression $e_{q,p}^T (e_{p,p}^Q)^* e_{p,f}^Q$, appear in the set D^c. By equal choice, this argument extends if other global actions are also enabled along with c. □

Theorem 2. *Let A be a product system with a conflict-equivalent matching. Then we can compute a connected expression for the language of A with an equal choice pairing of actions.*

Proof. Let A be a product system with a conflict-equivalent matching. Enumerate the global actions $a, b, \ldots$. Say the $matching(a)$ has n tuples.

We construct a new product system A' where, for the places in the j'th tuple of the $matching(a)$, we change the label of the outgoing a-moves to a^j;

similarly for the places in tuples of the $matching(b)$; and so on. We now have a new product system where the letter a of the alphabet has been replaced by the set $\{a^1, \ldots, a^n\}$; the letter b has been replaced by another set; and so on, obtaining a new distribution Σ'. By definition of a matching, the various labels do not interfere with each other, so we have a matching with the new alphabet, conflict-equivalent if the previous one was. Runs which were consistent with the matching continue to be consistent with the new matching. Again by the definition of matching, the new system A' has separation of labels. Hence we can apply Lemma 2.

From the Lemma 2 we get a connected expression $e' = fsync(s_1, \ldots, s_k)$ for the language of A' over Σ' where every regular expression has unique sites. From the proof of the Lemma 2 we get for every sequential system A'_i in the product, for the global actions $a^1, \ldots, a^n$, tuples $D'(a^j) = \Pi_{i \in loc(a)} D'_i(a^j)$ which are sites for a^j in the expression s_i, for every j. Now substitute a for every letter $a^1, \ldots, a^n$ in the expression, each tuple D' is isomorphic to a tuple D of sites for a in e and the sites are disjoint from one another. We let $pairing(a)$ be the partition formed by these tuples. Do the same for b obtaining $pairing(b)$. Repeat this process until all the global actions have been dealt with. The result is an expression e with pairing of actions. If the matching was conflict-equivalent, the pairing has equal choice.

The runs of A have to use product places in $pre(a)$ for global action a, define

$$L = Lang(A) \cap \Sigma^* a \Sigma^* = \bigcup_{R \in pre(a)} Pref_a^R(Lang(A))\; a\; Suf_a^R(Lang(A)).$$

The renaming of moves depends on the source place, so L is isomorphic to

$$L' = Lang(A') \cap \left(\sum_j (\Sigma')^* a^j (\Sigma')^* \right) = \bigcup_{j=1,n} Pref_{a^j}(Lang(A')) a^j Suf_{a^j}(Lang(A')).$$

Keeping Proposition 6 in our hands, the Lemma 2 ensures that $Lang(A') = Lang(e')$ and the expression e' has unique a^j-sites forming a block $D'(j)$. Then L' can be written as $\bigcup\limits_{j=1,n} Pref_{a^j}^{D'(j)}(Lang(e')) a^j Suf_{a^j}^{D'(j)}(Lang(e'))$. When we rename the a^j back to a we have a partition of $pairing(a)$ into sets D such that

$$L = \bigcup_{D \subseteq pairing(a)} Pref_a^D(Lang(e))\; a\; Suf_a^D(Lang(e)).$$

If all runs of A were consistent with the $matching(a)$, the product states in $pre(a)$ would all be in the $matching(a)$, and we obtain that the expression e is consistent with the $pairing(a)$.   □

Example 11. Let Σ be a distributed alphabet and $(\Sigma_1 = \{a\}, \Sigma_2 = \{a\})$ be a distribution of Σ. Consider a product system $A = (A_1, A_2)$ with matching, defined over Σ, as shown in Fig. 6. A matching relation for global action a is: $matching(a) = \{(D_1, D_4), (D_2, D_5), (D_3, D_6)\}$.

Let $w = (D_1, D_4), y = (D_2, D_5)$ and $b = (D_3, D_6)$. Hence, we have new alphabet $\Sigma' = \{a_w, a_y, a_b\}$ with distribution $\Sigma'_1 = \{a_w, a_y, a_b\}$ and $\Sigma'_2 = \{a_w, a_y, a_b\}$. We now have a new product system $A' = (A'_1, A'_2)$ in which each action labelled a of has been replaced by an action from $\{a_w, a_y, a_b\}$; Again by the definition of matching, the new system A' has separation of labels. Hence we can apply Lemma 2, to get a connected expression $e' = \text{fsync}((a_w a_y a_b)^* a_w a_y a_b, (a_w a_y a_b)^*)$ defined over Σ', language equivalent to A' and have unique sites. Derivatives for $s'_1 = (a_w a_y a_b)^* a_w a_y a_b$ and $s'_2 = (a_w a_y a_b)^* a_w a_r a_b$ are shown in the Fig. 5. Since e' has unique actions, for action a_w, there is only one block in the partitions of a_w-sites of s'_1 and s'_2: $Part_{a_w}(s'_1)$ and $Part_{a_w}(s'_2)$, and for remaining global actions a_y, a_b also. For action a_w partition set is: $Part_{a_w}(s'_1) = \{D'_1\}$, $Part_{a_w}(s'_2) = \{D'_4\}$, for action a_y: $Part_{a_y}(s'_1) = \{D'_2\}$, $Part_{a_y}(s'_2) = \{D'_5\}$, and, for action a_b: $Part_{a_b}(s'_1) = \{D'_3\}$, $Part_{a_b}(s'_2) = \{D'_6\}$.

Now we replace each a_w, a_y and a_b in e' by action a to get expression $e = \text{fsync}((aaa)^* aaa, (aaa)^*)$ defined over Σ. For blocks D'_i we get respective blocks D_i, as shown in Fig. 1. And, pairing relation for a is: $pairing(a) = \{(D_1, D_4), (D_2, D_5), (D_3, D_6)\}$.

6   Applying the Kleene Result to Nets

We now wish to see how the Kleene result between expressions and product systems proved in Theorems 1 and 2 can be applied to net systems. First some definitions.

Definition 11. *A labelled net N is a tuple (S, T, F, λ), where S is a set of places, T is a set of transitions labelled by the function $\lambda : T \to \Sigma$ and $F \subseteq (T \times S) \cup (S \times T)$ is the flow relation. It will be convenient to define $loc(t) = loc(\lambda(t))$.*

Elements of $S \cup T$ are called **nodes** of N. Given a node z of net N, set ${}^\bullet z = \{x \mid (x, z) \in F\}$ is called **pre-set** of z and $z^\bullet = \{x \mid (z, x) \in F\}$ is called **post-set** of z. Given a set Z of nodes of N, let ${}^\bullet Z = \bigcup_{z \in Z} {}^\bullet z$ and $Z^\bullet = \bigcup_{z \in Z} z^\bullet$. We only consider nets in which every transition has nonempty pre- and post-set.

Definition 12. *Let $N' = (S \cap X, T \cap X, F \cap (X \times X))$ be a subnet of net $N = (S, T, F)$, generated by a nonempty set X of nodes of N. N' is called a* **component** *of N if,*

- *For each place s of X, ${}^\bullet s, s^\bullet \subseteq X$ (the pre- and post-sets are taken in N),*
- *For all transitions $t \in T$, we have $|{}^\bullet t| = 1 = |t^\bullet|$ (N' is an S-net [DE95]),*
- *Under the flow relation, N' is connected.*

A set C of components of net N is called **S-cover** *for N, if every place of the net belongs to some component of C. A net is* **covered by components** *if it has an S-cover.*

Note that our notion of component does not require strong connectedness and so it is different from notion of S-component in [DE95], and therefore our notion of S-cover also differs from theirs.

Fix a distribution $(\Sigma_1, \Sigma_2, \ldots, \Sigma_k)$ of Σ. The next definition appears in several places for unlabelled nets, starting with [Hac72].

Definition 13. *A labelled net $N = (S, T, F, \lambda)$ is called* **S-decomposable** *if, there exists an S-cover $\mathcal{C}$ for N, such that for each $T_i = \{\lambda^{-1}(a) \mid a \in \Sigma_i\}$, there exists S_i such that the induced component (S_i, T_i, F_i) is in $\mathcal{C}$.*

Now from S-decomposability we get an S-cover for net N, since there exist subsets $S_1, S_2, \ldots, S_k$ of places S, such that $S = S_1 \cup S_2 \cup \ldots S_k$ and $^\bullet S_i \cup S_i^\bullet = T_i$, such that the subnet (S_i, T_i, F_i) generated by S_i and T_i is an S-net, where F_i is the induced flow relation from S_i and T_i.

6.1 Free Choice Nets

Definition 14 ([DE95]). *Let x be a node of a net N. The* **cluster** *of x, denoted by $[x]$, is the minimal set of nodes containing x such that*

- *if a place $s \in [x]$ then $s^\bullet$ is included in $[x]$, and*
- *if a transition $t \in [x]$ then $^\bullet t$ is included in $[x]$.*

A cluster C is called **free choice** *(FC) if all transitions in C have the same pre-set. A net is called* **free choice** *if all its clusters are free choice.*

In a labelled N, for a cluster $C = (S_C, T_C)$ define the a-labelled transitions $C_a = \{t \in T_C \mid \lambda(t) = a\}$. If the net has an S-decomposition generated by S_i, we associate a post-product $\pi(t) = \Pi_{i \in loc(a)}(t^\bullet \cap S_i)$ with every such transition t. This is well defined since by the S-net condition every transition will have at most one post-place in S_i. Let $post(C_a) = \bigcup_{t \in C_a} \pi(t)$. We also define the post-projection of the cluster $C_a[i] = C_a{}^\bullet \cap S_i$ and the **post-decomposition** $postdecomp(C_a) = \Pi_{i \in loc(a)} C_a[i]$.

Clearly $post(C_a) \subseteq postdecomp(C_a)$. The following definition appears in [Pha14b], and provides the way to direct product representability.

Definition 15 ([Pha14b]). *An S-decomposable net $N = (S, T, F, \lambda)$ is said to be* **distributed choice** *if, for all global actions a in Σ and for all clusters C of N, $postdecomp(C_a) \subseteq post(C_a)$.*

6.2 Net Systems and Their Languages

For our results we are only interested in 1-bounded (or condition/event) nets, where a place is either marked or not marked. Hence we define a marking as a function from the states of a net to $\{0, 1\}$.

A transition t is **enabled** in a marking M if all places in its pre-set are marked by M. In such a case, t can be fired to yield the new marking $M' = (M \setminus {}^\bullet t) \cup t^\bullet$. We write this as $M[t\rangle M'$ or $M[\lambda(t)\rangle M'$.

A **firing sequence** (finite or infinite) $\lambda(t_1)\lambda(t_2)\ldots$ is defined by composition, from $M_0[t_1\rangle M_1[t_2\rangle \ldots$ For every $i \leq j$, we say that M_j is **reachable** from M_i. A net system (N, M_0) is **live** if, for every reachable marking M and every transition t, there exists a marking M' reachable from M which enables t.

Definition 16. *For a labelled net system* $(N, M_0, \mathcal{G})$*, its **language** is defined as* $Lang(N, M_0, \mathcal{G}) = \{\lambda(\sigma) \in \Sigma^* \mid \sigma \in T^* \text{ and } M_0[\sigma\rangle M, \text{ for some } M \in \mathcal{G}\}$.

If a net (S, T, F, λ) is 1-bounded and S-decomposable then a marking can be written as a k-tuple from its components $S_1 \times S_2 \times \ldots \times S_k$. It is known [Zie87,Muk11] that if we do not enforce the "direct product" condition below we get a larger subclass of languages.

Definition 17. *An **S-decomposable labelled net system** $(N, M_0, \mathcal{G})$ is an S-decomposable labelled net* $N = (S, T, F, \lambda)$ *along with an initial marking* M_0 *and a set of markings* $\mathcal{G} \subseteq \wp(S)$*, which is a **direct product**: if* $\langle q_1, q_2, \ldots q_k \rangle \in \mathcal{G}$ *and* $\langle q_1', q_2', \ldots q_k' \rangle \in \mathcal{G}$ *then* $\{q_1, q_1'\} \times \{q_2, q_2'\} \times \ldots \times \{q_k, q_k'\} \subseteq \mathcal{G}$.

6.3   From Product Systems to Net Systems

From a product system we can straightforwardly construct a net.

Definition 18 (Product to Net). *Given a product system* $A = \langle A_1, \ldots, A_k \rangle$ *over distribution* Σ*, we can produce a net system* $(N = (S, T, F, \lambda), M_0, \mathcal{G})$ *as follows:*

- $S = \cup_i P_i$*, the set of places.*
- $T = \cup_a T_a$*, where* T_a *is* $\Rightarrow_a$*, the set of a-labelled global moves.*
- *The labelling function* λ *labels by* a *the transitions in* T_a*.*
- *The flow relation* $F = \{(p, g), (g, q) \mid g \in T_a, g[i] = \langle p, a, q \rangle, i \in loc(a)\}$*.*
- $M_0 = \{p_1^0, \ldots, p_k^0\}$*, the initial product state.*
- $\mathcal{G} = G_1 \times \cdots \times G_k$*, the set of final product states.*

Since a global action a can be in every component A_i of the product system and there can be an arbitrary number n_i of a-labelled choices in each component, the resulting a-cluster in the net has $n_1 \times \cdots \times n_k$ transitions which can be exponential in the size of the product system.

Here is what this construction yields.

Theorem 3 ([Pha14b,Pha14a]). *In the construction of net system* $(N, M_0, \mathcal{G})$ *in Definition 18,* N *is S-decomposable, satisfies the distributed choice property, and with* $Lang(N, M_0, \mathcal{G}) = Lang(A)$*. Further, if all runs of* A *are consistent with a conflict-equivalent matching of labels, we can choose* $T' \subseteq T$ *such that the subnet* N' *generated by* T' *is a free choice net and* $(N', M_0, \mathcal{G})$ *accepts the same language.*

Example 12. For the product system shown in Fig. 6 we construct a net as shown in Fig. 7. It is free choice and language equivalent to product system A. Set of final markings for this net is $M_f = \{(d_6, D_4)\}$. Hence, we get a language equivalent free choice net system for the connected expression $e = fsync((aaa)^*aaa, (aaa)^*)$ of Example 7. This net has distributed choice property.

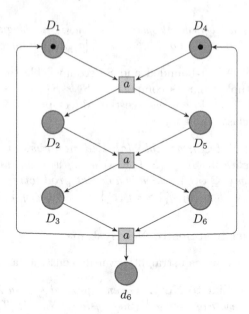

Fig. 7. Net system constructed from $A = (A_1, A_2)$ over Σ of Fig. 6.

6.4   S-decomposable Net Systems to Product Systems with Matching

For a net which is 1-bounded and S-decomposable it might have many S-covers for it. And, in an S-cover each component of it need not have only one token in it. For live and 1-bounded free choice nets, there exist at least one S-cover in which each component have only one token in it [DE95]. In this paper, when we say that a 1-bounded net is S-decomposable we refer to one such S-cover in which each component has only one token in it. Taking this S-cover it is easy to construct a product system.

Definition 19 (Net to Product).   *Given a 1-bounded and S-decomposable labelled net system* $(N, M_0, \mathcal{G})$, *with* $N = (S, T, F, \lambda)$ *the underlying net and* $N_i = (S_i, T_i, F_i)$ *the components in the S-cover, for i in* $\{1, 2, \ldots, k\}$, *we define a product system:*

- $P_i = S_i$, p_i^0 *the unique state in* $M_0 \cap P_i$.
- $\rightarrow_i = \{\langle p, \lambda(t), p' \rangle \mid t \in T_i$ *and* $(p, t), (t, p') \in F_i$, *for* $p, p' \in P_i\}$. *For each* $t \in T_i$, *we know that, there exist places* $p, p' \in S_i$ *such that* (p, t) *and* (t, p') *belong to* F_i.
- *So we get sequential system* $A_i = \langle P_i, \rightarrow_i, p_i^0 \rangle$ *and the product system* $A = \langle A_1, A_2, \ldots, A_k \rangle$ *over distributed alphabet* Σ.
- $G = \{(M \cap P_1, \ldots, M \cap P_k) \mid M \in \mathcal{G}\}$. *If* $\mathcal{G}$ *was a direct product set of final markings, we can define* $G_i = \{M \cap P_i \mid M \in \mathcal{G}\}$ *and set G to be their product* $G_1 \times \cdots \times G_k$.

The distributed choice property yields the following results. The references below provide counterexamples when the distributed choice condition is not met.

Theorem 4 ([Pha14b,Pha14a]). *When the given net N satisfies the distributed choice property, the construction of the product system A in Definition 19 preserves language, that is, when restricted to runs consistent with a matching, $\text{Lang}(N, M_0, \mathcal{G}) = \text{Lang}(A)$. Further, since the net is free choice, the matching is conflict-equivalent, making A an FC-matching product.*

Example 13. Let Σ be a distributed alphabet and $(\Sigma_1 = \{a\}, \Sigma_2 = \{a\})$ be a distribution of Σ. Consider the free choice net as shown in Fig. 7. It has distributed choice property, and an S-decomposition is $\{D_1, D_2, D_3, d_6\}$ and $\{D_4, D_5, D_6\}$. A set of final markings for this net is $M_f = \{(d_6, D_4)\}$. As one may expect this produces the language equivalent product system A shown in Fig. 6.

6.5   Conclusion

In earlier work [LMP11], we showed that a graph-theoretic condition called "structural cyclicity" enables us to extract syntax from a conflict-equivalent product system. In the present work we have generalized this condition so that we can deal with a larger class of product systems with a conflict-equivalent matching. Using [Pha14b,Pha14a] we obtain a Kleene characterization for the class of labelled free choice nets with the distributed choice property using a pairing condition on connected expressions.

Acknowledgements. We thank the referees of the PNSE workshop and the referees of ToPNOC, who urged us to improve the presentation of the proofs of the main theorems and to correct and clarify our results. We would also like to thank Jörg Desel for his patience as editor of the ToPNOC special issue.

References

[Ant96]   Antimirov, V.: Partial derivatives of regular expressions and finite automaton constructions. Theor. Comput. Sci. **155**(2), 291–319 (1996)

[Arn94]   Arnold, A.: Finite Transition Systems. Prentice-Hall, UK (1994)

[Brz64]   Brzozowski, J.A.: Derivatives of regular expressions. JACM **11**(4), 481–494 (1964)

[DE95]   Desel, J., Esparza, J.: Free Choice Petri Nets. Cambridge University Press, New York (1995)

[GR92]   Garg, V.K., Ragunath, M.T.: Concurrent regular expressions and their relationship to Petri nets. Theor. Comput. Sci. **96**(2), 285–304 (1992)

[Gra81]   Grabowski, J.: On partial languages. Fund. Inform. **IV**(2), 427–498 (1981)

[Hac72]   Hack, M.H.T.: Analysis of production schemata by Petri nets. Project Mac report TR-94. MIT (1972)

[LMP11]   Lodaya, K., Mukund, M., Phawade, R.: Kleene theorems for product systems. In: Holzer, M., Kutrib, M., Pighizzini, G. (eds.) DCFS 2011. LNCS, vol. 6808, pp. 235–247. Springer, Heidelberg (2011)

[LRR03] Lodaya, K., Ranganayakulu, D., Rangarajan, K.: Hierarchical structure of 1-safe petri nets. In: Saraswat, V.A. (ed.) ASIAN 2003. LNCS, vol. 2896, pp. 173–187. Springer, Heidelberg (2003)

[LS05] Lombardy, S., Sakarovitch, J.: How expressions can code for automata. RAIRO Theor. Inform. Appl. **39**(1), 217–237 (2005)

[LS10] Lombardy, S., Sakarovitch, J.: Corrigendum. RAIRO Theor. Inform. Appl. **44**(3), 339–361 (2010)

[LW00] Lodaya, K., Weil, P.: Series-parallel languages and the bounded width property. Theor. Comput. Sci. **237**(1–2), 347–380 (2000)

[Mir66] Mirkin, B.G.: An algorithm for constructing a base in a language of regular expressions. Eng. Cybern. **5**, 110–116 (1966)

[MR02] Mohalik, S., Ramanujam, R.: Distributed automata in an assumption-commitment framework. Sādhanā **27**(Part 2), 209–250 (2002)

[Muk11] Mukund, M.: Automata on distributed alphabets. In: D'Souza, D., Shankar, P. (eds.) Modern Applications of Automata Theory, pp. 257–288. World Scientific, Singapore (2011)

[MY60] McNaughton, R., Yamada, H.: Regular expressions and state graphs for automata. IEEE Trans. IRS **EC–9**, 39–47 (1960)

[Pha14a] Phawade, R.: Direct product representation of labelled free choice nets. Int. J. Comput. Appl. **99**(16), 1–8 (2014)

[Pha14b] Phawade, R.: Labelled Free Choice Nets, finite Product Automata, and Expressions. Ph.D. thesis, Homi Bhabha National Institute (2014, submitted)

[PL14] Phawade, R., Lodaya, K.: Kleene theorems for labelled free choice nets. In: Proceedings of the 8th PNSE. CEUR-WS, Tunis, vol. 1160, pp. 75–89 (2014)

[SH96] Straub, P.A., Carlos Hurtado, L.: Business process behaviour is (almost) free-choice. In: Proceedings of CESA, Lille, pp. 9–12. IEEE (1996)

[TY14] Thiagarajan, P.S., Yang, S.: Rabin's theorem in the concurrency setting: a conjecture. Theor. Comput. Sci. **546**, 225–236 (2014)

[Zie87] Zielonka, W.: Notes on finite asynchronous automata. Inform. Theor. Appl. **21**(2), 99–135 (1987)

Symbolic Model Checking of Security Protocols for Ad hoc Networks on any Topologies

Mihai Lica Pura[1](✉) and Didier Buchs[2]

[1] Military Technical Academy, Bucharest, Romania
puramihai@gmail.com
[2] Centre Universitaire d'Informatique, University of Geneva, Carouge, Switzerland

Abstract. Petri nets have proved their effectiveness in modeling and formal verification of a large number of applications: control systems, communication protocols, application workflows, hardware design, etc. In the present days, one important focus of computer science is on security and secure communications. The use of Petri nets for verifying security properties is not a mature field due to a lack of convenient modeling and verification capabilities. So far, in the Petri Net field there is only CPN Tools that is mature enough for modeling, using the colored Petri nets formalism. Nevertheless such verifications cannot be performed on large systems as CPN Tools is based on an exhaustive way of computing the semantics of a model. In this paper we present the use of AlPiNA, another candidate for this task. AlPiNA is a symbolic model checker that uses the formalism of algebraic Petri nets. We have used it successfully for modeling ad hoc networks and for verifying security protocols designed for this type of networks. As a case study and benchmark we have chosen the ARAN secure routing protocol. We managed to find all the attacks that were already reported for this protocol. To our knowledge this work is also the first successful attempt to use Petri nets for model checking the security properties of ad hoc networks protocols.

Keywords: Model checking · Ad hoc networks · Algebraic petri nets

1 Introduction

Place/Transition nets are a modeling language that proved its effectiveness in modeling a large variety of systems based on concurrent processes. Over the years, the initial Petri net formalism was enriched in order to simplify the specification of more and more complex systems. Among many others, two of the applications targeted were the model checking of security protocols and of the ad hoc network protocols (but not ad hoc network security protocols). To the best of our knowledge, model checking the security protocols specially designed for ad hoc networks has not been reported yet.

Ad hoc networks are a novel approach to assuring communications. The communications networks that are now in use are based on an infrastructure

---

This work has been partially supported by the SCIEX SARPOT project.

M. Koutny et al. (Eds.): ToPNoC X, LNCS 9410, pp. 109–130, 2015.
DOI: 10.1007/978-3-662-48650-4_6

composed of devices like switches, hubs, gateways, routers, and so on. Ad hoc networks aim to assure communications without the use of any infrastructure. In such networks there are no other devices, except the (usually mobile) ones that actually form it, and want to communicate. And they will also act as the infrastructure devices from a classical network, by routing the messages of all the other nodes. Such a behavior is assured by specially designed ad hoc routing protocols. So there is a need to describe abstract dynamic structures for the specification of the routes in a dynamic topology.

One of the enrichments of P/T nets dedicated specifically to data based functionalities is High Level Petri Nets (HLPN). In HLPN the tokens have different types and these types are part of a many-sorted algebra [27]. The possibility to use other types than the usual black tokens made it possible to use HLPN in modeling and verification of security protocols. Colored Petri Nets (CPN) were the first concrete realization of HLPN that were used for model checking security properties [2]. But besides CPN, there are other implementations of HLPN. The difference between them stands in the way the many-sorted algebra is defined. In CPN the many-sorted algebra is defined using the CPN ML language, which was built upon the standard ML.

For modeling ad hoc networks we focus on the model checker AlPiNA [3,4]. AlPiNA implements HLPN by algebraic Petri nets (APN), in which the colored tokens are defined using algebraic abstract data types (AADT) [1]. Like all the other model checkers, the focus of AlPiNA is to handle the state explosion problem in order to perform verification on real size system models. When using HLPN, the state space explosion has one more dimension (the data) than in the case of P/T nets. HLPN are more expressive and as a consequence, the state space of a HLPN model is in general much bigger. AlPiNA addresses this problem by using symbolic techniques based on several layers of Data Decision Diagrams, Set Decision Diagrams and Sigma Decision Diagrams [1]. In addition, some optimizations specific to the APN formalism (algebraic clustering, partial algebraic unfolding) [5] are supported. The tool can be downloaded from [5]. In this paper we will present the modeling of ad hoc networks and the verification of ARAN (Authenticated Routing for Ad Hoc Networks [6]) security protocol with APNs, and the advantages of AlPiNA for performing these tasks, in terms of modeling the protocol itself, as well as the possible attackers.

The rest of the paper is organized as follows. The second section presents the use of Petri nets in literature for modeling ad hoc networks and verifying properties related to them. In the third section we describe the use of algebraic Petri nets and AlPiNA for modeling ad hoc networks and the ARAN protocol. The fourth section contains the presentation of our results regarding verification of routing information correctness for ARAN. The last section contains conclusions.

2   The Use of Petri Nets in Modeling Ad hoc Networks

Petri nets already proved their effectiveness in modeling ad hoc networks. So far, researchers have used Fuzzy Petri nets, Stochastic Petri nets and Colored

Petri nets to model ad hoc networks. The purpose of these models was to obtain qualitative or quantitative information about the behavior of applications and protocols in the context of ad hoc networks. As far as we know, algebraic Petri nets were never used so far to model ad hoc networks.

It is important to state for which reasons we have chosen algebraic Petri nets to model security protocols for ad hoc networks. For this we will compare them with the formalisms used by the most important model checkers designed for verifying security properties: AVISPA, Casper & FDR2, and CPN Tools. The main one is the nondeterministic character of this formalism. AVISPA uses automata as specification formalism, which lacks nondeterminism. But nondeterminism is a must when modeling ad hoc routing protocols, because they use distributed algorithms which are nondeterministic by nature. The second reason is the high level of the algebraic Petri net specification. When compared to process algebra (communicating sequential processes used by Casper & FDR2) and colored Petri nets, algebraic Petri nets are more expressive and thus more simple to use. The third reason is the fact that modeling with algebraic Petri nets is actually done at two levels: first at the level of the Petri net, and second at the algebraic level. This allows for a separation between the interactions of the components of the system and the description of these components. The interactions between the parts of the system will be specified at the Petri net level, and the behavior of each part will be specified at the algebraic level. This would not be possible if algebraic specifications or process algebras would be used. In the case of ad hoc routing protocols, the Petri net will describe the interactions between the nodes, the network and the adversary, and algebraic specifications will be used to describe the behavior of the nodes, of the routing protocol and of the adversary. This means that when implementing different routing protocols, modifications have to be made only at the algebraic level, but not at the Petri net level, where the interactions are the same, no matter what protocol is used.

We will continue by presenting some of the latest published results concerning the use of Petri nets in ad hoc network research.

2.1 Modeling for Quantitative Evaluation

The research presented in [7] uses Fuzzy Petri Nets for modeling and analyzing the QoS dimension in order to evaluate how to manage congestion in wireless ad hoc networks. The networks itself, the nodes, the communication protocol are not actually modeled. In [8] Fuzzy Petri Nets are used to represent the multicast routing in an ad hoc network and to calculate multicast trees. The authors only model the topology of the network but not the actual routing protocol.

In [9] the authors present how to use Stochastic Petri Nets to model ad hoc networks. An ad hoc network is modeled by a single node, for which a proper amount of traffic is generated. By measuring how the node behaves under the given traffic, using suitable metrics, some conclusions can be obtained regarding a whole network with a given number of nodes like the modeled one. In [10] Stochastic Petri Nets are used to model mobility of ad hoc networks, but the actual ad hoc network is not modeled, neither the ad hoc routing, only an application level protocol that takes into account the fact that the nodes are moving between different geographic regions. Thus the authors are able to obtain quantitative data about the specified performance indices.

The authors of [11,12] use Colored Petri Nets. They propose models for the nodes of the network, for the routing protocol AODV (Ad Hoc On-Demand Distance Vector Routing) [12] and DSR (Dynamic Source Routing) [11] and for the behavior of the ad hoc network. The purpose of the modeling was to conduct a comparison between the two ad hoc routing protocols mentioned above, from the point of view of their efficiency (number of generated overhead packets, data packet delivery delay). In [13] Colored Petri Nets are used to model and to compare another pair of routing protocols, AOMDV (Ad Hoc On-Demand Multipath Distance Vector Routing) and DSR. In [14], Colored Petri Nets are used to model and validate the specification of a multicast routing protocol for ad hoc networks called DYMO (Dynamic MANET On-Demand). The properties that the authors specify and verify are all related to the correctness of the protocol: establishments of routes and correct processing of the routing messages.

2.2   Modeling for Qualitative Evaluation

From the point of view of model checking security protocols, HLPN were the only type of Petri nets used for this purpose. For example, [2,15] present work using CPN to model check confidentiality and authentication for TMN authenticated key exchange protocol. In [16] CPN are used to verify Andrew secure RPC protocol. Bouroulet et al. presents in [26] a framework for the specification and verification of security protocols, based on HLPN. In all these papers, HLPN help to find attacks over the considered protocols, even some that were previously unknown. But as far as we know, no Petri nets were used to model check the security protocols of ad hoc networks. So our paper is the first presentation using algebraic Petri nets to model ad hoc networks and to do model checking of security properties for specific ad hoc network protocols.

In the next sections, we will present the state of the art of modeling ad hoc networks with the help of Petri nets. Modeling an ad hoc network implies modeling the following elements: the nodes and the topology of the network.

2.3   Modeling the Nodes

For modeling the nodes of an ad hoc network, a single approach was used by all the researchers. The nodes were modeled by their behavior in the considered protocol or application. The Petri net contains a single instance of a node's behavior. But this behavior is parameterized with the identity of a node. The identities of the nodes, which are part of the considered network, are placed inside a special place. When the state space is calculated, all these identities are considered as executing the modeled behavior [11].

2.4   Modeling the Topology

When modeling the topology of the ad hoc networks, two aspects should be taken into consideration. The first one is how to model the actual topology of the network at a given time. The second aspect is how to model the mobility of the nodes, which implies the modeling of the dynamicity of the topology. Both aspects influence the modeling of the way messages travel through the network. Based on the current topology, a message transmitted by a node should only be received by the other nodes which are in the coverage area of the transmitting node. So far, researches have proposed three ways for modeling the topology.

1. In [11–13] the network topology was modeled by an approximation mechanism. Let us assume that the network has n nodes. When a node A sends a broadcast message, it actually sends n-1 copies of the message to a place that stores them in order to distribute them to the corresponding nodes. Based on a probability that represents how many nodes are in the coverage area of A, a certain number of these messages will be forwarded to other nodes, and the remaining messages will be dropped. In the case of unicast messages, they are sent only to the corresponding nodes. The authors of [12] call this model a topology approximation mechanism and prove through simulation that it can indeed mimic the mobility of a mobile ad hoc network (MANET).
2. In [14] the wireless mobile ad hoc network is modeled by two parts: a part that handles the transmission of the packets, and another part that handles the mobility of the nodes. The transmission of the packets is done based on the current topology of the network, which is explicitly represented in the following way: each node A has an adjacency list of nodes. Each node from this list is a node that is in the coverage area of A, and thus can receive packets from it. Based on the information from these lists, the transmission part of the model of the ad hoc network sends the packets to the appropriate nodes. The mobility part of the model is responsible with making modification to the topology. At the beginning of the validation, there is an initial topology and also the possible topology changes. Based on these changes, the mobility part modifies the topology as the validation continues.
3. The authors of [17,18] use reconfigurable algebraic higher-order net systems in order to model mobility for the ad hoc networks. The idea is to apply graph transformation (rewriting of the model) to algebraic nets. That is, the net gets reconfigured at run time in order to simulate the mobility of the nodes in an ad hoc network. The modeling is abstracted from the network layer, and the considered application is modeled in terms of work-flows.

3   Using Algebraic Petri Nets for Ad hoc Networks

3.1   Algebraic Petri Nets Definition

An APN is a HLPN where algebraic abstract data types are used. The structure of the net is the structure of a Place/Transition net, but algebraic values are used as tokens. Also, the transitions can have guards that are pairs of algebraic terms that allow the firing of the respective transitions. In the following a sketch of the model components are given, more details can be found in [1].

Definition 1. *Let* $\Sigma = \langle S, F \rangle$ *be a signature and* X *be a* S*-sorted set of variables. The set of* **terms of** Σ **over** X *is a* S*-sorted set* $T_{\Sigma,X}$*, where each set* $(T_{\Sigma,X})_s$ *is inductively defined as follows:*

- *each variable* $x \in X_s$ *is a term of sort* s*, i.e.,* $x \in (T_{\Sigma,X})_s$*;*
- *each constant* $f \in F_{\epsilon,s}$ *is a term of sort* s*, i.e.,* $f \in (T_{\Sigma,X})_s$*;*
- *for all operations that are not a constant* $f \in F_{w,s}$*, with* $w = s_1 \ldots s_n$*, and for all n-tuple of terms* $(t_1 \ldots t_n)$ *such that all* $t_i \in (T_{\Sigma,X})_{s_i} (1 \le i \le n)$*,* $f(t_1 \ldots t_n) \in (T_{\Sigma,X})_s$*.*

Definition 2. *Let* $\Sigma = \langle S, F \rangle$ *be a signature. The* **multiset extension of** Σ *is noted* $[\Sigma] = \langle S', F' \rangle$*, such that:*

- $S' = S \cup \{[s] | \forall s \in S\}$*;*
-

$$F' = F \cup_{s \in S} \begin{cases} \emptyset_s : & \epsilon \to [s] \\ [\_]_s : & s \to [s] \\ +_s : & [s], [s] \to [s] \\ -_s : & [s], [s] \to [s]. \end{cases}$$

Definition 3. *An* **algebraic Petri net specification** *is a 5-tuple* $N{-}SPEC = < Spec, T, P, X, AX >$*, where:*

- *Spec* $=< \Sigma, X', E >$ *is an algebraic specification extended in* $< [\Sigma], X', E >$*, where* $\Sigma = \langle S, F \rangle$*;*
- T *is the set of transition names;*
- P *is the set of place names and there is a function* $\tau : P \to S$ *which associates a sort to each place;*
- X *is a* S*-sorted set of variables;*
- *AX is a set of axioms (see below).*

Definition 4. *Given an algebraic Petri net specification* $N - SPEC =< Spec, T, P, X, AX >$*, an* **axiom** *in* AX *is a 4-tuple* $< t, Cond, In, Out >$ *such that:*

- $t \in T$ *is the transition name for which the axiom is defined;*
- *Cond* $\subseteq T_{\Sigma,X} \times T_{\Sigma,X}$ *is a set of equalities attached to the transition name* t *for this axiom; Cond is satisfied if and only if all the equalities from the set are satisfied;*
- $In = (In_p)_{p \in P}$ *is a* P*-sorted set of terms such that* $\forall p \in P, In_p \in (T_{[\Sigma],X})_{[\tau(p)]}$ *is the label of the arc from place* p *to transition* t*;*
- $Out = (Out_p)_{p \in P}$ *is a* P*-sorted set of terms such that* $\forall p \in P, Out_p \in (T_{[\Sigma],X})_{[\tau(p)]}$ *is the label of the arc from transition* t *to place* p*.*

In AlPiNA, the input of a transition is a set that can only contain variables and closed terms [4]. However, this limitation has no effect over the complexity of the systems that can be modeled and verified. It just reduces the complexity of the computations.

In order to provide a semantics to a specification $N - SPEC$, we can define the set of reachable states $StN - SPEC(M)$ from a given marking M. In this paper we do not need its precise definition; please consult [1] for more details.

3.2 Case Study: ARAN Secure Routing Protocol

In order to present our methodology for modeling ad hoc networks, we have taken as case study the ARAN secure routing protocol. We have chosen it because it is simple, well known and it is the state of the art regarding secure routing in ad hoc networks. The purpose of ARAN is to provide a route path for any node in the network. It is an implicit routing protocol, which means that it will not respond with the whole path, but only with the identity of the next node in the path. ARAN uses digital signatures to assure authentication and integrity for the exchanged routing information.

ARAN uses two message types: route discovery and route response. Each message is signed by its source node. As it travels to its destination, the signed message is also cosigned by each intermediate node, after eliminating the signature of the previous intermediary, if it exists. Each node validates the received message by validating the signature(s) from the message. If the signature(s) are not valid, the message is discarded. Otherwise, the intermediary node broadcasts the message, if it is a route discovery message, or unicast it, if it is a route response message. When a route discovery message reaches destination, the node will respond with a route response message. When a route response reaches destination, the node will modify its routing table accordingly. Also, each intermediary node that receives a route response for a route discovery that he processed, will also update its routing table. Each route from the routing table has a given lifetime. When no traffic has occurred on an existing route for that route's lifetime, the route is deactivated. When data is received for an inactive route, the recipient node will demand a new route request for the targeted destination node. So topology changes will determine route inactivation in some nodes' routing tables, which will further determine new route requests for the destination. For more information regarding the protocol, please consult [6].

The modeling of ARAN implies the modeling of the following elements: the nodes, the ad hoc network, the adversary and the protocol operation. The general model for ARAN is given in Fig. 1. The algebraic Petri net designed for modeling this protocol is presented throughout the paper in Figs. 3 and 5. For a better understanding of the explanations, it is worth mentioning that these figures present different parts of the same APN, and that they have to be seen together, in order to understand the general idea of our model. The only missing part is that for modeling the attacker, but we think that the explanation provided is simple enough to understand the corresponding APN part. We will now continue with the presentation of all the parts of the model.

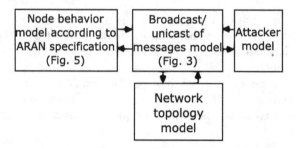

Fig. 1. ARAN general model

3.3 Modeling the Nodes

A node of the ad hoc network is modeled as a AADT *Node*. Each node has an identity which is unique in the ad hoc network. Each node has also a routing table and some other structures needed for the operation of the considered ad hoc routing protocol. Because ARAN uses digital signatures, each node also has a pair of public/private keys and a digital certificate. In addition, each node knows the public key of the certification authority that issued his certificate.

Since all the nodes are identical, they all behave the same way. So in the actual Petri net, all the nodes are tokens inside the place called *Nodes*. Here is the main part of the AADT *Node* in the case of ARAN:

```
Generators
node: Identity, RouteDiscoveryRequests, RouteDiscoveryRequests,
        RoutingTable, Nonce, Certificate, PrivateKey,
        PublicKey -> Node;
Operations
get_identity: Node -> Identity;
. . .
Axioms
get_identity(node($i, $rdr, $rp, $rt, $n, $c, $priv, $pub))=$i;
. . .
```

All the elements used by the *node* generator are other AADTs that define (in this order): the identity of the node, a list with the route discovery requests that were already broadcasted, a list with the route discovery responses that were already forwarded, a lists with the routes, the current value for the nonce used in the messages, the certificate of the node, the private key of the node, and the public key of the certification authority that issues certificates for the nodes.

3.4 Modeling the Topology

An ad hoc network can be defined as a directed graph. The nodes of the graph are the nodes of the ad hoc network, and the arcs represent the fact that two

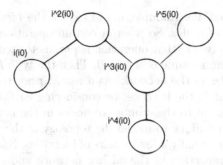

Fig. 2. An example of an ad hoc network topology

nodes can communicate directly through their wireless devices. So the topology of an ad hoc network can be represented as a graph. We modeled it as the AADT *Topology*, which is in fact a list of pairs of node identities, and represents the arc list that defines the graph. We have assume that the connections are bidirectional, so if the list constains the pair of identities *(a, b)*, representing the fact that the node with identity *a* can communicate with the node with identity *b*, it will also contain the pair *(b, a)*. The actual topology is contained in a variable of the type *Topology*. Its value can be given in two different ways. Depending on the type of properties that will be verified, the first or the second approach will be preferred. The first way is to give the value explicitly. In this case, the model will represent the exact ad hoc network that has that topology. For example, the topology of the ad hoc network given in Fig. 2, will be defined by the next term (where *i0* is the generator of the AADT *Identity*, which models the unique identifier for each of the nodes):

```
cons(pairIdentityIdentity(i(i0), i^2(i0)),
cons(pairIdentityIdentity(i^2(i0), i(i0)),
cons(pairIdentityIdentity(i^2(i0), i^3(i0)),
cons(pairIdentityIdentity(i^3(i0), i^2(i0)),
cons(pairIdentityIdentity(i^3(i0), i^4(i0)),
cons(pairIdentityIdentity(i^4(i0), i^3(i0)),
cons(pairIdentityIdentity(i^3(i0), i^5(i0)),
cons(pairIdentityIdentity(i^5(i0), i^3(i0)), empty))))))))
```

The second way is to not assign any value to the variable. This way it will be a free variable. Then, with the use of domain unfolding, AlPiNA will generate for that variable all the possible values within a given range. We will next explain how this works and the impact of such a choice.

3.5   Using Unfolding to Model Topology

Unfolding is used for the verification process in order to let the user define the part of the domain of a data type that will be taken into consideration when the state space is computed. For example, in our model, the *Identity* AADT is used for the identification of nodes. So when a certain operation must be done for all the nodes in the network, that operation is parameterized with a variable of type *Identity* for which no value is specified. Then the type *Identity* is unfolded to the number of nodes in the network. As a result, prior to building the state space, AlPiNA will unfold the Petri net by considering for that *Identity* variable all the possible values, up to the number of nodes in the network. Let us show how we can use this technique to model the topology of the ad hoc networks.

Topology AADT is actually a list of pairs of identities. Each pair of identities represents a direct connection in the ad hoc network and it is defined by the AADT *PairIdentityIdentity*. So the definition of the type *Topology* is based on the type *PairIdentityIdentity*, which is based on the type *Identity*. As a result, in order to unfold *Topology*, one needs to unfold also the other two types. Unfolding of a data type is specified by the name of the type, and the limit that will be considered for the domain. Here is an example of unfolding specification for *Topology* and for its dependencies.

```
Identity : TOTAL;
PairIdentityIdentity : TOTAL;
Topology : 3;
```

The type *Identity* is unfolded to the number of nodes in the network; the type *PairIdentityIdentity* is totally unfolded. That means that all the possible pairs that can be created with the identities of the nodes in the network will be taken into consideration. *Topology* is then unfolded up to the specified depth. In the example above, the specified depth is three. So in this specific case, AlPiNA will take into consideration all the lists with at most three pairs that can be constructed with the pairs obtained by unfolding *PairIdentityIdentity* type. This way, we have actually defined all the topologies that a network can have with the given number of nodes, and in which there are at most three nodes which can directly communicate.

The number of topologies that will be taken into consideration in a non deterministic way, through the above unfolding mechanism, depends on the number n of nodes in the network, and on the number m of direct connections between them. This value represents the number of combinations of pairs that can be formed with n identities, taken m at a time. If $m < n-1$, the network is never connected, but the structure may evolve with time. Likewise if $2m < n$, some nodes are isolated, but they may change with time. As the values for n and m increase, this value is rapidly increasing too. Unfortunately, the topology of the network cannot be abstracted, nor parameterized because of the way message exchange is done in wireless networks. In the case of a broadcast, the nodes which should receive the message can be determined only from the topology. Likewise, in the case of unicast or multicast, the topology is the only information regarding the fact that a node should receive the message or not. In conclusion, the topologies have to be taken into consideration explicitly.

Let us consider an example. If the ad hoc network has three nodes: A, B, and C, it means that for *Identity* all these three values will be considered. Next, because *PairIdentityIdentity* is totally unfolded, the following values will be considered for it: AB, AC, BA, BC, CA, and CB. As a result, Topology can have the following values:

(1) {},
(2) {AB}, {AC}, {BA}, {BC}, {CA}, {CB},
(3) {AB, AC}, {AB, BA}, {AB, BC}, {AB, CA}, {AB, CB},
. . . ,
(4) {AB, BA, BC}, {AB, BA, CA}, {AB, BA, CB},
. . .

One could notice that, because we have assumed the connections are bidirectional, pairs like $\{AB\}$ and $\{BA\}$, or the group of pairs like $\{AB, BA, BC\}$ and $\{AB, BA, CB\}$ are equivalent, in the sense that they represent the same topology (equivalent topologies). This is due to the way the unfolding mechanism is actually implemented in AlPiNA, mechanism over which the user has no control. As a consequence, AlPiNA will take into consideration the same topology several times, as equivalent topologies are generated by the unfolding.

With (1) we consider the topology in which none of the nodes have direct wireless connections. With (2) we consider the possible topologies in which only two nodes can communicate directly, the third one being outside the communication range with each of the other two. With (3) we consider the possible topologies in which there are two groups of two nodes which can reach each other. And with (4) we consider all the topologies in which there are three groups of two nodes which can communicate with each other.

If the same value is considered for the topology for a whole protocol run, it means that after considering all these values, the protocol will be verified for all the possible static topologies for three nodes. Let us consider the following example. If the same topology $\{AB, BA, CB\}$ is considered for all the message exchanges in the protocol run, it means that the protocol was verified for that static topology.

When different values for the topology are successively considered in the same protocol run, it means that the protocol is verified over a dynamic topology. So because of the fact that the order in which each of these values is considered is non deterministic, the verification will be made for all the possible dynamic topologies and for all the possible node movements in each of the topologies. To exemplify this feature, let us assume that, in the same protocol run, when sending a message, the considered topology is $\{AB, BA, CB\}$ (first configuration), but when the next message is sent, the value considered for the topology is $\{AB, BA\}$ (second configuration). This means that between the sending of the two messages, node C has left the coverage area of B, so it can no longer communicate with B. In this case the protocol was verified for a dynamic topology evolving from the first configuration to the second one.

Because it is a list, *Topology* is an unbounded data type. So unfolding its entire domain is impossible. But AlPiNA allows the partial unfolding up to a given bound on the number of elements, as we explained above. It is important to state that this second way of defining the topology of the network is particular to AlPiNA and it works thanks to a special characteristic of the verification algorithm called partial net unfolding. Partial net unfolding means that it is not mandatory to unfold all the types, and the user can choose only the type that it needed to be unfolded [1].

When the topology is defined as a closed term, AlPiNA will compute the state space for the given algebraic Petri net N, starting from the initial marking. If M_0 is the initial marking, then the state space computed for a given topology can be written as:

$$St_N(M_0). \tag{1}$$

When the topology is defined by unfolding, the algebraic Petri net is parameterized by a free variable of type Topology. If $tp is the name of this variable, then the parameterized algebraic Petri net can be written as:

$$N(\$tp). \tag{2}$$

By unfolding, AlPiNA will instantiate the variable $tp with each of the possible values of the topology, as explained above, thus computing a set of algebraic Petri nets, one for each value:

$$N = \cup_{x \in T_{\Sigma, Topology}} N(x). \tag{3}$$

The obtained Petri net is the net over which the model checking will be performed. As defined above, it is a reunion of a number of Petri nets equal to the number of network topologies that can be constructed with the given number of nodes. All these Petri nets are identical, except the part concerning the topology. So, when they will be reunited, the identical parts will overlap and the distinct topologies will become a multiset of terms that will be considered when the state space will be constructed. The topology is used for message transmission to determine what nodes will receive a broadcast message and if a unicast message can indeed be received by its destination node. We will describe this part of the Petri net in more detail in the next section. Having several values for the topology means that when a message has to be distributed to the receivers, all the possible topologies will be taken into consideration, thus resulting in multiple possibilities. Each of these possibilities will lead to a different path in the state space of the model. At the end of the state space computation, it will represent all the possible message exchanges between the nodes, no matter how they can be arranged to form a wireless ad hoc network and no matter how they move inside this network.

When computing the state space, AlPiNA will actually compute the set of state spaces such that each state space corresponds to a value for the topology. We can write this as follows:

$$St_N(M_0) = \cup_{x \in T_{\Sigma, Topology}} St_{N(x)}(M_0). \tag{4}$$

As it will be presented in Sect. 4, the security properties that we have model checked with AlPiNA were expressed through an invariant property. In order to check such a property, AlPiNA starts by computing the state space of the algebraic Petri net provided as input. Then, it checks if the specified property is true for each of the states. If it is, then the property holds for the model. If not, the property does not hold for the model, and a counter-example is provided.

If the topology is defined as a closed term, checking a property for the model implies checking the property for the state space computed for the corresponding APN.

$$St_N(M_0) \models invariant\ property \tag{5}$$

If the topology is defined by unfolding, checking a property for all models implies checking it for the set of state spaces generated by instantiating the topology variable with all the possible values.

$$(5) \Leftrightarrow \cup_{x \in T_{\Sigma,Topology}}(St_{N(x)}(M_0) \models invariant\ property) \tag{6}$$

So we will check the invariant on all instances; finding a contradiction will mean there is one topology evolution that contradicts the invariant. If the invariant is satisfied on the whole model it means that it is obviously satisfied in each instance. It seems heavy to do it on all topologies (static and dynamic) but fortunately it remains tractable due to the large possible sharing of topologies in the behavioral computations.

3.6 Modeling the Network

The message exchange in an ad hoc network has special characteristics, because all the nodes act like routers. When a node transmits a message, it is received only by the nodes which have a direct connection to that node at that point. Then, each of the nodes which received the message, processes it according to the routing protocol, and then retransmits it. This process continues until the message gets to the destination or the emission fails. Another aspect that must be taken into consideration is the fact that messages can be of unicast or broadcast type. If a message is unicast, it will be processed only by the node to which it is intended. If a message is broadcast, it should be processed by all the nodes which can receive it directly at that point, according to the present topology.

All the messages transmitted by the nodes are represented by the tokens from the place called *Transmitted Packets* (Fig. 3). The transitions *Packet is Unicast* and *packet is Multicast*, which model the behavior of the network, process these tokens and put the output tokens in the place called *Received Packets* (Fig. 3), from where the nodes can take them for processing (see Fig. 5) and so on.

In order to have in the High level Petri net model the behavior presented above, we need to model accordingly two elements: the format of the messages exchanged by the nodes and the network itself. Regarding the format of the messages, besides the fields that a message has according to the considered routing protocol, we added two extra fields: a field that stores the identity of the previous node that transmitted it (*prev*), and a field that represents the identity of the node which should receive the message (*next*). If next field contains the value *i0*, then it means that the message is broadcast. Otherwise the message is unicast. The structure of the AADT *Packet* is provided in Fig. 4. The modeling

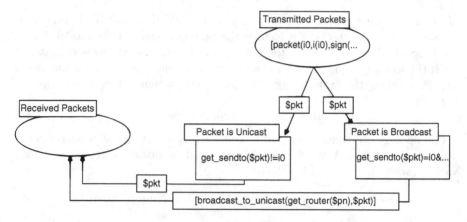

Fig. 3. The model for the Ad Hoc network operation

Identity of the node that sent the message	Identity of the node that should process the message/ Broadcast message	Signature(s)			
		Message type (route discovery request/route discovery response)	Destination node	Nonce	Certificate(s)

Fig. 4. The model for the ARAN messages

of the transmission/reception of a message is given in Fig. 3. All the messages transmitted by the nodes are stored in the place called *Transmitted Packets*. From here they are processed in order to provide the behavior explained in the previous paragraph. First we check if the message is unicast or broadcast. If it is unicast, no other processing is required (transition *Packet is unicast*) so the message is placed in the *Received Packets* place from where the destination node can pick it up for processing.

If the message is broadcast (transition *Packet is broadcast*), we search in the topology for all the identities of the nodes which can receive the message according to it, and we produce the same number of copies for the message, but with the next field filled with the corresponding identity. To verify in the APN if a certain node with identity i can receive a message, we search the variable of type *Topology* if it contains a pair of identities formed by the identity stored in *prev* and by i.

It is worth mentioning that this model of broadcast has an atomicity problem caused by some limitations of the Petri nets. Unfortunately there is no better way of modeling it with the current formalism. The problem is the fact that all the copies of the broadcasted message should reach all the destination nodes at the same time, as if they would be produced in the same transition. This is not possible to model, so, as a result, given the non determinism of the Petri net, other transitions could be fired before all the copies reach the destination nodes. This could be solved by an extension of the Petri net, as the one proposed in [20]. The LLAMAS (Language for Advanced Modular Algebraic Systems) model proposed here is based on the old ideas of CO-OPN [25] and it uses synchronization between transitions in order to provide a better control of the atomicity. By using such synchronization it would be possible to force the correct transmission of a broadcast message by preventing any other transition to fire before the transition that handles the broadcast fires all the possible times, handling all the tokens that represent the copies of the broadcasted message for each intended node. Such a mechanism will also have an impact over the combinatorial explosion by eliminating possibilities that have no meaning in the real ad hoc networks.

3.7   Modeling the Adversary

The model that we used for the adversary was the Dolev-Yao model [21]. In this model it is presumed that the adversary can perform the following operations:

- he can intercept all the messages transmitted in the network (1);
- he can generate new messages based on the knowledge he obtained from the intercepted messages (2);
- he can transmit messages (without modifying them) in the name of any node in the network (3);
- he can prevent a node from receiving a message that was meant for it, with the purpose of sending it another message (4).

So far we have only implemented attack types (1), (3) and (4). As a consequence, cryptographic security properties like authentication, confidentiality and integrity cannot be checked. On the contrary, correctness properties can be checked and we will present how in Sect. 4. To implement attack types (1), (3) and (4), the adversary was modeled as having access to all the messages exchanged in the network (places *Transmitted Packets* and *Received Packets* in Fig. 3). Thus he can perform the following actions: he can intercept all the messages (attack type (1)), he can retransmit a message (without modifying it) to another node than the node it was meant for (attack type (3)), and he can drop a message and thus prevent a node to receive it (attack type (4)) with the purpose of replacing the dropped message with another one.

Implementing a new attack type in this configuration is very simple. We will next present the principle of plugging a new attack type by exemplifying an attack of type (2). We will start by describing the implementation used for the replay attack. The attacker has access to all the messages that travel through the network, being able to use the tokens from the place *Transmitted Packets* which represents all the messages created by the nodes. The modifications that the attacker performs over the messages are modeled by the operation *change_sendto* that changes the intended destination of a message to the identity of each of the other nodes present in the network. The modified messages are then reintroduced

in the network by being put to place *Received Packets*. For exemplification pur-
poses, we next present the axiom for the *change_sendto* operation (*packet* is the
generator of the AADT that models the messages. Its structure was explained in
Sect. 3.6. One can see that the identity of the intended destination node (*next*)
is changed with another identity (*i*).):

```
change_sendto($i, packet($next,$prev,$signature,$certificate))=
packet($i,$prev,$signature,$certificate);
```

To plug in a new attack type one has to define a similar transition, that uses a
new operation of the type *change_sendto*. These are the only modifications that
have to be done. Next, the new operation has to be defined and its axioms have
to be provided. To implement a fabrication attack of type (2) one has to define
a new operation, e.g. *fabricate_message*, and to define axioms such that it will
generate new messages based on the previous messages seen by the attacker. In
order to obtain such a behavior, the attacker would have to memorize all the
information he can extract from the messages that travel through the network.
So *fabricate_message* operation would have to also extract information from the
messages and to manage the collection of extracted information. To resume,
fabricate_message would have to have two arguments: the current message and
the collection of extracted information, and would have to return a new message. The axiomatic definition of *fabricate_message* would have to address the
following: extraction of the information sent in clear; memorizing the extracted
information in the collection; and finally, generation of new messages based on
all the possible combinations of the information stored in the collection. One can
observe that plugging in a new attack type has only minor implications for the
Petri net, and that the heavy part is modeled by the axioms of the used AADTs.

3.8   ARAN Operation

When modeling ARAN, we have focused on the most important part of the
protocol - route discovery. As one can see from Fig. 5, the behavior of a node
that participates in a route discovery was modeled with two transitions. The
transition *REP Packet at source* corresponds to the fact that the node that initiated the route request receives the response message. The transition *Packet
processing* corresponds to all the other processing that a node has to do: broadcast of a route request message by an intermediary node, reception of the route
request message by the targeted node, validation of the digital signature(s) from
the message, response to a route request message by the destination node, and
the unicast of a response to a route discovery message. The actual behavior is
implemented by axioms in the AADTs that define the nodes, the messages, the
certificates, and the cryptographic operations. The conceptual difference between
the two transitions is the presence of the place called *Witness Nodes I*. The purpose of *Witness Nodes I* will be explained in the following paragraph.

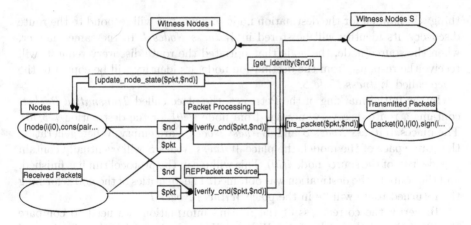

Fig. 5. The model for the node behavior in ARAN

4   Verification of Security Properties for ARAN

The security objectives of ARAN are to provide authentic and correct routing information. Thus, the security properties that have to be verified are authentication of the nodes which participate in the route discovery, and integrity and correctness of the exchanged routing information. ARAN was already modeled and verified using different tools, and we will only cite the latest paper on the subject, [22]. ARAN is successful in assuring authentication and integrity, but an intruder can disturb it by replaying attacks and can propagate incorrect information about the topology of the network. In order to validate our modeling method using AlPiNA, we wanted to see if we will obtain the same results as the ones already reported by previous research.

The security property that we have verified is correctness of routing information. Authentication and integrity were not considered for reasons explained in Sect. 3. To present what correctness of routing information means, we will use an example. As presented, our model is capable of handling dynamic topologies, but to keep the explanation simple for this example only, we will consider the static topology depicted in Fig. 2. If $i(i0)$ is the initiator node, and $i^5(i0)$ is the destination node, then the expected path between them that should be returned by the protocol is: $i(i0)$, $i^2(i0)$, $i^3(i0)$, and $i^5(i0)$. We say that the protocol provided correct routing information, if and only if for each route discovery request made by node $i(i0)$ for node $i^5(i0)$, the protocol will always return the above path. In all the other cases the routing information would not be correct.

In order to verify routing information correctness, we reduced the model of the intruder so that it will only use the possibility of replay attacks. Also, we added to the Petri net the places *Witness Nodes I* and *Witness Nodes S*. Their role will be presented next. Each time an intermediary node along the routing path from the source node to the destination node processes a message related to the discovery process, its identity is stored in *Witness Nodes I*. The same thing will happen for the destination node too: when it will respond to the route discovery, its identity will be stored in *Witness Nodes I*. In the same manner, when the source node, the node that initiated the route discovery request, will receive the response from the destination node, its identity will be copied to the place called *Witness Node S*.

In the initial marking of the Petri net, the place called *Transmitted Packets* contains a route discovery message from node $i(i0)$ for the destination $i^5(i0)$. The places *Witness Nodes S* and *Witness Nodes I* are empty. When generating the state space of the model, the place *Witness Nodes S* will eventually contain the identity of the source node $i(i0)$. This will mean the protocol run has finished, and the route to the destination was obtained. The identities of the nodes forming the returned route will be in the place *Witness Nodes I*.

To verify the correctness of the routing information, we need to compare the identities of the nodes from *Witness Nodes I* place with the identities of the nodes from the actual path in the considered topology. Using the property specification language available in AlPiNA, we have specified this property in the following way: If the number of nodes in the place *Witness Nodes S* is equal to one it implies that the number of nodes in the place *Witness Nodes I* is equal to the number of nodes in the path from the considered topology (noted with *value* in the below specification). Here is the specification of this property in AlPiNA's property specification language:

```
(card($x in WitnessNodesS) = 1 ) =>
       (card($y in WitnessNodesI) = value );
```

If the property holds when model checking is performed, it means the protocol provided correct routing information. Otherwise, the routing information is incorrect and AlPiNA will display a counter-example: content for the place *Witness Nodes I* that contains a different number of nodes. Based on this counterexample, we can reconstruct the attack performed by the intruder.

After performing the model checking we have seen that the protocol does not always provide correct routing information, meaning that the intruder was able to mount an attack on it (in concordance with [22]).

Returning to the example we have considered when explaining how the verification is done, when model checking the protocol for this topology, the place *Witness Nodes I*, contains $\{i^2(i0)\}$, or $\{i^3(i0)\}$, or $\{i^5(i0)\}$, or $\{i^2(i0), i^3(i0), i^5(i0)\}$. Only the last value for *Witness Nodes I* corresponds to a correct run of the protocol. The other values represent incorrect routing information that the intruder manages to propagate in the network by replaying attacks. For example, if place *Witness Nodes I* contains $\{i^5(i0)\}$, it means that the intruder managed to replay the route discovery message sent by $i(i0)$ to $i^5(i0)$, and prevented node $i^2(i0)$ from receiving it. In this way $i^5(i0)$ believes it has a direct connection with A, and responds accordingly. The intruder does the same with the route response message from $i^5(i0)$ (Table 1).

The table above presents quantitative information regarding the verification of routing information correctness, as previously described, in comparison with

Table 1. Quantitative information

Tool name	Tool's performance for ARAN		
	Number of nodes	*Time (s)*	No of states
AlPiNA	4 (all nodes attacked)	0.95	436
	5 (all nodes attacked)	3.70	4655
	6 (all nodes attacked)	80.82	77239
	7 (all nodes attacked)	110.95	79131
	8 (all nodes attacked)	20.22	11637
	9 (all nodes attacked)	32.92	15500
	10 (all nodes attacked)	44.06	19363
AVISPA	4	0.05	–
	5	0.07	–

another model checker called AVISPA, used in [22], where the authors reported the same verification results as ours. The variable of the runs is the number of nodes, besides the adversary, in the topology of the ad hoc network that is taken into consideration. For some of the cases, AlPiNA was unable to compute the state space for all the possible attacks. So we limited the number of nodes which were attacked to some maximum value, which is provided in the table between parentheses, in the same cell as the number of nodes.

AVISPA uses an on-the-fly model checking technique in which attacks are searched for without a prior computation of the state space. On the contrary, AlPiNA first computes the state space in a symbolic manner, and only then makes the search for attacks. As a consequence, the values provided for AVISPA represent the time of finding the replaying attack for the considered specification, while in the case of AlPiNA, the time column represents the time of computing the entire state space of the considered model. These values cannot be directly compared, but they reveal the fact that AlPiNA is capable of handling the whole state space of the specifications verified with AVISPA, but with the limitation on the number of attacked nodes. AlPiNA is capable of handling state spaces of 1-2 millions of states, but in this case, because of the atomicity problem presented at the end of Subsect. 3.6, starting with 7 nodes, all being attacked, the size of the state spaces goes directly to more millions of states than AlPiNA can handle. This is the reason of using these limitations and also the reason for the fact that the biggest size of the state space in the table is a little less than 80000. So more research is needed regarding these aspects, in order to find a solution to overcome the limitations and to be able to make verifications for more general cases. Only this way one will be sure that no possible attacked is missed.

In [22], the authors state they were unable to check the protocol for more than five nodes, because of the state space explosion. But using AlPiNA, we managed to model check the protocol for ten nodes (with 5 nodes attacked). It is worth mentioning that these results are also superior to the ones reported in other papers like [23,24], where the maximum number of considered nodes is six. Although these papers describe the application of model checking techniques to other protocols than ARAN, the difference in the maximum number of nodes from the considered topologies is still important, because dealing with the topologies is the heavy part of the model checker, and not the protocol operation itself, as we have shown in the third section.

5   Conclusions and Future Work

In this paper we have presented a proof of concept for the use of algebraic Petri nets for modeling ad hoc networks and for verifying correctness properties for security protocols specially designed for this type of networks, with the use of AlPiNA, a symbolic model checker based on APNs. As far as we know this is the first report of using Petri nets for verifying security properties of the protocols designed for ad hoc networks.

As one can see from the figures we have provided, the Petri net that models the ad hoc network and the security protocol is very simple and clear and has a very small number of places. For example, the model for ARAN has six places. The heavy part of the model is represented by the AADTs that were defined. Thus AlPiNA combines the powerful symbolic model checking with the easy to use APN formalism, providing a good user experience, but also with the ability to master state space explosion, at the price of some limitations.

The limitations of our approach refer to the fact that fabrication attacks were not considered. Fabrication refers to the ability of the intruder to create and send new messages, based on what he previously learned from the network. Our model for the adversary is able to use the messages learned from the network, but cannot create new messages. Because it is a symbolic model checker, when an attack is found, AlPiNA cannot provide attack traces. This makes it very difficult to model fabrication attacks, because of the lack of feedback from the tool. But we plan to address this limitation by developing a technique for inversing transitions in an APN, and thus providing attack traces and the necessary feedback.

The model and the verification performed for ARAN secure routing protocol discovered the attack that was previously reported for this protocol. This indicates the validity of the method, but most importantly, it indicates that AlPiNA can be used with success for verifying security protocols.

As future work, we have proposed to perform a quantitative comparison between CPN Tools and AlPiNA in order to see the actual performance improvement brought by the latter. Also we will work on proposing an extension to the current APN model, that will be more adequate to the modeling of distributed protocols, in general, and which, in particular, will be able to handle broadcast and similar operations in a correct manner. Another future work direction is to modify the modeling of the topology, such that equivalent topologies will be eliminated from the verification, thus reducing the state space and increasing the performance of the model checking.

References

1. Hostettler, S.P.: High-level Petri net model checking: the symbolic way, Ph.D. thesis, University of Geneva (2011)
2. Permpoontanalarp, Y., Sornkhom, P.: A new colored petri net methodology for the security analysis of cryptographic protocols. In: The 10th Workshop and Tutorial on Practical Use of Colored Petri Nets and the CPN Tools, Denmark, pp. 81–100 (2009)
3. Buchs, D., Hostettler, S., Marechal, A., Risoldi, M.: AlPiNA: a symbolic model checker. In: Lilius, J., Penczek, W. (eds.) PETRI NETS 2010. LNCS, vol. 6128, pp. 287–296. Springer, Heidelberg (2010)
4. Hostettler, S.P., Marechal, A., Linard, A., Risoldi, M., Buchs, D.: High-level petri net model checking with AlPiNA. Fundamenta Informaticae, **113**(3–4), August 2011, ISSN **0169–2968**, 229–264 (2011)
5. AlPiNA tool web page, 10 March 2015. http://alpina.unige.ch/
6. Sanzgiri, K., Dahill, B.: A secure routing protocol for ad hoc networks. In: Proceedings of the 10th IEEE International Conference on Network Protocols, pp. 78–87 (2002)
7. Khoukhi, L., Cherkaui, S.: Intelligent solution for congestion control in wireless ad hoc networks. In: WONS 2006: Third Annual Conference on Wireless On-demand Network Systems and Services, pp. 10–19 (2006)
8. Chiang, T-C., Huang, Z-M.: Multicast routing representation in ad hoc networks using fuzzy petri nets. In: Proceedings of the 18th International Conference on Advanced Information Networking and Application, vol. 2, p. 420 (2004)
9. Zhang, C., Zhou, M.: A stochastic petri net approach to modeling and analysis of ad hoc network. In: Proceedings of the International Conference on Information Technology: Research and Education, pp. 152–156 (2003)
10. Beccuti, M., De Pierro, M., Horvath, A., Horvath, A., Farkas, K.: A mean field based methodology for modeling mobility in ad hoc networks. In: IEEE 73rd, Vehicular Technology Conference (VTC Spring), 2011, pp. 1–5 (2011)
11. Prasad, P., Singh, B., Sahoo, A.K.: Validation of Routing Protocol for Mobile Ad Hoc Networks using Colored Petri Nets, bachelor thesis. National Institute of Technology, Rourkela (2009)
12. Xiong, C., Murata, T., Tsai, J.: Modeling and simulation of routing protocol for mobile ad hoc networks using colored petri nets. Proc. Conf. Appl. Theory Petri Nets Formal Meth. Software Eng. De-fence Syst. **12**, 145–153 (2002)
13. Jamali, M.A.J., Khosravi, T.: Validation of ad hoc on-demand multipath distance vector using colored petri nets. Int. Conf. Comput. Softw. Model. Singap. **14**, 29–34 (2011)
14. Espensen, K.L., Kjeldsen, M.K., Kristensen, L.M.: Modelling and initial validation of the DYMO routing protocol for mobile ad-hoc networks. In: van Hee, K.M., Valk, R. (eds.) PETRI NETS 2008. LNCS, vol. 5062, pp. 152–170. Springer, Heidelberg (2008)
15. Permpoontanalarp, Y., Changkhanak, A.: Security Analysis of the TMN protocol by using colored petri nets: on-the-fly trace generation method and homomorphic property In: The 8th International Joint Conference on Computer Science and Software Engineering (JCSSE), pp. 63–68 (2011)
16. Yang, X.: Modeling and analysis of security protocols using colored petri nets. J. Comput. **6**(1), 19–27 (2011)

17. Golas, U., Hoffman, K., Ehrig, H., Rein, A., Padberg, J.: Functional analysis of algebraic higher-order net systems with applications to mobile ad-hoc networks. Bulletin EATCS **101**, 148–160 (2010)
18. Padberg, J., Ehrig, H., Ribeiro, L.: Formal modeling and analysis of flexible processes in mobile ad-hoc networks. Bulletin EATCS, 128–132 (2007)
19. Ehrig, H., Mahr, B.: Fundamentals of Algebraic Specification 1: Equations and Initial Semantics. Monographs in Theoretical Computer Science, An EATCS Series. Springer, Heidelberg (1985)
20. Ayar, A., Marin, M.: Unifying the syntax and semantics of modular extensions of Petri nets, Ph.D. thesis, University of Geneva (2013)
21. Dolev, D., Yao, A.: On the security of public key protocols. IEEE Trans. Inf. Theory **29**(2), 198–208 (1983)
22. Benetti, D., Merro, M., Vigano, L.: Model checking ad hoc network routing protocols: ARAN vs. endairA. In: The 8th IEEE International Conference on Software Engineering and Formal Methods (SEFM), pp. 191–202 (2010)
23. Viana, A.C., Maag, S., Zaidi, F.: One step forward: linking wireless self-organising networks validation techniques with formal testing approaches, ACM Comput. Surv., **43**(2), article no. 7, April 2011
24. Chen, Z., Zhang, D., Zhu, R., Ma, Y., Yin, P., Xie, F.: A review of automated formal verification of ad hoc routing protocols for wireless sensor networks. Sens. Lett. **11**(5), 752–764 (2013)
25. Biberstein, O., Buchs, D., Guelfi, N.: Object-oriented nets with algebraic specifications: the CO-OPN/2 formalism. In: Agha, G., De Cindio, F., Rozenberg, G. (eds.) APN 2001. LNCS, vol. 2001, p. 73. Springer, Heidelberg (2001)
26. Bouroulet, R., Devillers, R., Klaudel, H., Pelz, E., Pommereau, F.: Modeling and analysis of security protocols using role based specifications and petri nets. In: van Hee, K.M., Valk, R. (eds.) PETRI NETS 2008. LNCS, vol. 5062, pp. 72–91. Springer, Heidelberg (2008)
27. Vautherin, J.: Un modèle algébrique, basé sur les réseaux de Petri, pour l'étude des systèmes parallèles, Ph.D. thesis, Université de Paris-Sud, LRI (1985)

Symbolic Search of Insider Attack Scenarios from a Formal Information System Modeling

Amira Radhouani[1,2,3,5]([✉]), Akram Idani[1,2], Yves Ledru[1,2],
and Narjes Ben Rajeb[3,4]

[1] LIG, University of Grenoble Alpes, 38000 Grenoble, France
amira.radhouani@imag.fr
[2] LIG, CNRS, 38000 Grenoble, France
[3] LIP2-LR99ES18, 2092 Tunis, Tunisia
[4] INSAT, Carthage University, Tunis, Tunisia
[5] FST, Tunis-El Manar University, Tunis, Tunisia

Abstract. The early detection of potential threats during the modelling and design phase of a Secure Information System is required because it favours the design of a robust access control policy and the prevention of malicious behaviours during system execution. This paper deals with internal attacks which can be made by people inside the organization. Such attacks are difficult to detect because insiders have authorized system access and also may be familiar with system policies and procedures. We are interested in finding attacks which conform to the access control policy, but lead to unwanted states. These attacks are favoured by policies involving authorization constraints, which grant or deny access depending on the evolution of the functional Information System state. In this context, we propose to model functional requirements and their Role Based Access Control (RBAC) policies using B machines and then to formally reason on both models. In order to extract insider attack scenarios from these B specifications, our approach first investigates symbolic behaviours. Then, the use of a model-checking tool allows to exhibit, from a symbolic behaviour, an observable concrete sequence of operations that can be followed by an attacker. In this paper, we show how this combination of symbolic analysis and model-checking allows to find out such insider attack scenarios.

Keywords: Information system · B-Method · RBAC · Attack scenario · Model checking · Symbolic search

1 Introduction

Developing secure Information Systems is an active research area addressing a wide range of challenges mostly interested in how to prevent external attacks such as intrusion, code injection, denial of service, identity fraud, etc. Insider attacks are less addressed despite they may cause much more damage than external intrusions because an insider is above all a trusted entity. Intrinsically it is given means to violate a security policy, either by using legitimate

© Springer-Verlag Berlin Heidelberg 2015
M. Koutny et al. (Eds.): ToPNoC X, LNCS 9410, pp. 131–152, 2015.
DOI: 10.1007/978-3-662-48650-4_7

access, or by obtaining unauthorized access. This paper deals especially with Role Based Access Control (RBAC) concerns with the aim to exhibit potential insider threats from a formal modelling of secure Information Systems. We are interested in finding attacks which conform to the access control policy, but lead to unwanted states. These attacks are favoured by policies involving authorization constraints, which grant or deny access depending on the evolution of the functional Information System state. To identify such attacks at the model level, on the one hand, we need to link the security model to the functional model of the information system, and on the other hand, to build tools taking into account the dynamic evolution of the IS state.

In [14], we discussed shortcomings of existing approaches in this context, and showed the advantages of using a formal specification assisted by animation tools. This paper goes a step further than our previous works by taking advantage of model-checking and proof tools in order to automatically find insider attack scenarios composed of a sequence of actions modifying the functional state to satisfy the authorization constraint.

This paper is an extended version of [19]. It is organized as follows: In Sect. 2 we give an overview of our approach and its underlying methodology. In Sect. 3 we present a simple example that illustrates our contribution. Section 4 defines semantics and technical aspects. In Sect. 5 we propose a symbolic search that automates generation of attack scenarios and we discuss results of its application on the given example. In Sect. 6 we compare our approach to some related work. Finally, we draw conclusions and perspectives.

2   Overall Approach

Bridging the gap between formal (*e.g.* Z, B, VDM . . .) techniques [22] and graphical languages such as UML has been a challenge since several years. On the one hand, formal techniques allow reasoning assisted by proof and model-checking tools, and on the other hand, graphical techniques allow visualization and better understanding of the system structure. These complementary aspects are useful to ensure a software development process based on notations with precise syntax and semantics and which allows to structure a system graphically. Most existing research works [3,11,20] in this context have been focused only on modelling and validation of functional aspects which are initially described by various kinds of UML diagrams (class, state/transition, sequence, . . .) and then translated into a formal specification. These works have shown the interest of linking formal and graphical paradigms and also the feasibility of such translations.

In our work, we adopt a similar approach in order to graphically model and formally reason on both functional and security models. We developed the B4MSecure[1] platform [13] in order to translate a UML class diagram associated to a SecureUML model into B specifications [1] which is a state-based formal development method which allows to model either static and dynamic behaviour

---

[1] http://b4msecure.forge.imag.fr/.

of a System. Static behaviour is designed by means of set of variables and constants. Whereas, dynamic behaviour is expressed by means of operations which perform actions according to a given specification if called whithin a given precondition.

The resulting B specifications illustrated in Fig. 1 follow the separation of concerns principle in order to be able to validate both models separately and then validate their interactions.

The functional B model on the left hand side of Fig. 1 is issued from a conceptual class diagram. It integrates all basic operations generated automatically (constructors, destructors, setters, getters, . . .) and also additional user-defined operations which are integrated into the graphical model and specified using the B syntax. This functional specification can be further improved by adding invariants and carrying out proof of correction with the help of AtelierB prover.

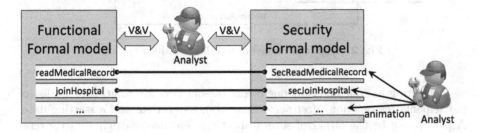

Fig. 1. Validation of functional and security models

The security model, on the right hand side of Fig. 1 is dedicated to control the access to functional operations with respect to access control rules defined in the SecureUML model. The security formal model allows to validate RBAC well-formedness rules such as no role hierarchy cycles, and separation of duty properties (SoD) such as assignment of conflicting roles to users. . .

This paper assumes that validation of both models in isolation is done: operations of functional model don't violate invariant properties, and the security model is robust. Such validation activities are widely discussed in the literature [18]. However, currently available validation approaches do not take sufficiently into account interactions between both models which result from the fact that authorisation constraints expressed in the security model also refer to information of the functional model. In fact, security policies often depend on dynamic properties based on the functional system state. For example, a bank customer may transfer funds from his account, but if the amount is greater than some limit the transfer must be approved by his account manager. Access control decisions depend then on the satisfaction of authorization constraints in the current system state. Dynamic evolution of the functional state impacts these constraints and may lead to a security vulnerability if it opens an unexpected access. In this paper we use validation tools (prover and model-checker) in order to search for malicious sequences of operations by analysing authorization constraints.

3   A Simple Example

In this section we use a running example issued from [4] and which deals with a SecureUML model associated to a functional UML class diagram.

3.1   Functional Model

The functional UML class diagram (presented in Fig. 2) describes a meeting scheduler dedicated to manage data about two entities: Persons and Meetings.

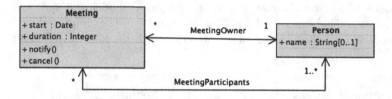

Fig. 2. Functional model of meeting scheduler system

A meeting has one and only one owner (association *MeetingOwner*), a list of participants (association *MeetingParticipants*), a duration, and a starting date. A person can be the owner of several meetings and may participate to several meetings. Operations *notify* and *cancel* are user-defined, and allow respectively to send messages to participants and to delete a meeting after notifying their participants by e-mail. Constructors, setters and getters are implicitly defined for both classes and both associations.

3.2   Access Control Rules

The access control model is given in Fig. 3 using the secureUML syntax. It features three different roles:

- **SystemUser:** defines persons who are registered on the system and then have permission **UserMeetingPerm** which allows them to create and read meetings. Deletion and modification of meetings (including operation *cancel*) are granted to system users by means of permission **OwnerMeetingPerm**, featuring an authorization constraint checking that the user who tries to run these actions is the meeting owner.
- **Supervisor:** defines system users with more privileges because they can run actions notify and cancel on any meeting even if they are not owners.
- **SystemAdministrator:** having a full access on entity Person, an administrator manages system users. Full access grants him the right to create a new person, remove or modify an existing one. Furthermore, a system administrator has only a read access on meetings: he is not expected to create or modify meetings.

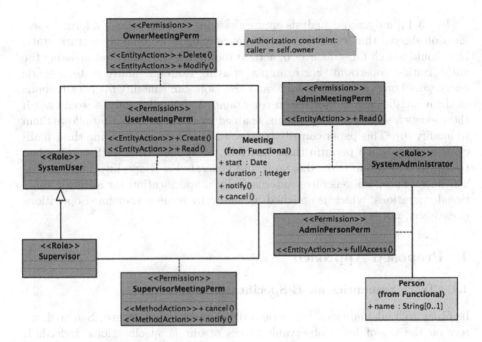

Fig. 3. Security model of meeting scheduler system

3.3 Validation

This example is intended to be validated in [4] based on a set of static queries that investigate a given system state in order to grasp some useful information like *"which user can perform an action on a concrete resource in a given state"*.

Authorization constraint associated to **OwnerMeetingPerm** requires information from the functional model because it deals with the *MeetingOwner* association. In the rest of this article, we consider three users John, Alice and Bob such that user assignments are as defined by Fig. 4 and a given initial state in which Alice is owner of meeting m_1, Bob is a participant of m_1. In such a state, the above static query establishes that only Alice is allowed to modify or delete m_1 because she is the owner of m_1.

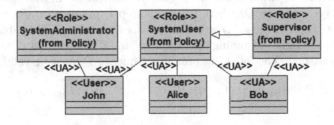

Fig. 4. Users assignement

In [13,14] a dynamic analysis approach based on animation of a formal specification showed that validation should not only be based on a given static state, but should search for sequences of actions modifying this state and breaking the authorization constraint. For example, starting from the above state, a static query would only report that John, and also Bob, can't modify m_1 because none of them satisfies the authorization constraint. A dynamic analysis would ask if there exists a sequence of operations enabled by John, or Bob, that allows them to modify m_1. This paper contributes towards automatically finding these malicious sequences. To perform these analysis, we applied the B4MSecure tool to the UML and SecureUML diagrams and generated a B specification counting 946 lines. This tool generates automatically a specification for all basic functional operations, which is enriched manually by some user-defined operations (*i.e.* cancel, notify).

4   Proposed Approach

4.1   Trace Semantics for B Specifications

In order to find malicious behaviours of an operational secure IS model, we rely on the set of finite observable traces of our B specifications. Indeed, B specifications can be approached by means of a trace semantics composed of an initialization substitution *init*, a set of operations $\mathcal{O}$ and a set of state variables $\mathcal{V}$. We note *val* a possible state predicate allowed by the invariant and *op* an operation from $\mathcal{O}$. A functional behaviour is an observable sequence $\mathcal{Q}$

$$\mathcal{Q} \mathrel{\hat{=}} init \; ; \; op_1 \; ; \; op_2 \; ; \; \dots \; ; \; op_m$$

such that $\forall i.(i \in 1..m \Rightarrow op_i \in \mathcal{O})$ and there exists a sequence $\mathcal{S}$ of state predicates which does not violate invariant properties:

$$\mathcal{S} \mathrel{\hat{=}} val_0 \; ; \; val_1 \; ; \; \dots \; ; \; val_m$$

in which val_0 is an initial state, and op_i is enabled from state val_{i-1} and state val_i is reached by op_i, starting from state val_{i-1}.

The security model filters functional behaviours by analysing access control premises which are triplets (u, R, c) where u is a user, R is a set of possible roles assigned to u, and c is an authorization constraint. An observable secure behaviour is a sequence $\mathcal{Q}$, where for every step i, premise (u_i, R_i, c_i) is valid (expressed as $(u_i, R_i, c_i) \models true$). This means that roles R_i activated by user u_i grant him the right of running operation op_i and if a constraint c_i exists, then it must be satisfied. The following premises sequence $\mathcal{P}$ must be valid for $\mathcal{Q}$:

$$\mathcal{P} \mathrel{\hat{=}} (u_1, R_1, c_1) \; ; \; (u_2, R_2, c_2) \; ; \; \dots \; ; \; (u_m, R_m, c_m)$$

4.2 Tools to Exhibit Behaviours from B Specifications

Model-checking and symbolic proof techniques are of interest in order to exhibit a relevant behaviour from an operational B specification. Proof techniques deal with infinite systems and can prove constraint satisfiability, or establish that some operation can be enabled from an abstract state predicate. Model-checking is based on model exploration of finite systems, and can be used to find a sequence of actions leading to a given state or property. In our approach, we combine both techniques in order to overcome their shortcomings: complexity of proofs for the first one, and state explosion for the second one. In this sub-section, we illustrate both tools.

Model checking and animation (the ProB tool). ProB [16] is an animation and a model-checker of B specifications that explores the concrete state space of the specification and generates accessibility graphs. Then, every predicate val_i (where $i \in \{0, 1, \ldots, m\}$) of sequence S is a valuation of variables issued from V. For example, starting from an initial state val_0 where:
$V = \{person, meeting, meetingOwner, meetingParticipants\}$ and such that:

$$val_0 \;\hat{=}\; person = \emptyset$$
$$\wedge meeting = \emptyset$$
$$\wedge meetingOwner = \emptyset$$
$$\wedge meetingParticipant = \emptyset$$

and having $\mathcal{O} = \{personNew, meetingNew, meetingAddParticipants, \ldots\}$, the scenario of Table 1 is successfully animated using ProB. Column "reached states" gives only modified B variables from the previous step.

Table 1. Animation of a normal scenario with ProB

step	Sequence $\mathcal{Q}$	Reached states S	RBAC premises $\mathcal{P}$
1	personNew	person = {Alice}	John SystemAdministrator no constraint
2	personNew	person = {Alice, Bob}	John SystemAdministrator no constraint
3	meetingNew	meeting = $\{m_1\}$ meetingOwner = {(Alice, m_1)}	Alice SystemUser no constraint
4	meetingAddParticipants	meetingParticipants = {(m_1, Bob)}	Alice SystemUser Constraint: Alice is the owner of m_1

In step 1, the tool animates operation *personNew* which modifies variable person (initially equal to $\emptyset$) and this action was performed by user John using role SystemAdministrator without need of authorization constraint. In step 4, the tool adds participant Bob to the meeting m_1 by animating operation meetingAddParticipants, after verification that authorization constraint is True for Alice using role SystemUser. Indeed, Alice is the owner of m_1.

Symbolic Proof (The GeneSyst Tool). ProB is useful to animate scenarios identified during requirements analysis, or to exhaustively explore a finite subset of state space. As we are interested in finding malicious scenarios that exhibit a potential internal attack, the ProB technique may be useful only if it explores the right state space subset in the right direction, which is not obvious for infinite systems. Symbolic proof techniques, such as that of GeneSyst [7], are more interesting because they allow to produce symbolic transition systems that represent a potentially infinite set of values and a set of predicate states. Such tools reason on the enabledness properties of an operation *op* from a symbolic state E and the reachability properties of a symbolic state F by *op* from E. In [7], three enabledness properties and three reachability properties are defined in terms of the following proof obligations, where E and F are two disjoint state predicates and x is the set of variables of the system:

(1) always enabled: $\forall x.E \Rightarrow Pre(op)$
(2) never enabled: $\forall x.E \Rightarrow \neg Pre(op)$
(3) possibly enabled: $\exists x.E \wedge Pre(op)$
(4) always reached: $\forall x.E \wedge Pre(op) \Rightarrow [Action(op)]F$
(5) never reachable: $\forall x.E \wedge Pre(op) \Rightarrow [Action(op)]\neg F$
(6) possibly reached: $\exists x.E \wedge Pre(op) \Rightarrow \neg[Action(op)]\neg F$

Where $Pre(op)$ is a predicate representing the preconditions under which the operation *op* becomes feasible [2], and $Action(op)$ is a generalized substitution [1] representing its action.

The first three proof obligations deals with enabledness property. Proof obligation (1) means that whenever the state E is satisfied, the precondition of the operation *op* is true, then *op* is always enabled from E. Whereas, according to the proof obligation (2), the *op* precondition is false when E is satisfied which means that *op* can never be enabled from E. Proof obligation (3) means that there exists a subset in E from which the precondition is satisfied, then *op* is possibly enabled from E.

In the generalized substitution theory, formula $[S]R$ means that substitution S always establishes predicate R, and $\neg[S]\neg R$ means that substitution S may establish predicate R. Hence, proof (4) means that F is always reached by the operation *op* from E. Proof (5) means that F is never reached by actions of *op* from state E. Finally, proof (6) means that state F can be reached by actions of *op*, when the operation precondition is true in state E. Note that reachability properties do not make sense if the enabledness property is not proved.

Let us consider, for example, the functional operation $meetingNew$:

$$meetingNew(m, p) \hat{=} PRE\ m \notin meeting \land p \in person\ THEN$$
$$meeting := meeting \cup \{m\}$$
$$||\ meetingOwner := meetingOwner \cup \{(m \mapsto p)\}$$
$$END$$

This operation adds a new meeting m and links it to an owner p. If we define states E and F such that:

$$E \hat{=} meetingOwner[\{m_1\}] = \emptyset$$
$$F \hat{=} meetingOwner[\{m_1\}] \neq \emptyset$$

Then, proof obligation produced by GeneSyst for property (6) was successfully proved showing that operation $meetingNew$ when enabled from a state where m_1 does not exist and there exists at least one person in the system, may lead to a state where m_1 is created and has an owner.

As illustrated above, our work will focus on proof (6) which states the reachability of a target state from an initial one by some operations that are proved enabled from this one according to proof (3). We assume it is sufficient to decide whether an operation is potentially useful for a malicious behaviour. Proofs (4) and (5) can be used if one would like to assume that a state can never be reached, or it is always reached, by an operation.

4.3   Malicious Behaviour

Based on the security requirements, several operations are identified as critical. For example, security requirements have identified the integrity of meeting information as critical. Therefore, operations which perform unauthorized modifications of meeting informations (e.g. $MeetingSetStart$) are identified as critical.

A malicious behaviour executed by a user u, regarding authorization constraints, is an observable secure behaviour Q with m steps such that:

- op_m is a critical operation to which an authorization constraint c_m is associated.
- user u is malicious and would like to run op_m by misusing his roles R_u.
- val_0 : is an initial state where $(u, R_u, c_m) \models false$
- for every step i $(i \in 1..m)$ premise $(u, R_u, c_i) \models true$

In other words, malicious user u is not initially allowed to execute the critical operation, but he is able to run a sequence of operations leading to a state from which he can execute this operation. In our investigation we assume that user u executes this malicious sequence without collusion with another user. This problem will be tackled in further work.

Section 3.3 gave an example where neither Bob nor John are allowed to run a modification operation, such as $meetingSetStart$ which modifies attributes of class Meeting, from the initial state due to the authorization constraint. This initial state is:

$$val_0 \; \hat{=} \; person = \{Alice, Bob\}$$
$$\wedge \; meeting = \{m_1\}$$
$$\wedge \; meetingOwner = \{(Alice \mapsto m_1)\}$$
$$\wedge \; meetingParticipant = \{(m_1 \mapsto Bob)\}$$

In the following, we denote as $init_0$ the sequence of operations leading to val_0 as presented in Table 1. We used the model-checking facility of ProB in order to explore exhaustively the state space and automatically find a path starting from val_0 and leading to a state where operation $meetingSetStart$ becomes permitted to John. We asked ProB to find a sequence where John becomes the owner of m_1:

$$meetingOwner(m_1) = John$$

After exploring more than 1000 states, ProB found a scenario in which John executes sequentially operations personNew, personAddMeetingOwner and meetingSetStart. Indeed, this dynamic analysis takes advantage of the fact that John, as a system administrator, has a full access to entity Person. This permission allows him to create, modify, read and delete any instance of class Person. First, using his system administration role, he creates an instance John of class Person that corresponds to him by running operation $personNew(John)$. Then he adds meeting m_1 to the set of meetings owned by John, by running operation $personAddMeetingOwner(John, m_1)$ which is a basic modification operation of class Person. These two actions allowed him to become the owner of m_1 and then he was able to modify the meeting of Alice using his system user role.

Like all model-checking techniques, when ProB explores exhaustively the state space, it faces the combinatorial explosion problem which depends on the number of operations provided to the tool and the state space size. In order to address this problem, our approach proposes a symbolic search which finds a sequence of potentially useful operations on which the model-checker should be focused.

5   Symbolic Search

The proposed symbolic search is performed by an algorithm (Fig. 5) that looks for an observable symbolic sequence $\mathcal{Q} \hat{=} init_0 \; ; \; op_1 \; ; \; \ldots \; ; \; op_m$ such that operations are not instantiated. The searched sequence is executed by a user u, where (u, R_u, c_m) is not valid for a critical operation op_m in the initial state val_0 but becomes valid for state val_{m-1} where op_m can be enabled. It is a backward search algorithm, starting from the goal state val_{m-1} from which the critical operation op_m can be enabled: $val_{m-1} \hat{=} c_m \wedge Pre(op_m)$; and working backwards until the initial state val_0 is encountered. The algorithm ends when sequence $\mathcal{Q}$ is found or when all operations are verified without encountering the initial state. We consider that val_0 is a completely valuated state such as the one where Alice is the owner of m_1, and Bob is a participant to m_1. This prevents the initial state from being included in both states val_{m-1} and val_{m-2}, which would never verify the condition of the while loop.

```
1.  Q ≜ op_m;
2.  val_{m-1} ≜ c_m ∧ Pre(op_m);
3.  val_{m-2} ≜ ¬val_{m-1};
4.  Opset ≜ O;
5.  while (val_0 ⇏ val_{m-1} and val_{m-1} ⊭ false and Opset ≠ ∅) do
6.          choose any o_i ∈ Opset where
7.              (u, R_u, c_i) ⊨ true ∧
8.              ∃x.val_{m-2} ∧ Pre(o_i) ∧        //PO3
9.              ∃x.val_{m-2} ∧ Pre(o_i) ⇒ ¬[Action(o_i)]¬val_{m-1}  //PO6
10.         do
11.             Q ≜ o_i ; Q ;
12.             val_{m-1} ≜ val_{m-2} ∧ Pre(o_i);
13.             val_{m-2} ≜ val_{m-2} ∧ ¬Pre(o_i);
14.             Opset ≜ Opset \ {o_i};
15.         else
16.             raise exception: No sequence found;
17.         enddo
18. endwhile
19. if val_0 ⇒ val_{m-1} then
20.         Q ≜ init ; Q ;
21. else
22.         raise exception: No sequence found;
23. endif
```

Fig. 5. A symbolic search proof based algorithm

5.1 Termination

Termination of our algorithm is ensured by the termination of the while loop conditions:

$$val_0 \not\Rightarrow val_{m-1} \text{ and } val_{m-1} \not\models false \text{ and } Opset \neq \emptyset$$

- $val_0 \not\Rightarrow val_{m-1}$: means that the initial state is not yet encountered. If the initial state is included in val_{m-1} ($val_0 \Rightarrow val_{m-1}$), then our algorithm concludes that a sequence is found.
- $val_{m-1} \not\models false$: means that precondition of the last computed operation is not reduced to false. If this condition becomes false, then the algorithm concludes that there is no further state enabling the last computed operation, and then it raises exception "no sequence found".
- $Opset \neq \emptyset$: means that there still exist operations that are not exploited. Every operation is called at the most once in a symbolic sequence because the algorithm iteratively removes operations from set $Opset$ ($Opset \triangleq Opset \setminus \{o_i\}$). Hence, when a sequence is found, the maximum size of a computed scenario is n such that n is the system operations number. This last condition guarantees termination when none of the previous conditions becomes false after exploiting all operations.

5.2   Completeness

Although our algorithm succeeds in finding attacks (see Sect. 5.4), it lacks completeness in two cases. First, since operations are deleted from set $Opset$ as soon as they are used, it is not able to extract attack scenarios in which an operation occurs more than once. Second, the algorithm expects operations to have non trivial preconditions, and may stop too early if the sequence includes operations with $true$ as a precondition. In fact, the algorithm builds symbolic states step by step. Based on the precondition of the extracted operation on a given step it infers the previous states as follows:

$$val_{m-1} \,\hat{=}\, val_{m-2} \wedge Pre(o_i);$$
$$val_{m-2} \,\hat{=}\, val_{m-2} \wedge \neg Pre(o_i);$$

Due to the precondition negation, the algorithm stops when it extracts an operation without precondition (i.e. $Pre(o_i)\hat{=}true$). Consequently, the algorithm may extracts just a part of an existing sequence.

However, experiments shows that it does well for many case studies and it is able to extract symbolic sequences that don't include repetition of operations or operations without precondition or operations with the same preconditions. Because of these restrictions, we propose to combine the symbolic search with model checking. Thus, the symbolic sequence found by our algorithm is then used to guide a model-checker which will instantiate the parameters of operations, and may identify sequences with operation repetition.

5.3   Step by Step Illustration

We take advantage of abstraction and step by step we refine the val_{m-2} symbolic state:

1. At the first step of the algorithm, the state space is represented by two symbolic states: the first one val_{m-1} includes all states where the authorization constraint c_m is true and which are enabling op_m, and the second one val_{m-2} is the negation of val_{m-1} which is then $\neg c_m \vee \neg Pre(op_m)$. As they are two disjoint state predicates, we conduct proofs (3) and (6) in order to find an operation o_i that belongs to $\mathcal{O}$ and which is possibly enabled from val_{m-2} and reaches the first state val_{m-1} and such that premise (u, R_u, c_i) is valid. If o_i does not exist, then no sequence could be found for the expected attack and we can try proof (5) for each operation attesting that all operations never reach val_{m-1} from val_{m-2}. Figure 6 provides a state machine diagram that illustrates this first iteration. In this representation, states are predicates and transitions are symbolic operations.

2. At the second step of the algorithm, if proofs (3) and (6) succeed for some operation op_{m-1}, then an observable sequence may exist, leading to the critical operation where access control premise (u, R_u, c_m) is valid. If val_0 is inside $Pre(o_i)$ then the algorithm stops. Otherwise, as showed in Fig. 7, the algorithm looks inside state val_{m-2} in order to find out the previous operations

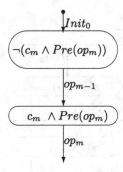

Fig. 6. First iteration algorithm illustration

that can be invoked in the attack scenario. State val_{m-2} is partitioned into two sub-states which are:

$$val_{m-2} \wedge Pre(op_{m-1}) \equiv \neg(c_m \wedge Pre(op_m)) \wedge Pre(op_{m-1})$$

$$val_{m-2} \wedge \neg Pre(op_{m-1}) \equiv \neg(c_m \wedge Pre(op_m)) \wedge \neg Pre(op_{m-1})$$

Then, we look for operations that reach the first sub-state from the second one.

3. The algorithm proceeds iteratively (Fig. 8) by partitioning the second state into two sub-states until either it finds a state that includes the initial state, which corresponds to a successful search, or fails the search because val_{m-1} is empty or all operations have been invoked once. In the best case, our algorithm gives some symbolic attack scenario, which consists of sequence $(init_0 ; op_n ; op_{n+1} ; \dots ; op_m)$ invoked by the same user u and where:

$$val_{n-1} \hat{=} \neg(c_m \wedge Pre(op_m)) \wedge \neg Pre(op_{m-1}) \wedge \neg Pre(op_{m-2}) \wedge \dots \wedge Pre(op_n)$$

and such that $val_0 \Rightarrow val_{n-1} \wedge \forall i.(i \in (n..m) \Rightarrow (u, R_u, c_i) \models true)$

5.4 Application

We apply our algorithm to the meeting scheduler example starting from the following initial state val_0:

$$
\begin{aligned}
val_0 \;\hat{=}\; &person = \{Alice, Bob\} \\
&\wedge\ meeting = \{m_1\} \\
&\wedge\ meetingOwner = \{(Alice \mapsto m_1)\} \\
&\wedge\ meetingParticipant = \{(m_1 \mapsto Bob)\}
\end{aligned}
$$

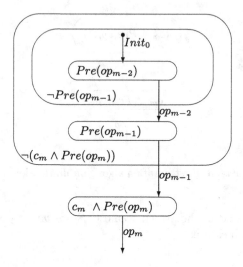

Fig. 7. Second iteration algorithm illustration

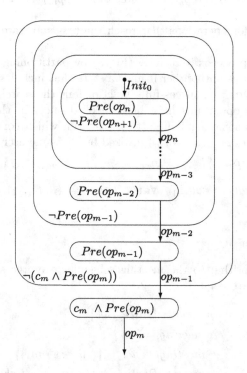

Fig. 8. Last iteration algorithm illustration

In this state user John is not allowed to modify meeting m_1 because the authorization constraint allows modification only by the owner of m_1. A malicious scenario would lead to a state where John becomes able to execute a modification operation such as operation $meetingSetStart$ on meeting m_1. In this state we have to verify:

$$Pre(meetingSetStart(m_1, start)) \hat{=} m_1 \in meeting$$
$$\text{and } (John, SystemUser, MeetingOwner(m_1) = John) \models true$$

1. First iteration: considering the following symbolic states

$$val_{m-1} \hat{=} (MeetingOwner(m_1) = John) \wedge m_1 \in Meeting$$
$$val_{m-2} \hat{=} \neg val_{m-1}$$

we have:
- $val_0 \not\Rightarrow val_{m-1}$ because, in state val_0, $MeetingOwner(m_1) = Alice$, and
- proof (6) is discharged automatically by AtelierB prover for the operations $meetingNew$ which may be executed by $John$ as system user, and $personAddMeetingOwner$ as system administrator. In addition, by conducting manual proofs, we were able to demonstrate that $meetingNew$ satisfies the proof obligation for the instantiation $meetingNew(m_1, John)$ and $personAddMeetingOwner$ leads to val_{m-1} if and only if it is executed with $(John, m_1)$ parameters.

   We also conduct proof (5) to verify that all other operations never reach val_{m-1} from val_{m-2}. Then, we may go on with the second iteration of the algorithm for each of these two operations.

2. Second iteration: we partition state val_{m-2} into two sub-states:

$$val_{m-3} \hat{=} val_{m-2} \wedge \neg Pre(op_{m-1})$$
$$val_{m-2} \hat{=} val_{m-2} \wedge Pre(op_{m-1})$$

- **case 1:** we choose $op_{m-1} = meetingNew(m_1, John)$, and then we have:
  - $Pre(meetingNew(m_1, John)) \hat{=} m_1 \notin meeting \wedge John \in person$, and
  - $val_0 \not\Rightarrow val_{m-2}$ because $John \notin person$

  In this case, the algorithm does not find an operation permitted to John leading to a state where operation $meetingNew$ becomes enabled. Indeed, no operation satisfies proof obligation (6). In the other side, proof obligation (5) succeeds for all operations. Our algorithm concludes that there does not exist an attack scenario invoking $meetingNew$ as step $m - 1$. (Fig. 9).
- **case 2:** we choose $op_{m-1} = personAddMeetingOwner(John, m_1)$ and then we have:
  - $Pre(personAddMeetingOwner(John, m_1)) =$
    $$m_1 \in meeting \wedge John \in person \wedge (John, m_1) \notin MeetingOwner$$
  - $val_{m-2} \hat{=} \neg(m_1 \in meeting \wedge meetingOwner\{(m_1)\} = John) \wedge$
    $$m_1 \in meeting \wedge John \in person \wedge (John, m_1) \notin MeetingOwner$$
    $$\hat{=} m_1 \in meeting \wedge John \in person \wedge (John, m_1) \notin MeetingOwner$$

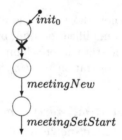

Fig. 9. No state enabling operation *meetingNew* is found

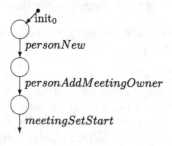

Fig. 10. Symbolic malicious scenario for user John.

- $val_{m-3} \mathrel{\hat=} \neg(m_1 \in meeting \land meetingOwner\{(m_1)\} = John) \land$
  $\neg(m_1 \in meeting \land John \in person \land (John, m_1) \notin MeetingOwner)$
  $\mathrel{\hat=} m_1 \notin meeting \lor (meetingOwner\{(m_1)\} \neq John \land John \notin person)$

- $val_0 \not\Rightarrow val_{m-2}$ because $John \notin person$

In this case, proof (6) succeeds for operation *personNew* which means that if *personNew* is executed, it may lead to a state where *meetingNew* can be enabled. *personNew* may be executed by *John* as system administrator.

3. Third iteration: we partition state val_{m-3} into two sub-states:

$$val_{m-3} \mathrel{\hat=} val_{m-3} \land Pre(personNew(John))$$
$$\mathrel{\hat=} John \notin person \land (m_1 \notin meeting \lor meetingOwner\{(m_1)\} \neq John)$$

This stops normally the algorithm because in this case $val_0 \Rightarrow val_{m-3}$. Figure 10 presents the full symbolic scenario that allows John to modify Alice's meeting.

5.5   Discussion

Technically, our approach applies the GeneSyst tool in order to produce proof obligations and then asks the AtelierB prover to discharge them automatically. As the resulting scenarios are symbolic and based on "possibly reached proofs", the analyst can conclude that attacks may exist but he can not guarantee their existence for the concrete system. An interesting contribution of our proof-based symbolic sequences, besides the fact that they draw the analyst's attention to potential flaws, is that they give useful inputs to the model-checker. Indeed, a model-checking tool can be used to exhibit, from a symbolic behaviour, an observable concrete sequence of operations that can be followed by an attacker. For example, based on the symbolic sequence of Fig. 10, ProB was able to extract the malicious concrete scenario represented in Fig. 11a. In order to reduce significantly the state space, we can ask ProB to explore only operations found in the symbolic malicious scenarios. For our example, when trying only operations personNew, personAddMeetingOwner and meetingSetStart, ProB exhibits a concrete attack scenario after visiting a dozen of states which shows a significant speed up with respect to our initial ProB attempts (involving more than 1000 states).

Our technique was able to extract another scenario (Fig. 11b) which can be executed by user Bob holding the supervisor role from the same initial state, in order to steal the ownership of m_1. In this scenario, Bob first cancels the meeting and then he recreates it before applying the critical operation.

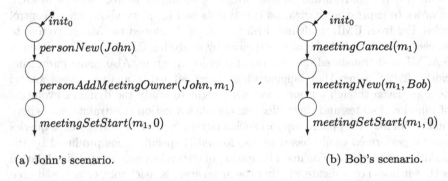

(a) John's scenario.   (b) Bob's scenario.

Fig. 11. Observable concrete scenarios produced by ProB

The first scenario, done by user John, is made possible by the full access permission to class Person, associated to role SystemAdministrator, which includes the right to modify association ends. This attack affects meeting integrity. One solution can be to add a SSD (Static Separation of Duties) constraint between roles SystemAdministrator and SystemUser. John will then still be able to become owner of the meeting, but will not be able to log in as SystemUser in order to modify it.

The second scenario done by Bob was possible due to role Supervisor which gives him the right to cancel a meeting, and then, as a SystemUser he can recreate it in order to become its owner. This scenario does not point out a flaw since whenever a meeting is cancelled it should be legitimate that a user can start a new meeting with the same identifier as the cancelled one.

Our algorithm was able to extract all possible sequences leading to the state that enables the critical operation. The security breaches that our technique is looking for, are issued from flaws in the conceptual logic of the security policy. Then, the produced sequences don't violate the access control policy, but they must be checked carefully by the security analyst in order to decide whether it is an attack scenario (*e.g.* attack Fig. 11a done by John) or a legitimate access (*e.g.* scenario Fig. 11b performed by Bob).

6   Related Work

Several research works have been devoted to the validation of access control policies. They are mainly focused on detecting external intrusion. Recently, the interest to insider attacks grew leading to two categories of validation: stateless and dynamic access control validation.

Stateless access control validation is dedicated to validate security policies in a given state without taking into account the dynamic evolution of the IS states. Among these works we can cite the SecureMova tool [4] which models security policies using SecureUML and OCL expressions. In the same context Kuhlmann et al. [10] took advantage on the USE tool to model RBAC policies in OCL in order to express authorization constraints and to query about access control rules. Far from UML modeling, Fisler et al. [8] developed the Margrave tool to answer the same kind of stateless queries by analysing RBAC models written in XACML and translated into a form of decision-diagram. Also, some interesting works [21,23] using Alloy language have been defined to analyse access control policies. Even though authors have not sought to study the dynamic evolution of functional states and their effect on the authorization constraints, we believe that a tool like Alloy could support such analysis. Note that such stateless queries can be performed easily based on the formal B specifications produced by the B4MSecure platform. The main limitation of a stateless access control validation is that it does not indicate whether the given state is reachable, or not, and then it may lead to incomplete conclusions.

Dynamic access control validation attempts to identify strategies followed by malicious users to counter some security rules by taking advantage of the IS states evolution. In [14], a dynamic analysis is done interactively with the help of a Z animator, but it requires user insight and may miss some possible flaws. In [24,25] authors proposed a backward algorithm to find a strategy allowing the attacker to reach a target state. A plain model-checking approach is proposed in order to check specifications written in the RW (Read-Write) language. On the one hand, the proposed algorithm suffers from scalability for the verification of complex specifications because of combinatorial explosion of the state space; and on the other hand, the RW language is poor compared to B because it doesn't express complex functional behaviours. The authors propose a contribution towards identifying strategies involving multiple users in coalition. This aspect is not covered in this paper and is planned for further work. A similar approach is proposed in [9] in order to validate access control policies of web-based collaborative systems. Even though their experiments show that they achieve better results compared to the approach in [24,25], it is still a model-checker solution that can not deal with policies of huge size.

Becker et al. [6] approach is the most similar approach to ours. Indeed, they proposed a Hoare-style proof system based on a Logic for State-Modifying (SMP) in which they express reachability properties in terms of pre and post-conditions. They reason about an abstract set of target states that satisfy some constraint. They also implemented a backward algorithm that extracts the sequence of operations leading to the goal state. Their algorithm is also able to compute the minimal sequence. However, the use of a logic-based language like SMP is not adequate for the context of Information Systems with a need to express complex functional behaviours. Moreover, the use of a proof system on a symbolic model may produce a sequence which cannot be reproduced in the concrete model. To circumvent this shortcoming we proposed in our approach to combine both proofs and model-checking techniques.

Our proof based symbolic search is achieved by assessing reachability properties [7] of functional operations. Other works proposed to explore this kind of properties in order to reason on sequences of B operations. In [17], the authors proposed two approaches to prove reachability properties in a B formal information system modelling. In the first one, they used substitution refinement techniques based on Morgan's specification statement, and in the second one, they proposed an algorithm that produces a proof obligation to be discharged automatically by AtelierB in order to prove whether a given sequence of operations reaches (or not) a defined state. The proposed techniques may help for our work since it is a proposal to simplify proofs and make them easier for AtelierB. However, unlike our approach, they don't search sequences leading to a goal state from an initial one. Their approach starts from a given sequence of operations, and tries to prove its reachability.

7   Conclusion

We described in this paper a symbolic search approach that can extract insider malicious behaviours from a formal Information System modelling. The meeting scheduler example was discussed in several articles [4,5]. However, they do not report the attack scenarios presented in this paper. This is due to the fact that dynamic evolution of the functional state is not taken into account. Contributions of this paper showed how dynamic analysis, assisted by proofs and model-checking, is useful to find out potential threats. In addition, thanks to our algorithm, proofs and model checking tools, our method can be automated in order to extract attack scenarios breaking some authorization constraint. We also applied our approach on the case study that we proposed in [12] and we were able to find, automatically, the discussed threat. Currently we are looking for application on a real case study, issued from the ANR-Selkis project[2], and

---

[2] http://lacl.univ-paris12.fr/selkis.

which deals with a medical information system involving various authorization constraints [15].

Our approach is automated by exploiting tools B4MSecure[3], GeneSyst[4], AtelierB[5] and ProB[6]. B4MSecure translates functional and security graphical models into B specification, from which we automatically produce proof obligations on enabledness and reachability properties by taking advantage of the GeneSyst tool. Then, these proof obligations are discharged automatically using the AtelierB prover. When a symbolic scenario is found, ProB is used to explore the concrete state space focusing on operations issued from the symbolic scenario. Currently, we are working on a new tool that implements our algorithm and integrates all other tools mentioned previously in order to have a complete automated solution. The main limitation of our work is that sometimes, when proof obligations are complex, AtelierB fails to prove them automatically. Interactive proofs are then required, but they may be pretty difficult for the analyst. One naive solution is to keep operations for which proofs don't succeed automatically in order to be exploited further using the model-checker. A more interesting solution is to focus on other kinds of proof obligations. For example, one can try to prove that an operation op is never enabled from a state E and/or op never reaches a state F. Applying these proofs to the meeting scheduler example we were able to eliminate half of the operations after proving automatically that they cannot be involved in the attack scenario.

Acknowledgments. This work is supported by the french MESR. The authors would like to thank the anonymous reviewers for their valuable comments which contributes to improve this paper.

References

1. Abrial, J.-R.: The B-Book: Assigning Programs to Meanings. Cambridge University Press, Cambridge (1996)
2. Abrial, J.-R., Mussat, L.: Introducing dynamic constraints in B. In: Bert, D. (ed.) B 1998. LNCS, vol. 1393, pp. 83–128. Springer, Heidelberg (1998)
3. Anastasakis, K., Bordbar, B., Georg, G., Ray, I.: UML2Alloy: a challenging model transformation. In: Engels, G., Opdyke, B., Schmidt, D.C., Weil, F. (eds.) MODELS 2007. LNCS, vol. 4735, pp. 436–450. Springer, Heidelberg (2007)
4. Basin, D., Clavel, M., Doser, J., Egea, M.: Automated analysis of security-design models. Inf. Softw. Technol. **51**, 815–831 (2009)
5. Basin, D., Doser, J., Lodderstedt, T.: Model driven security: from UML models to access control infrastructures. ACM Trans. Softw. Eng. Methodol. **15**(1), 39–91 (2006)
6. Becker, M.Y., Nanz, S.: A logic for state-modifying authorization policies. ACM Trans. Inf. Syst. Secur. **13**(3), 20:1–20:28 (2010)

---

[3] http://b4msecure.forge.imag.fr.
[4] http://perso.citi.insa-lyon.fr/nstouls/?ZoomSur=GeneSyst.
[5] http://www.atelierb.eu/.
[6] http://www.stups.uni-duesseldorf.de/ProB.

7. Bert, D., Potet, M.-L., Stouls, N.: GeneSyst: a tool to reason about behavioral aspects of B event specifications. Application to security properties. In: Treharne, H., King, S., Henson, M., Schneider, S. (eds.) ZB 2005. LNCS, vol. 3455, pp. 299–318. Springer, Heidelberg (2005)

8. Fisler, K., Krishnamurthi, S., Meyerovich, L.A., Tschantz, M.C.: Verification and change-impact analysis of access-control policies. In: Proceedings of the 27th International Conference on Software Engineering, ICSE 2005, pp. 196–205. ACM, New York (2005)

9. Koleini, M., Ryan, M.: A knowledge-based verification method for dynamic access control policies. In: Qin, S., Qiu, Z. (eds.) ICFEM 2011. LNCS, vol. 6991, pp. 243–258. Springer, Heidelberg (2011)

10. Kuhlmann, M., Sohr, K., Gogolla, M.: Employing UML and OCL for designing and analysing role-based access control. Math. Struct. Comput. Sci. 23(4), 796–833 (2013)

11. Lano, K., Clark, D., Androutsopoulos, K.: UML to B: formal verification of object-oriented models. In: Boiten, E.A., Derrick, J., Smith, G. (eds.) IFM 2004. LNCS, vol. 2999, pp. 187–206. Springer, Heidelberg (2004)

12. Ledru, Y., Idani, A., Milhau, J., Qamar, N., Laleau, R., Richier, J.-L., Labiadh, M.-A.: Taking into account functional models in the validation of IS security policies. In: Salinesi, C., Pastor, O. (eds.) CAiSE Workshops 2011. LNBIP, vol. 83, pp. 592–606. Springer, Heidelberg (2011)

13. Ledru, Y., Idani, A., Milhau, J., Qamar, N., Laleau, R., Richier, J.-L., Labiadh, M.-A.: Validation of IS security policies featuring authorisation constraints. Int. J. Inf. Syst. Model. Des. (IJISMD) 6, 24–46 (2014)

14. Ledru, Y., Qamar, N., Idani, A., Richier, J.-L., Labiadh, M.-A.: Validation of security policies by the animation of Z specifications. In: Proceedings of the 16th ACM Symposium on Access Control Models and Technologies, SACMAT 2011. ACM, New York (2011)

15. Ledru, Y., Idani, A., Richier, J.-L.: Validation of a security policy by the test of its formal B specification - a case study. In: 3rd International Workshop on Formal Methods in Software Engineering (FormaliSE 2015), Colocated with International Conference on Software Engineering, pp. 13–22. IEEE Computer Society (2015)

16. Leuschel, M., Butler, M.: ProB: a model checker for B. In: Araki, K., Gnesi, S., Mandrioli, D. (eds.) FME 2003. LNCS, vol. 2805, pp. 855–874. Springer, Heidelberg (2003)

17. Mammar, A., Frappier, M.: Proof-based verification approaches for dynamic properties: application to the information system domain. Formal Aspects Comput. 27(2), 335–374 (2015)

18. Qamar, N., Ledru, Y., Idani, A.: Evaluating RBAC supported techniques and their validation and verification. In: 6th International Conference on Availability, Reliability and Security (ARES 2011). IEEE Computer Society, Vienna, Autriche, August 2011

19. Radhouani, A., Idani, A., Ledru, Y., Rajeb, N.B.: Extraction of insider attack scenarios from a formal information system modeling. In: 5th International Workshop on Formal Methods for Security (FMS) (2014)

20. Snook, C., Butler, M.: UML-B: formal modeling and design aided by UML. ACM Trans. Softw. Eng. Methodol. 15(1), 92–122 (2006)

21. Toahchoodee, M., Ray, I., Anastasakis, K., Georg, G., Bordbar, B.: Ensuring spatio-temporal access control for real-world applications. In: Proceedings of the 14th ACM Symposium on Access Control Models and Technologies, SACMAT 2009, pp. 13–22. ACM, New York (2009)

22. Woodcock, J., Larsen, P.G., Bicarregui, J., Fitzgerald, J.: Formal methods: practice and experience. ACM Comput. Surv. **41**(4), 19:1–19:36 (2009)

23. Zao, J., Wee, H., Chu, J., Jackson, D.: RBAC schema verification using lightweight formal model and constraint analysis. In: Proceedings of the 8th ACM Symposium on Access Control Models and Technologies, SACMAT 2003. ACM (2003)

24. Zhang, N., Ryan, M.D., Guelev, D.P.: Evaluating access control policies through model checking. In: Zhou, J., López, J., Deng, R.H., Bao, F. (eds.) ISC 2005. LNCS, vol. 3650, pp. 446–460. Springer, Heidelberg (2005)

25. Zhang, N., Ryan, M., Guelev, D.P.: Synthesising verified access control systems through model checking. J. Comput. Secur. **16**(1), 1–61 (2008)

Modelling and Analysis Mobile Systems Using π-calculus (EFCP)

Victor Khomenko(✉) and Vasileios Germanos

Newcastle University, Newcastle upon Tyne NE1 7RU, UK
{Victor.Khomenko,V.Germanos}@ncl.ac.uk

Abstract. Reference passing systems, like mobile and reconfigurable systems are common nowadays. The common feature of such systems is the possibility to form dynamic logical connections between the individual modules. However, such systems are very difficult to verify, as their logical structure is dynamic. Traditionally, decidable fragments of π-calculus, e.g. the well-known Finite Control Processes (FCP), are used for formal modelling of reference passing systems. Unfortunately, FCPs allow only 'global' concurrency between processes, and thus cannot naturally express scenarios involving 'local' concurrency inside a process, such as multicast. In this paper we propose Extended Finite Control Processes (EFCP), which are more convenient for practical modelling. Moreover, an almost linear translation of EFCPs to FCPs is developed, which enables efficient model checking of EFCPs.

Keywords: π-calculus · Finite control process · Extended finite control process · Reconfigurable systems · Mobile systems · Model checking

1 Introduction

Many contemporary systems enjoy a number of features that significantly increase their power, usability and flexibility:

- *Dynamic reconfigurability*: The overall structure of many existing systems is flexible. Nodes in ad-hoc networks can dynamically appear or disappear; individual cores in Networks-on-Chip can be temporarily shut down to save power; resilient systems have to continue to deliver (reduced) functionality even if some of their modules develop faults.
- *Logical mobility*: Mobile systems permeate our lives and are becoming ever more important. Ad-hoc networks, where devices like mobile phones and laptops form dynamic connections are common nowadays, and the vision of pervasive (ubiquitous) computing [1], where several devices are simultaneously engaged in interaction with the user and each other, forming dynamic links, is quickly becoming a reality.
- *Dynamic allocation of resources*: It is often the case that a system has several instances of the same resource (e.g., network servers or processor cores in a microchip) that have to be dynamically allocated to tasks depending on the current workload, power mode, priorities of the clients, etc.

© Springer-Verlag Berlin Heidelberg 2015
M. Koutny et al. (Eds.): ToPNoC X, LNCS 9410, pp. 153–175, 2015.
DOI: 10.1007/978-3-662-48650-4_8

The common feature of such systems is the possibility to form dynamic logical connections between the individual modules. It is implemented using *reference passing*. A module can become aware of another module by receiving a *reference* (e.g., in the form of a network address) to it, which enables subsequent communication between these modules. This can be thought of as a new (logical) *channel* dynamically created between these modules. We will refer to such systems as *Reference Passing Systems* (RPS).

As people are increasingly dependent on the correct functionality of RPSs, the cost incurred by design errors in such systems can be extremely high. However, even the conventional concurrent systems are notoriously difficult to design correctly because of the complexity of their behaviour, and reference passing adds another layer of complexity due to the logical structure of the system becoming dynamical. Hence, computer-aided formal verification has to be employed in the design process to ensure the correct behaviour of RPSs. However, validation of such systems is almost always limited to simulation/testing, as their formal verification is very difficult due to either the inability of the traditional verification techniques to express reference passing[1] (at least in a natural way) or by poor scalability of the existing verification techniques for RPSs.

This is very unfortunate: As many safety-critical systems must be resilient (and hence reconfigurable), they are often RPSs and thus have very complicated behaviour. Hence, for such systems the design errors are both very likely and very costly, and formal verification must be an essential design step. This paper addresses this problem by developing a formalism that can specify RPSs and make their formal verification feasible.

There is a number of formalisms that are suitable for specification of RPSs. The main considerations and trade-offs in choosing an appropriate formalism are its expressiveness and the tractability of the associated verification techniques. Expressive formalisms (like π-calculus [2] and Ambient Calculus [3]) are Turing powerful and so not decidable in general. Fortunately, the ability to pass references *per se* does not lead to undecidability, and it is possible to put in place some restrictions (e.g., finiteness of the control) that would guarantee decidability, while still maintaining a reasonable modelling power.

Finite Control Processes (FCP) [4] are a fragment of π-calculus, where the system is constructed as a parallel composition of sequential entities (threads). Each sequential entity has a finite control, and the number of such entities is bounded in advance. The entities communicate synchronously via channels, and have the possibility to create new channels dynamically and to send channels via channels.

As π-calculus is the most well-known formalism suitable for RPS specification, we fix FCPs (as a natural decidable and reasonably expressive fragment of π-calculus) as the primary RPS specification formalism, from which a new extension will be derived.

---

[1] Some existing tools like SPIN allow to send channels via channels; however, they do not allow dynamic creation of new channels, which is often essential in RPSs.

One common feature of RPSs is *multicast*. That is, data can be transmitted from one source to more than one destination concurrently. Using FCPs to model such systems is inconvenient because local concurrency inside the thread is forbidden. Thus, we propose a new subclass of π-calculus, the *Extended Finite Control Processes* (EFCP), that allows to model multicast in a natural way and is still amenable to model checking.

The formal verification of RPSs expressed as EFCPs can be done in stepwise manner. Firstly, a translation from EFCP to FCP is performed as explained in this paper. The size of the resulting FCP is quadratic in the worst case, but often linear in practice (see Sect. 4.4). Then, the resulting FCP can be translated to a Petri net of polynomial size [5], and for the latter there are already efficient verification techniques.

2   Basic Notions

In π-calculus [6,7] and FCPs [4], threads communicate via synchronous message exchange. The key idea of the formalism is that messages and the channels they are sent on have the same type: they are just *names* from some set $\Phi \stackrel{\text{df}}{=} \{a, b, x, y, i, f, r, \ldots\}$, which are the simplest entities of the π-calculus. This means a name that has been received as message in one communication may serve as channel in a later interaction. To communicate, processes consume *prefixes* π of the form

$$\pi ::= \overline{a}\langle b \rangle \mid a(x) \mid \tau.$$

The *output prefix* $\overline{a}\langle b \rangle$ sends name b along channel a. The *input prefix* $a(i)$ receives a name that replaces i on channel a. The input and output actions are called *visible actions* and prefix τ stands for a *silent action*.

Threads, also called *sequential processes*, are constructed as follows. A *choice process* $\sum_{i \in I} \pi_i.S_i$ over a finite set of indices I executes a prefix π_i and then behaves like S_i. The special case of choices over an empty index set $I = \emptyset$ is denoted by $\mathbf{0}$ — such a process has no behaviour. Moreover, when $|I| = 1$ we drop Σ. We use $\odot$ to refer to iterated prefixing, e.g. $\overline{a_1}\langle b_1 \rangle.\overline{a_2}\langle b_2 \rangle.\overline{a_3}\langle b_3 \rangle.\overline{a_4}\langle b_4 \rangle.\mathbf{0}$ can be written as $\left(\odot_{i=1}^4 \overline{a_i}\langle b_i \rangle \right).\mathbf{0}$. A *restriction* $\nu r : S$ generates a name r that is different from all other names in the system. We denote a sequence of restrictions $\nu r_1 \ldots \nu r_k$ by $\nu\tilde{r}$ with $\tilde{r} = r_1 \ldots r_k$. To implement parameterised recursion, we use *calls to process identifiers* $K\lfloor\tilde{a}\rfloor$. We defer the explanation of this construct for a moment. To sum up, FCP *threads* take the form

$$S ::= K\lfloor\tilde{a}\rfloor \mid \sum_{i \in I} \pi_i.S_i \mid \nu r : S.$$

A *finite control process (FCP)* F is a parallel composition of a fixed number of threads:

$$F ::= \nu\tilde{a} : (S_1 \mid \ldots \mid S_n).$$

Note that in FCPs the *parallel composition* operator | is allowed at the top level, but not inside the threads, whereas in general π-calculus there is no such restriction. We use Π to denote iterated parallel composition, e.g. the above definition of an FCP can be re-written as $F ::= \nu\tilde{a} : \prod_{i=1}^{n} S_i$.

Our presentation of parameterised recursion using calls $K\lfloor\tilde{a}\rfloor$ follows [7]. Process identifiers K are taken from some set $\Psi \stackrel{\text{df}}{=} \{H, K, L, \ldots\}$ and have a *defining equation* $K(\tilde{f}) := S$. Here S can be understood as the implementation of identifier K. The process has a list of *formal parameters* $\tilde{f} = f_1, \ldots, f_k$ that are replaced by *factual parameters* $\tilde{a} = a_1, \ldots, a_k$ when a call $K\lfloor\tilde{a}\rfloor$ is executed. Note that both lists $\tilde{a}$ and $\tilde{f}$ have the same length. When we talk about an *FCP specification* F, we mean process F with all its defining equations.

To implement the replacement of $\tilde{f}$ by $\tilde{a}$ in calls to process identifiers, we use *substitutions*. A substitution is a function $\sigma : \Phi \to \Phi$ that maps names to names. If we make domain and codomain explicit, $\sigma : A \to B$ with $A, B \subseteq \Phi$, we require $\sigma(a) \in B$ for all $a \in A$ and $\sigma(x) = x$ for all $x \in \Phi \setminus A$. We use $\{\tilde{a}/\tilde{f}\}$ to denote the substitution $\sigma : \tilde{f} \to \tilde{a}$ with $\sigma(f_i) \stackrel{\text{df}}{=} a_i$ for $i \in \{1, \ldots, k\}$. The *application of substitution* σ to S is denoted by $S\sigma$ and defined in the standard way [7].

Input prefix $a(i)$ and restriction νr *bind* the names i and r, respectively. The *set of bound names* in a process $P = S$ or $P = F$ is $bn\,(P)$. A name which is not bound is *free*, and the *set of free names* in P is $fn\,(P)$. We permit $\alpha-conversion$ of bound names. Therefore, w.l.o.g., we make the following assumptions common in π-calculus theory and collectively referred to as *no clash* (**NOCLASH**) [5] henceforth. For every π-calculus specification, we require that:

- a name is bound at most once;
- a name is used at most once in formal parameter lists;
- the sets of bound names, free names and formal parameters are pairwise disjoint;
- if a substitution $\sigma = \{\tilde{a}/\tilde{x}\}$ is applied to P then $bn\,(P)$ and $\tilde{a} \cup \tilde{x}$ are disjoint.

Assuming (**NOCLASH**), the names occurring in a π-calculus specification F can be partitioned into the following sets:

$\mathcal{P}$ public names that are free in F;
$\mathcal{R}$ names bound by restriction operators;
$\mathcal{I}$ names bound by input prefixes;
$\mathcal{F}$ names used as formal parameters in defining equations.

The *size* of a π-calculus specification is defined as the size of its initial term plus the sizes of the defining equations. The corresponding function $\|\cdot\|$ measures the number of channel names, process identifiers, the lengths of parameter lists, and the number of operators in use:

$$\|\mathbf{0}\| \stackrel{\text{df}}{=} 1$$

$$\|K\lfloor\tilde{a}\rfloor\| \stackrel{\text{df}}{=} 1 + |\tilde{a}|$$

$$\|\nu r : P\| \stackrel{\text{df}}{=} 1 + \|P\|$$

$$\|K(\tilde{f}) := S\| \overset{\mathrm{df}}{=} 1 + |\tilde{f}| + \|S\|$$

$$\|\textstyle\sum_{i \in I} \pi_i.S_i\| \overset{\mathrm{df}}{=} 3|I| - 1 + \sum_{i \in I} \|S_i\|$$

$$\|\prod_{i=1}^{n} S_i\| \overset{\mathrm{df}}{=} n - 1 + \sum_{i=1}^{n} \|S_i\|$$

It is not so simple to define reduction on terms of π-calculus, because two subterms of a process-term may interact despite the fact that they may not be adjacent. To define the behaviour of a process and the reduction on process terms, we rely on a relation called *structural congruence* $\equiv$. It is the smallest congruence where α-*conversion* of bound names is allowed, $+$ and $|$ are commutative and associative with $\mathbf{0}$ as the neutral element, and the following laws for restriction hold:

$$\nu x : \mathbf{0} \equiv \mathbf{0}$$

$$\nu x : \nu y : P \equiv \nu y : \nu x : P$$

$$\nu x : (P \,|\, Q) \equiv P \,|\, (\nu x : Q) \text{ if } x \notin \mathit{fn}\,(P)$$

The behaviour of π-calculus processes is determined by the *reaction relation* $\rightarrow$. The reaction relations are defined by inference rules [6,7]:

(Tau) $\tau.S + M \rightarrow S$ (React) $(x(y).S + M) \,|\, (\overline{x}\langle z \rangle.S' + N) \rightarrow S\{z/y\} \,|\, S'$

(Res) $\dfrac{P \rightarrow P'}{\nu a : P \rightarrow \nu a : P'}$ (Struct) $\dfrac{P \rightarrow P'}{Q \rightarrow Q'}$ if $P \equiv Q$ and $P' \equiv Q'$

(Par) $\dfrac{P \rightarrow P'}{P \,|\, Q \rightarrow P' \,|\, Q}$ (Const) $K\lfloor \tilde{a} \rfloor \rightarrow S\{\tilde{a}/\tilde{f}\}$ if $K(\tilde{f}) := S$

The rule (Tau) is an axiom for silent steps. (React) describes the communication of two parallel threads, consuming their send and receive actions respectively and continuing as a process, where the name y is substituted by z in the receiving thread S. (Const) describes identifier calls, likewise using a substitution. The remaining rules define $\rightarrow$ to be closed under structural congruence, parallel composition and restriction. By $\mathcal{R}(F)$ we denote the set of all processes reachable from F. The *transition system* of FCP F factorises the reachable processes along structural congruence.

2.1   Normal Form Assumptions

We require that the sets of process identifiers called (both directly from F and indirectly from defining equations) by different threads are disjoint. This restriction corresponds to the notion of a *safe* FCP [8] and can be achieved by replicating some defining equations. The resulting specification is bisimilar with F and has the size $O(n\|F\|) = O(\|F\|^2)$. We illustrate the construction on the following example of an FCP specification (left) together with its replicated version (right):

$$K(f_1, f_2) := \tau.L(f_1, f_2)$$
$$L(f_3, f_4) := \tau.K(f_3, f_4)$$

$$K^1(f_1^1, f_2^1) := \tau.L^1(f_1^1, f_2^1)$$
$$L^1(f_3^1, f_4^1) := \tau.K^1(f_3^1, f_4^1)$$
$$K^2(f_1^2, f_2^2) := \tau.L^2(f_1^2, f_2^2)$$
$$L^2(f_3^2, f_4^2) := \tau.K^2(f_3^2, f_4^2)$$
$$K^3(f_1^3, f_2^3) := \tau.L^3(f_1^3, f_2^3)$$
$$L^3(f_3^3, f_4^3) := \tau.K^3(f_3^3, f_4^3)$$

$$K\lfloor a, b \rfloor \mid K\lfloor b, c \rfloor \mid L\lfloor a, c \rfloor \qquad\qquad K^1\lfloor a, b \rfloor \mid K^2\lfloor b, c \rfloor \mid L^3\lfloor a, c \rfloor$$

Intuitively, in the resulting FCP specification each thread has its own set of defining equations. This normal form is applicable also to EFCPs introduced in Sect. 4.2.

2.2   Match and Mismatch Operators

The match and mismatch operators are a common extension of π-calculus [5]. Intuitively, the process $[x = y].P$ behaves as P if x and y refer to the same channel, and as $\mathbf{0}$ otherwise, and the process $[x \neq y].P$ behaves as P if x and y refer to different channels, and as $\mathbf{0}$ otherwise.

2.3   Polyadic Communication

Polyadic communication can be used to make modelling more convenient. Using polyadic communication *tuples* of names can be exchanged in a single reaction. More precisely, a sending prefix $\overline{a}\langle x_1 \dots x_m \rangle$ (with $m \geq 0$) and a receiving prefix $a(y_1 \dots y_n)$ (with $n \geq 0$ and all y_i being different names) can synchronise iff $m = n$, and after synchronisation each y_i is replaced by x_i, $\{y_i/x_i\}$. Formally,

$$(\text{React})\,(a(\tilde{y})\;;\;P_1 + Q_1)\,|(\overline{a}\langle \tilde{x} \rangle\;;\;P_2 + Q_2) \to P_1\{\tilde{x}/\tilde{y}\}\,|\,P_2\ if\ |\,\tilde{y}\,| = |\,\tilde{x}\,|\,.$$

3   Extended Finite Control Processes

This section introduces the *Extended Finite Control Processes* (*EFCP*), which add new features to FCPs, in particular limited local concurrency within a thread, while still allowing one to formally verify such systems. Thus, practical modelling of reconfigurable systems becomes more convenient.

The threads in an FCP can communicate synchronously via channels, and are able to create new channels dynamically and send channels via channels. However, FCP threads are *sequential* processes, without any 'local' concurrency inside them. This makes FCPs too restrictive when one wants to model scenarios involving local concurrency within a thread, for instance, in case of routing protocols in multi-core processor systems. An essential feature of such protocols is multicast, i.e. the ability of a core to send a datum to several destinations concurrently.

EFCPs are sufficient for modelling many practical reconfigurable systems. Moreover, since an efficient translation from FCPs to safe Petri nets exists [5], it can be reused for EFCPs (via an intermediate translation to FCPs). Hence efficient formal verification algorithms for Petri nets can be used to verify EFCPs.

For example, the following process is an FCP, which is a parallel composition of three sequential processes (threads):

$$K_1 := a(x) \; . \; \overline{x}\langle b \rangle \; . \; \mathbf{0}$$
$$K_2 := \nu u : \overline{a}\langle u \rangle \; . \; \overline{w}\langle u \rangle \; . \; \mathbf{0}$$
$$K_3 := w(t) \; . \; t(v) \; . \; \mathbf{0}$$
$$K_1 \,|\, K_2 \,|\, K_3$$

Note that in FCPs the parallel composition operator '|' can be used only in the initial term, i.e. the threads are fully sequential and their number is bounded in advance.

To be able to model a wide range of RPSs, a higher degree of freedom in the syntax is required to specify their various behavioural scenarios. To that end, an extension of FCPs, the EFCP, is introduced, which allows local concurrency and replaces the prefixing operator '.' with a more powerful *sequential composition* operator ';'. The full EFCP syntax is defined in Sect. 3.1, and an example is given below.

$$K_1 := \nu r : \left((\overline{a}\langle r \rangle \,|\, \overline{b}\langle r \rangle) \; ; \; (r(x) \,|\, r(y)) \right)$$
$$K_2 := a(z) \; ; \; \overline{z}\langle c \rangle$$
$$K_3 := b(w) \; ; \; \overline{w}\langle d \rangle$$
$$K_1 \,|\, K_2 \,|\, K_3$$

3.1   The Syntax of Extended Finite Control Processes

To define the EFCP syntax the notion of *finite processes* is required. Such processes have special syntax ensuring that the number of actions they can execute is bounded in advance.

The arguments of the parallel composition operator, when used inside a thread, are limited to finite processes only. Similarly, the left hand side of sequential composition must be a finite process, but the right hand side is not required to be such.

This new subcalculus is defined by a context-free grammar consisting of two sub-grammars, one for the *finite executed processes* and one for generic processes.

Definition 1 (Grammar for Finite Processes).

$$F ::= \mathbf{0} \;\mid\; \pi \;\mid\; F + F \;\mid\; F \,|\, F \;\mid\; \nu \tilde{r} : F \;\mid\; F \; ; \; F$$

The syntax of generic processes includes that of finite processes, but also allows for extra features like recursive definitions.

Definition 2 (EFCP Grammar). *Let F be a finite process defined above. The syntax of an EFCP thread is then*

$$P ::= K\lfloor \tilde{x} \rfloor \mid F \mid P + P \mid \nu \tilde{r} : P \mid F \ ; P$$

An EFCP specification is comprised of a set of defining equations of the form $K(\tilde{f}) := P$ and an initial term of the form $\nu \tilde{r} : \prod_{i=1}^{n} P_i$, where P and all P_i are EFCP threads.

Note that an EFCP thread cannot contain the construction $P \mid P$ (only the initial term can have it), but it can contain $F \mid F$.

3.2 Structural Congruence and Operational Semantics

The structural congruence relation is used in the definition of the behaviour of a process term. The choice '+' and the parallel composition '|' are commutative and associative with $\mathbf{0}$ as the neutral element. Sequential composition ';' is associative with $\mathbf{0}$ as the neutral element, but not commutative.

Definition 3 (Structural Congruence). *The structural congruence $\equiv$ is the smallest congruence that satisfies the following axioms:*

Alpha-Convertion:

$$\nu r : P \equiv \nu r' : P\{r'/r\} \text{ if } r' \notin fn\,(P).$$
$$a(x) \ ; P \equiv a(x') \ ; P\{x'/x\} \text{ if } x' \notin fn\,(P).$$

Laws for Sequential Composition:

$$\mathbf{0} \ ; P \equiv P$$
$$F \ ; \mathbf{0} \equiv F$$
$$(F_1 \ ; F_2) \ ; P \equiv F_1 \ ; (F_2 \ ; P)$$

Laws for Restriction:

$$\nu r : \mathbf{0} \equiv \mathbf{0}$$
$$\nu \alpha : \nu \beta : P \equiv \nu \beta : \nu \alpha : P$$

Laws for Parallel Composition:

$$P_1 \mid (P_2 \mid P_3) \equiv (P_1 \mid P_2) \mid P_3$$
$$P_1 \mid P_2 \equiv P_2 \mid P_1$$
$$P \mid \mathbf{0} \equiv P$$

Laws for Summation:

$$P_1 + (P_2 + P_3) \equiv (P_1 + P_2) + P_3$$
$$P_1 + P_2 \equiv P_2 + P_1$$
$$P + \mathbf{0} \equiv P$$

Definition 4 (Structural Operational Semantics). *The transition system of EFCP is defined by the following rules:*

$$(\text{Seq}) \; \frac{F \to F'}{F \; ; \; Q \to F' \; ; \; Q} \qquad\qquad (\text{Tau}) \; \tau \; ; \; P + Q \to P$$

$$(\text{Res}) \; \frac{P \to P'}{\nu r : P \to \nu r : P'} \qquad (\text{Struct}) \; \frac{P \to P'}{Q \to Q'} \; \text{ if } P \equiv Q \text{ and } P' \equiv Q'$$

$$(\text{Par}) \; \frac{P \to P'}{P \,|\, Q \to P' \,|\, Q} \qquad (\text{Const}) \; K\lfloor \tilde{a} \rfloor \to P\{\tilde{a}/\tilde{f}\} \quad \text{ if } K(\tilde{f}) := P$$

$$(\text{React}) \, (x(y) \; ; \; P_1 + Q_1) \,|\, (\overline{x}\langle z \rangle \; ; \; P_2 + Q_2) \to P_1\{z/y\} \,|\, P_2$$

Note that these rules are similar to the π-calculus rules in Sect. 2 with the exception of the (Seq) rule expressing the semantics of our more powerful sequential composition operator ' ; '.

4   Translation of EFCPs to FCPs

In this section, a formal description of the new formalism is presented, and an almost linear translation from EFCP to FCP is introduced. The purpose of translating EFCP to FCP is for the latter to be translated to safe low-level Petri nets [8], for which efficient verification techniques can be applied.

4.1   Description

The translation has to eliminate the parallel composition operator inside threads and the use of sequential composition. Since an FCP consists of sequential processes (*threads*), any thread of an EFCP that is not sequential must be converted to a sequential one. This can be done by shifting all the concurrency to the initial term. Moreover, sequential composition has to be replaced by prefixing. To avoid blow up in size, new declarations are introduced during this process.

To ensure that the order of actions is preserved and that the context (binding of channel names) is correct, extra communication between threads may be required. New process definitions are introduced in two cases. The first is when local concurrency exists within a thread, e.g.:

$$K[x] := \nu r : ((\overline{a}\langle x \rangle \,|\, \overline{b}\langle r \rangle) \; ; \; \tau)$$
$$K\lfloor u \rfloor$$

The translation result is:

$$K[x] := \nu r : (\overline{begin_1}\langle x \rangle \, . \, \overline{begin_2}\langle r \rangle \, . \, end_1() \, . \, end_2() \, . \, \tau \, . \, \mathbf{0})$$
$$K_1 \quad := begin_1(x) \, . \, \overline{a}\langle x \rangle \, . \, \overline{end_1}\langle \rangle \, . \, K_1$$
$$K_2 \quad := begin_2(r) \, . \, \overline{b}\langle r \rangle \, . \, \overline{end_2}\langle \rangle \, . \, K_2$$
$$K\lfloor u \rfloor \,|\, K_1 \,|\, K_2$$

Here K_1 and K_2 are fresh PIDs and $begin_1$, $begin_2$, end_1, end_2 are fresh public names. Note that the necessary context is passed to the auxiliary FCP threads K_1 and K_2 using communication on $begin_1$ and $begin_2$.

The second case is when there is a sequential composition with a non-trivial left-hand side, e.g.:

$$K[x] := \nu r : \left(\underbrace{(\overline{a}\langle x\rangle + \overline{b}\langle r\rangle)}_{\text{l.h.s.}} \; ; \; \underbrace{(\overline{c}\langle x\rangle + \overline{d}\langle r\rangle)}_{\text{r.h.s.}} \right)$$

$$K\lfloor u\rfloor$$

This process is translated as follows:

$$
\begin{aligned}
K[x] \quad &:= \nu r : (\overline{a}\langle x\rangle \,.\, K_1\lfloor x, r\rfloor + \overline{b}\langle r\rangle \,.\, K_1\lfloor x, r\rfloor) \\
K_1[x, r] &:= \overline{c}\langle x\rangle \,.\, \mathbf{0} \,+\, \overline{d}\langle r\rangle \,.\, \mathbf{0} \\
K\lfloor u\rfloor
\end{aligned}
$$

Here K_1 is a fresh PID. Note that the initial term did not change and that the context is passed via parameters of a call.

4.2   Formal Definition of EFCP to FCP Translation

In this section, the translation is defined in a formal way. EFCP has the form

$$K_1[\tilde{x_1}] := P_1$$

$$\vdots$$

$$K_n[\tilde{x_n}] := P_n$$
$$\nu\tilde{r} : (Q_1 \,|\, \ldots \,|\, Q_k)$$

where the syntax of each P_i is given by Definitions 1 and 2, and we assume that no Q_i in the initial term uses '|' or ';'. Note that the EFCP is assumed to be safe and to satisfy **(NOCLASH)**. Safe EFCPs are defined similarly to safe FCPs, see Sect. 2.1.

Definition 5 (Translation). *The translation $[\![\cdot]\!]_B$ from EFCP to FCP is defined inductively on the syntactical structure of the EFCP. Here B is the parameter of the translation. It defines the* context, *i.e. the set of names that were bound prior to the occurrence of the term to be translated. The translation is applied to each process declaration separately:*

$$[\![K[\tilde{x}] := P]\!]_\emptyset \stackrel{\text{df}}{=} K[\tilde{x}] := [\![P]\!]_{\tilde{x} \cap fn(P)} \qquad \text{(Decl)}$$

Base Cases:

$$[\![\mathbf{0}]\!]_B \stackrel{\text{df}}{=} \mathbf{0} \qquad\qquad\qquad\qquad \text{(Stop)}$$

$$[\![\pi]\!]_B \stackrel{\text{df}}{=} \pi \,.\, \mathbf{0} \qquad\qquad\qquad \text{(Pref)}$$

$$[\![K\lfloor\tilde{x}\rfloor]\!]_B \stackrel{\text{df}}{=} K\lfloor\tilde{x}\rfloor \qquad\qquad \text{(Call)}$$

Parallel Composition:

$$\left[\!\!\left[\prod_{i=1}^{k} P_i\right]\!\!\right]_B \overset{\mathrm{df}}{=} \left(\bigodot_{i=1}^{n} \overline{begin_i}\langle B \cap fn\,(P_i)\rangle\right) . \bigodot_{i=1}^{n} end_i() \qquad \text{(Par)}$$

where $begin_i$ and end_i are fresh public names and K_i are fresh PIDs

$$K_i := begin_i(B \cap fn\,(P_i)).[\![P_i \; ; \; \overline{end_i}\langle\rangle \; ; \; K_i]\!]_{B \cap fn(P_i)}, \quad i = 1 \ldots k \; \prod_{i=1}^{k} K_i$$

is addedconcurrently to the initial term.

Restriction:

$$[\![\nu\tilde{r} : P]\!]_B \overset{\mathrm{df}}{=} \nu\tilde{r} : [\![P]\!]_{(B \cup \tilde{r}) \cap fn(P)} \qquad \text{(Restr)}$$

Choice Composition:

$$\left[\!\!\left[\sum_{i=1}^{k} P_i\right]\!\!\right]_B \overset{\mathrm{df}}{=} \sum_{i=1}^{k} [\![P_i]\!]_{B \cap fn(P_i)} \qquad \text{(Choice)}$$

Match and Mismatch:

$$[\![[a = x] \cdot P]\!]_B \overset{\mathrm{df}}{=} [a = x] \cdot [\![P]\!]_{B \cap fn(P)} \qquad \text{(Match)}$$

$$[\![[a \neq x] \cdot P]\!]_B \overset{\mathrm{df}}{=} [a \neq x] \cdot [\![P]\!]_{B \cap fn(P)} \qquad \text{(Mismatch)}$$

Sequential Composition Base Cases:

$$[\![\mathbf{0} \; ; \; P]\!]_B \overset{\mathrm{df}}{=} [\![P]\!]_B \qquad \text{(SeqStop)}$$

$$[\![\tau \; ; \; P]\!]_B \overset{\mathrm{df}}{=} \tau \cdot [\![P]\!]_B \qquad \text{(SeqTau)}$$

$$\left[\!\!\left[\overline{a}\langle\tilde{b}\rangle \; ; \; P\right]\!\!\right]_B \overset{\mathrm{df}}{=} \overline{a}\langle\tilde{b}\rangle.[\![P]\!]_{B \cap fn(P)} \qquad \text{(SeqSend)}$$

$$\left[\!\!\left[a(\tilde{b}) \; ; \; P\right]\!\!\right]_B \overset{\mathrm{df}}{=} a(\tilde{b}).[\![P]\!]_{(B \cup \tilde{b}) \cap fn(P)} \qquad \text{(SeqRec)}$$

Sequential Composition Inductive Cases:

$$\left[\!\!\left[\left(\sum_{i=1}^{k} P_i\right) \; ; \; P\right]\!\!\right]_B \overset{\mathrm{df}}{=} \left[\!\!\left[\sum_{i=1}^{k}\left(P_i \; ; \; K[B \cap fn\,(P)]\right)\right]\!\!\right]_B \qquad \text{(SeqChoice)}$$

where K is a fresh PID (not added to the initial process)

$$K[B \cap fn\,(P)] := [\![P]\!]_{B \cap fn(P)}$$

$$\left[\!\!\left[\left(\prod_{i=1}^{k} P_i\right) \; ; \; P\right]\!\!\right]_B \overset{\mathrm{df}}{=} \left[\!\!\left[\prod_{i=1}^{k} P_i\right]\!\!\right]_{B \cap \bigcup_{i=1}^{k} fn(P_i)} \cdot [\![P]\!]_{B \cap fn(P)} \qquad \text{(SeqPar)}$$

$$[\![(\nu\tilde{r} : P) \; ; \; P']\!]_B \overset{\mathrm{df}}{=} [\![\nu\tilde{r} : (P \; ; \; P')]\!]_B \qquad \text{(SeqRestr)}$$

4.3   An Example of Translation from EFCP to FCP

The following EFCP process models a client that communicates with a server.

$$C\lfloor url, ip \rfloor := \nu q : (\overline{url}\langle ip, q \rangle \; ; \; ip(a) \; ; \; C\lfloor url, ip \rfloor)$$
$$S\lfloor url' \rfloor := url'(ip', q') \; ; \; \nu x : ((\nu r : \overline{x}\langle r \rangle \; ; \; \tau \; ; \; r(a) \; ; \; \overline{ip'}\langle a \rangle) \, |$$
$$x(v) \; ; \; (\tau \; + \; \tau) \; ; \; \overline{v}\langle a' \rangle) \; ; \; S\lfloor url' \rfloor$$
$$\nu url'', ip'' : (S\lfloor url'' \rfloor \, | \, C\lfloor url'', ip'' \rfloor)$$

The server is located at some URL, $S\lfloor url' \rfloor$. A client can contact it by sending its IP address ip on the channel url. At the same time it sends a question, q, to the server, $\overline{url}\langle ip, q \rangle$. The client generates and sends a different question each time, thus q is a restricted name. The client's IP address and the question are received by the server and are stored as ip' and q', $url'(ip', q')$. The server runs two computational threads, which communicate with one another via a temporary internal channel x and produce an answer, and one of them sends the answer to the client on ip', $\nu x : ((\nu r : \overline{x}\langle r \rangle \; ; \; \tau \; ; \; r(a) \; ; \; \overline{ip'}\langle a \rangle) \, | \, x(v) \; ; \; (\tau \; + \; \tau) \; ; \; \overline{v}\langle a' \rangle)$, at which point the server repeats its behaviour by calling $S\lfloor url' \rfloor$. The client receives the answer, $ip(a)$, and is able to contact the server again, $C\lfloor url, ip \rfloor$.

This specification is a safe EFCP satisfying **(NOCLASH)**. Now, we translate it to FCP in a stepwise manner. First, the declaration of C is translated according to the rules of Definition 5:

$$
\begin{aligned}
&[\![C\lfloor url, ip \rfloor := \nu q : (\overline{url}\langle ip, q \rangle \; ; \; ip(a) \; ; \; C\lfloor url, ip \rfloor)]\!]_{\emptyset} && = by\ Decl \\
&C[url, ip] := [\![\nu q : (\overline{url}\langle ip, q \rangle \; ; \; ip(a) \; ; \; C\lfloor url, ip \rfloor)]\!]_{\{url, ip\}} && = by\ Restr \\
&C[url, ip] := \nu q : ([\![\overline{url}\langle ip, q \rangle \; ; \; ip(a) \; ; \; C\lfloor url, ip \rfloor]\!]_{\{url, ip, q\}}) && = by\ SeqSend \\
&C[url, ip] := \nu q : (\overline{url}\langle ip, q \rangle \; . \; [\![ip(a) \; ; \; C\lfloor url, ip \rfloor]\!]_{\{url, ip\}}) && = by\ SeqRec \\
&C[url, ip] := \nu q : (\overline{url}\langle ip, q \rangle \; . \; ip(a) \; . \; [\![C\lfloor url, ip \rfloor]\!]_{\{url, ip\}}) && = by\ Call \\
&C[url, ip] := \nu q : \overline{url}\langle ip, q \rangle \; . \; ip(a) \; . \; C\lfloor url, ip \rfloor
\end{aligned}
$$

Finally, client process has been converted to FCP. It is now the server's turn to be translated to FCP. Again, the same procedure is followed.

$$
\begin{aligned}
&[\![S\lfloor url' \rfloor := url'(ip', q') \; ; \; \nu x : ((\nu r : \overline{x}\langle r \rangle \; ; \; \tau \; ; \; r(a) \; ; \; \overline{ip'}\langle a \rangle) \, | \\
&\qquad x(v) \; ; \; (\tau \; + \; \tau) \; ; \; \overline{v}\langle a' \rangle) \; ; \; S\lfloor url' \rfloor]\!]_{\emptyset} && = by\ Decl \\
&S[url'] := [\![url'(ip', q') \; ; \; \nu x : ((\nu r : \overline{x}\langle r \rangle \; ; \; \tau \; ; \; r(a) \; ; \; \overline{ip'}\langle a \rangle) \, | \\
&\qquad x(v) \; ; \; (\tau \; + \; \tau) \; ; \; \overline{v}\langle a' \rangle) \; ; \; S\lfloor url' \rfloor]\!]_{\{url'\}} && = by\ SeqRec \\
&S[url'] := url'(ip', q') \; . \; [\![\nu x : ((\nu r : \overline{x}\langle r \rangle \; ; \; \tau \; ; \; r(a) \; ; \; \overline{ip'}\langle a \rangle) \, | \\
&\qquad x(v) \; ; \; (\tau \; + \; \tau) \; ; \; \overline{v}\langle a' \rangle) \; ; \; S\lfloor url' \rfloor]\!]_{\{ip', url'\}} && = by\ SeqRestr \\
&S[url'] := url'(ip', q') \; . \; [\![\nu x : (((\nu r : \overline{x}\langle r \rangle \; ; \; \tau \; ; \; r(a) \; ; \; \overline{ip'}\langle a \rangle) \, | \\
&\qquad x(v) \; ; \; (\tau \; + \; \tau) \; ; \; \overline{v}\langle a' \rangle) \; ; \; S\lfloor url' \rfloor)]\!]_{\{ip', url'\}} && = by\ Restr \\
&S[url'] := url'(ip', q') \; . \; \nu x : [\![((\nu r : \overline{x}\langle r \rangle \; ; \; \tau \; ; \; r(a) \; ; \; \overline{ip'}\langle a \rangle) \, | \\
&\qquad x(v) \; ; \; (\tau \; + \; \tau) \; ; \; \overline{v}\langle a' \rangle) \; ; \; S\lfloor url' \rfloor]\!]_{\{ip', x, url'\}} && = by\ SeqPar
\end{aligned}
$$

$$S[url'] := url'(ip',q') \cdot \nu x : ([[(\nu r : \overline{x}\langle r\rangle \; ; \; \tau \; ; \; r(a) \; ; \; \overline{ip'}\langle a\rangle)] \; |$$
$$x(v) \; ; \; (\tau + \tau) \; ; \; \overline{v}\langle a'\rangle]_{\{ip',x\}} \cdot [S\lfloor url'\rfloor]_{\{url'\}}) \qquad = by\,Call$$
$$S[url'] := url'(ip',q') \cdot \nu x : ([[(\nu r : \overline{x}\langle r\rangle \; ; \; \tau \; ; \; r(a) \; ; \; \overline{ip'}\langle a\rangle)] \; |$$
$$x(v) \; ; \; (\tau + \tau) \; ; \; \overline{v}\langle a'\rangle]_{\{ip',x\}} \cdot S\lfloor url'\rfloor) \qquad = by\,Par$$
$$S[url'] := url'(ip',q') \cdot \nu x : \overline{begin_1}\langle x, ip'\rangle \cdot \overline{begin_2}\langle x\rangle \cdot$$
$$end_1() \cdot end_2() \cdot S\lfloor url'\rfloor$$

Here $begin_1, begin_2, end_1, end_2$ are fresh public names, K_1 and K_2 are fresh PIDs, and $(K_1 \mid K_2)$ is added to the initial process.

$$K_1 := begin_1(x, ip') \cdot [\nu r : \overline{x}\langle r\rangle \; ; \; \tau \; ; \; r(a) \; ; \; \overline{ip'}\langle a\rangle \; ; \; \overline{end_1}\langle\rangle \; ; \; K_1]_{\{ip',x\}} \qquad = by\,Restr$$
$$K_1 := begin_1(x, ip') \cdot \nu r : [\overline{x}\langle r\rangle \; ; \; \tau \; ; \; r(a) \; ; \; \overline{ip'}\langle a\rangle \; ; \; \overline{end_1}\langle\rangle \; ; \; K_1]_{\{ip',x,r\}} \qquad = by\,SeqSend$$
$$K_1 := begin_1(x, ip') \cdot \nu r : \overline{x}\langle r\rangle \cdot [\tau \; ; \; r(a) \; ; \; \overline{ip'}\langle a\rangle \; ; \; \overline{end_1}\langle\rangle \; ; \; K_1]_{\{ip',r\}} \qquad = by\,SeqTau$$
$$K_1 := begin_1(x, ip') \cdot \nu r : \overline{x}\langle r\rangle \cdot \tau \cdot [r(a) \; ; \; \overline{ip'}\langle a\rangle \; ; \; \overline{end_1}\langle\rangle \; ; \; K_1]_{\{ip',r\}} \qquad = by\,SeqRec$$
$$K_1 := begin_1(x, ip') \cdot \nu r : \overline{x}\langle r\rangle \cdot \tau \cdot r(a) \cdot [\overline{ip'}\langle a\rangle \; ; \; \overline{end_1}\langle\rangle \; ; \; K_1]_{\{ip',a\}} \qquad = by\,SeqSend$$
$$K_1 := begin_1(x, ip') \cdot \nu r : \overline{x}\langle r\rangle \cdot \tau \cdot r(a) \cdot \overline{ip'}\langle a\rangle \cdot [\overline{end_1}\langle\rangle \; ; \; K_1]_{\emptyset} \qquad = by\,SeqSend$$
$$K_1 := begin_1(x, ip') \cdot \nu r : \overline{x}\langle r\rangle \cdot \tau \cdot r(a) \cdot \overline{ip'}\langle a\rangle \cdot \overline{end_1}\langle\rangle \cdot [K_1]_{\emptyset} \qquad = by\,Call$$
$$K_1 := begin_1(x, ip') \cdot \nu r : \overline{x}\langle r\rangle \cdot \tau \cdot r(a) \cdot \overline{ip'}\langle a\rangle \cdot \overline{end_1}\langle\rangle \cdot K_1$$

$$K_2 := begin_2(x) \cdot [x(v) \; ; \; (\tau + \tau) \; ; \; \overline{v}\langle a'\rangle \; ; \; \overline{end_2}\langle\rangle \; ; \; K_2]_{\{x\}} \qquad = by\,SeqRec$$
$$K_2 := begin_2(x) \cdot x(v) \cdot [(\tau + \tau) \; ; \; \overline{v}\langle a'\rangle \; ; \; \overline{end_2}\langle\rangle \; ; \; K_2]_{\{v\}} \qquad = by\,SeqChoice$$
$$K_2 := begin_2(x) \cdot x(v) \cdot [(\tau \; ; \; K_3\lfloor v\rfloor \; + \; \tau \; ; \; K_3\lfloor v\rfloor)]_{\{v\}} \qquad = by\,Choice$$

Here K_3 is a fresh PID (not added to the initial process).

$$K_2 := begin_2(x) \cdot x(v) \cdot ([\tau \; ; \; K_3\lfloor v\rfloor]_{\{v\}} \; + \; [\tau \; ; \; K_3\lfloor v\rfloor]_{\{v\}}) \qquad = by\,SeqTau$$
$$K_2 := begin_2(x) \cdot x(v) \cdot (\tau \cdot [K_3\lfloor v\rfloor]_{\{v\}} \; + \; \tau \cdot [K_3\lfloor v\rfloor]_{\{v\}}) \qquad = by\,Call$$
$$K_2 := begin_2(x) \cdot x(v) \cdot (\tau \cdot K_3\lfloor v\rfloor \; + \; \tau \cdot K_3\lfloor v\rfloor)$$

$$K_3[v] := [\overline{v}\langle a'\rangle \; ; \; \overline{end_2}\langle\rangle \; ; \; K_2]_{\{v\}} \qquad = by\,SeqSend$$
$$K_3[v] := \overline{v}\langle a'\rangle \cdot [\overline{end_2}\langle\rangle \; ; \; K_2]_{\emptyset} \qquad = by\,SeqSend$$
$$K_3[v] := \overline{v}\langle a'\rangle \cdot \overline{end_2}\langle\rangle \cdot [K_2]_{\emptyset} \qquad = by\,Call$$
$$K_3[v] := \overline{v}\langle a'\rangle \cdot \overline{end_2}\langle\rangle \cdot K_2$$

Finally, the resulting FCP is:

$$C[url, ip] := \nu q : \overline{url}\langle ip, q\rangle \cdot ip(a) \cdot C\lfloor url, ip\rfloor$$
$$S[url'] := url'(ip',q') \cdot \nu x : \overline{begin_1}\langle x, ip'\rangle \cdot \overline{begin_2}\langle x\rangle \cdot end_1() \cdot end_2() \cdot S\lfloor url'\rfloor$$
$$K_1 := begin_1(x, ip') \cdot \nu r : \overline{x}\langle r\rangle \cdot \tau \cdot r(a) \cdot \overline{ip'}\langle a\rangle \cdot \overline{end_1}\langle\rangle \cdot K_1$$
$$K_2 := begin_2(x) \cdot x(v) \cdot (\tau \cdot K_3\lfloor v\rfloor \; + \; \tau \cdot K_3\lfloor v\rfloor)$$

$K_3[v] := \overline{v}\langle a' \rangle . \overline{end_2}\langle\rangle . K_2$

$\nu url'', ip'' : (S\lfloor url'' \rfloor \mid C\lfloor url'', ip'' \rfloor \mid K_1 \mid K_2).$

4.4   Size of the Translation

One can easily check that every translation rule except (SeqChoice) yields a linear size result, and that (SeqChoice) yields at most quadratic result. This quadratic blow-up happens when it is necessary to pass a large number of bound names as parameters of a call, as shown in the following example.

$$K := a(\tilde{x}) ; \left(\sum_{i=1}^{N} \tau \right) ; \overline{b}\langle \tilde{x} \rangle$$
$$K$$

The translated process is:

$$K := a(\tilde{x}). \left(\sum_{i=1}^{N} \tau.K_1\lfloor \tilde{x} \rfloor \right)$$
$$K_1[\tilde{x}] := \overline{b}\langle \tilde{x} \rangle . \mathbf{0}$$
$$K$$

If $|\tilde{x}| = N$ then the size of the translated specification is quadratic, as N calls with N parameters each are created.

Note that this quadratic blow-up in (SeqChoice) is isolated, and the subsequent translation of these calls by the (Call) rule cannot create any further blow-up, and so the overall size of the translated process is at most quadratic. Furthermore, one needs a rather artificial process for this quadratic blow-up to occur, and we conjecture that for practical EFCP models the translation will usually be linear.

5   Case Study

In this section, the applicability of the proposed formalism and its translation to safe FCP is demonstrated using SpiNNaker [9] as a case study.

5.1   SpiNNaker Architecture

SpiNNaker is a massively parallel architecture designed to model large-scale spiking neural networks in real-time [10]. Its design is based around *ad-hoc* multi-core System-on-Chips, which are interconnected using a two-dimensional toroidal triangular mesh [10,11]. Neurons are modelled in software and their spikes generate packets that propagate through the on- and inter-chip communication fabric relying on custom-made on-chip multicast routers [12,13]. The aim of SpiNNaker project is to simulate a billion spiking neurons in real time [14–16]. The SpiNNaker architecture is illustrated in Fig. 1.

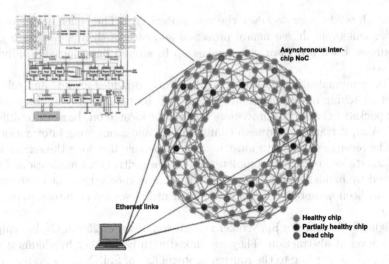

Fig. 1. The SpiNNaker architecture [17].

Every node of the network consists of a SpiNNaker Chip multiprocessor (CMP), which constitutes the basis of the system [18,19]. It comprises 20 processing cores and SDRAM memory. For the cores, synchronous ARM9 processors were used because of their high power efficiency [14]. One of the processors is called monitor processor and its role is to perform system management tasks

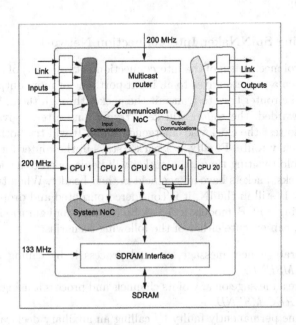

Fig. 2. The SpiNNaker chip organisation [20].

and to allow the user to track the on-chip activity. The other processors run independent event-driven neural processes and each of them simulates a group of neurons. Each processor core models up to around one thousand individual neurons.

The communication network-on-chip (NoC) provides an on- and off- chip packet switching infrastructure [20], see Fig. 2. Its main task is to carry neural-event packets between the processors that can be located on the same or different chips. Also, it transports system configurations and monitoring information [18, 20]. The receiver of the data must be able to manage how long the sender keeps the data stable in order to complete a Delay-Insensitive communication. This is achieved by handshaking. The receiver uses an acknowledgement to show that data has been accepted. The acknowledgement follows a return-to-zero protocol [18, 20].

Figure 3 illustrates a SpiNNaker system composed of 25 SpiNNaker chips at a high level of abstraction. They are linked with each other by channels (e.g., $c1$, $c2$, ...). According to the routing protocol [20] of SpiNNaker's system, every chip can generate and propagate a datum. Every chip is connected to six other chips by bidirectional links as shown in Fig. 3. This structure forms a Cartesian coordinate system. For instance, P_0 can communicate only with P_1, P_6, P_5, P_4, P_{24} and P_{20}. Thus, the communication happens in the first and third quadrant. Every chip has a pair of coordinates. These coordinates are needed for the routing plan of the system. It is possible for some chips to be faulty or congested. In such a case, an emergency routing plan is followed to bypass this kind of issues [21, 22]. Thus, the redundancy of the SpiNNaker chips enhances the fault tolerance of the system [23].

5.2   Modelling SpiNNaker Interconnection Network

The flow-control mechanism of the interconnection network (IN) of SpiNNaker is as follows. When a packet arrives to an input port, one or more output ports are selected, and the router tries to transmit the packet through them. If the packet cannot be forwarded, the router will keep trying, and after a given period of time it will also test the clockwise emergency route. It will try both the regular and the emergency route. Finally, if a packet stays in the router for longer than a given threshold (waiting time), the packet will be dropped to avoid deadlocks. To avoid livelocks, packets have an age field in their header. When two ages pass and the packet is still in the IN, it is considered outdated and dropped [10].

The following EFCP models a 5×5 SpiNNaker configuration. A healthy processor, *HP*, can execute either of the following scenarios:

- It can generate a new message, m, and process it by calling an auxiliary declaration *MSEND*.
- It can receive a message on any of its channels and process it using an auxiliary declaration *REC_MSEND*.
- It can become permanently faulty by calling an auxiliary declaration *FP*.

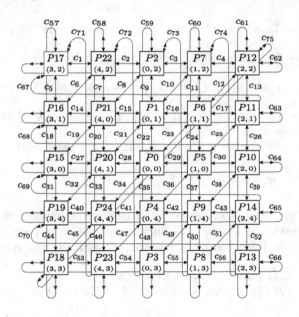

Fig. 3. SpiNNaker network topology [20].

The definition of *HP* has six formal parameters corresponding to the six channels connecting it to the neighbours, see Fig. 3. These parameters are named after points of the compass, e.g. 'n' stands for 'north', 'ne' stands for 'north-east', etc.

$$HP[n, ne, e, s, sw, w] := \nu m : MSEND\lfloor m, n, ne, e, s, sw, w\rfloor$$
$$+REC\_MSEND\lfloor n, n, ne, e, s, sw, w\rfloor$$
$$+REC\_MSEND\lfloor ne, n, ne, e, s, sw, w\rfloor$$
$$+REC\_MSEND\lfloor e, n, ne, e, s, sw, w\rfloor$$
$$+REC\_MSEND\lfloor s, n, ne, e, s, sw, w\rfloor$$
$$+REC\_MSEND\lfloor sw, n, ne, e, s, sw, w\rfloor$$
$$+REC\_MSEND\lfloor w, n, ne, e, s, sw, w\rfloor$$
$$+FP\lfloor n, ne, e, s, sw, w\rfloor$$

The auxiliary declarations are as follows:

$MSEND[m, n, ne, e, s, sw, w]$ sends message m on 0 or more of the channels and becomes $HP[n, ne, e, s, sw, w]$. In particular, the message can be consumed, forwarded or multicast. Clockwise emergency routes are used in case of negative acknowledgement *nack*.

$$MSEND[m, n, ne, e, s, sw, w] := \Bigg($$
$$\Big(\tau + \overline{n}\langle m\rangle ; n(a) ; ([a = ack] ; \tau + [a = nack] ; \overline{ne}\langle m\rangle ; ne(a))\Big) \Big|$$

$$\left(\tau + \overline{ne}\langle m \rangle \; ; \; ne(a) \; ; \; \left([a = ack] \; ; \; \tau + [a = nack] \; ; \; \overline{e}\langle m \rangle \; ; \; e(a) \right) \right) |$$

$$\left(\tau + \overline{e}\langle m \rangle \; ; \; e(a) \; ; \; \left([a = ack] \; ; \; \tau + [a = nack] \; ; \; \overline{s}\langle m \rangle \; ; \; s(a) \right) \right) |$$

$$\left(\tau + \overline{s}\langle m \rangle \; ; \; s(a) \; ; \; \left([a = ack] \; ; \; \tau + [a = nack] \; ; \; \overline{sw}\langle m \rangle \; ; \; sw(a) \right) \right) |$$

$$\left(\tau + \overline{sw}\langle m \rangle \; ; \; sw(a) \; ; \; \left([a = ack] \; ; \; \tau + [a = nack] \; ; \; \overline{w}\langle m \rangle \; ; \; w(a) \right) \right) |$$

$$\left(\tau + \overline{w}\langle m \rangle \; ; \; w(a) \; ; \; \left([a = ack] \; ; \; \tau + [a = nack] \; ; \; \overline{n}\langle m \rangle \; ; \; n(a) \right) \right)$$

$$\Big) \; ; \; HP \lfloor n, ne, e, s, sw, w \rfloor$$

$REC\_MSEND[c, n, ne, e, s, sw, w]$ receives a message on channel c and either negatively acknowledges ($nack$) it to simulate congestion or positively acknowledges (ack) it and then consumes, forwards or multicasts it by calling $MSEND$.

$$REC\_MSEND[c, n, ne, e, s, sw, w] := c(m) \; ; \; ($$
$$\overline{c}\langle nack \rangle \; ; \; HP \lfloor n, ne, e, s, sw, w \rfloor + \overline{c}\langle ack \rangle \; ; \; MSEND \lfloor m, n, ne, e, s, sw, w \rfloor$$
$$)$$

$FP[n, ne, e, s, sw, w]$ models a faulty process that does not send any messages and negatively acknowledges ($nack$) all the received messages.

$$FP[n, ne, e, s, sw, w] := ($$
$$n(m) \; ; \; \overline{n}\langle nack \rangle + ne(m) \; ; \; \overline{ne}\langle nack \rangle + e(m) \; ; \; \overline{e}\langle nack \rangle$$
$$+ s(m) \; ; \; \overline{s}\langle nack \rangle + sw(m) \; ; \; \overline{sw}\langle nack \rangle + w(m) \; ; \; \overline{w}\langle nack \rangle$$
$$) \; ; \; FP \lfloor n, ne, e, s, sw, w \rfloor$$

The initial term creates 25 concurrent instances of HP, $\prod_{i=1}^{25} HP \lfloor \ldots \rfloor$, and connects them by channels as shown in Fig. 3:

$$HP \lfloor c_{22}, c_{23}, c_{29}, c_{35}, c_{34}, c_{28} \rfloor \; | \; HP \lfloor c_9, c_{10}, c_{16}, c_{22}, c_{21}, c_{15} \rfloor \; |$$
$$HP \lfloor c_{59}, c_{73}, c_3, c_9, c_8, c_2 \rfloor \; | \; HP \lfloor c_{48}, c_{49}, c_{55}, c_{59}, c_{72}, c_{54} \rfloor \; |$$
$$HP \lfloor c_{35}, c_{36}, c_{42}, c_{48}, c_{47}, c_{41} \rfloor \; | \; HP \lfloor c_{24}, c_{25}, c_{30}, c_{37}, c_{36}, c_{29} \rfloor \; |$$
$$HP \lfloor c_{11}, c_{12}, c_{17}, c_{24}, c_{23}, c_{16} \rfloor \; | \; HP \lfloor c_{60}, c_{74}, c_4, c_{11}, c_{10}, c_3 \rfloor \; |$$
$$HP \lfloor c_{50}, c_{51}, c_{56}, c_{60}, c_{73}, c_{55} \rfloor \; | \; HP \lfloor c_{37}, c_{38}, c_{43}, c_{50}, c_{49}, c_{42} \rfloor \; |$$
$$HP \lfloor c_{26}, c_{68}, c_{64}, c_{39}, c_{38}, c_{30} \rfloor \; | \; HP \lfloor c_{13}, c_{67}, c_{63}, c_{26}, c_{25}, c_{17} \rfloor \; |$$
$$HP \lfloor c_{61}, c_{75}, c_{62}, c_{13}, c_{12}, c_4 \rfloor \; | \; HP \lfloor c_{52}, c_{70}, c_{66}, c_{61}, c_{74}, c_{56} \rfloor \; |$$
$$HP \lfloor c_{39}, c_{69}, c_{65}, c_{52}, c_{51}, c_{43} \rfloor \; | \; HP \lfloor c_{18}, c_{19}, c_{27}, c_{31}, c_{69}, c_{64} \rfloor \; |$$
$$HP \lfloor c_5, c_6, c_{14}, c_{18}, c_{68}, c_{63} \rfloor \; | \; HP \lfloor c_{57}, c_{71}, c_1, c_5, c_{67}, c_{62} \rfloor \; |$$
$$HP \lfloor c_{44}, c_{45}, c_{53}, c_{57}, c_{75}, c_{66} \rfloor \; | \; HP \lfloor c_{31}, c_{32}, c_{40}, c_{44}, c_{70}, c_{65} \rfloor \; |$$
$$HP \lfloor c_{20}, c_{21}, c_{28}, c_{33}, c_{32}, c_{27} \rfloor \; | \; HP \lfloor c_7, c_8, c_{15}, c_{20}, c_{19}, c_{14} \rfloor \; |$$
$$HP \lfloor c_{58}, c_{72}, c_2, c_7, c_6, c_1 \rfloor \; | \; HP \lfloor c_{46}, c_{47}, c_{54}, c_{58}, c_{71}, c_{53} \rfloor \; |$$
$$HP \lfloor c_{33}, c_{34}, c_{41}, c_{46}, c_{45}, c_{40} \rfloor$$

The above specification is an EFCP and below its translation to FCP is given. It has been obtained with the help of the developed tool EFCP2FCP. First of all, this EFCP must be translated to a safe EFCP. This is done automatically by the tool by replicating the process declarations, HP, $MSEND$, REC_MSEND, and FP, so that each of the 25 threads has its own copies of these declarations: HP^i, $MSEND^i$, REC_MSEND^i, FP^i, $i = 1 \ldots 25$. Also, the tool enforces the **(NOCLASH)** assumptions by renaming the formal parameters and bound names. However, below we disregard this renaming for the sake of clarity.

The translation of HP and REC_MSEND is straightforward as they do not use any special features of EFCP:

$$
\begin{aligned}
HP^i[n, ne, e, s, sw, w] := \nu m : \; & MSEND^i\lfloor m, n, ne, e, s, sw, w\rfloor \\
+ \; & REC\_MSEND^i\lfloor n, n, ne, e, s, sw, w\rfloor \\
+ \; & REC\_MSEND^i\lfloor ne, n, ne, e, s, sw, w\rfloor \\
+ \; & REC\_MSEND^i\lfloor e, n, ne, e, s, sw, w\rfloor \\
+ \; & REC\_MSEND^i\lfloor s, n, ne, e, s, sw, w\rfloor \\
+ \; & REC\_MSEND^i\lfloor sw, n, ne, e, s, sw, w\rfloor \\
+ \; & REC\_MSEND^i\lfloor w, n, ne, e, s, sw, w\rfloor \\
+ \; & FP^i\lfloor n, ne, e, s, sw, w\rfloor
\end{aligned}
$$

$$
\begin{aligned}
REC\_MSEND^i[c, n, ne, e, s, sw, w] := c(m) \; . \; (\\
\overline{c}\langle nack\rangle \; . \; HP^i\lfloor n, ne, e, s, sw, w\rfloor + \overline{c}\langle ack\rangle \; . \; MSEND^i\lfloor m, n, ne, e, s, sw, w\rfloor \\
)
\end{aligned}
$$

The translation of FP can be obtained by applying the (SeqChoice) rule:

$$
\begin{aligned}
FP^i[n, ne, e, s, sw, w] := \\
n(m).\overline{n}\langle nack\rangle.K_{FP^i}\lfloor n, ne, e, s, sw, w\rfloor + ne(m).\overline{ne}\langle nack\rangle.K_{FP^i}\lfloor n, ne, e, s, sw, w\rfloor \\
+ e(m).\overline{e}\langle nack\rangle.K_{FP^i}\lfloor n, ne, e, s, sw, w\rfloor + s(m).\overline{s}\langle nack\rangle.K_{FP^i}\lfloor n, ne, e, s, sw, w\rfloor \\
+ sw(m).\overline{sw}\langle nack\rangle.K_{FP^i}\lfloor n, ne, e, s, sw, w\rfloor + w(m).\overline{w}\langle nack\rangle.K_{FP^i}\lfloor n, ne, e, s, sw, w\rfloor \\
K_{FP^i}[n, ne, e, s, sw, w] := FP^i\lfloor n, ne, e, s, sw, w\rfloor
\end{aligned}
$$

Here K_{FP^i} is a fresh PID.

The translation of $MSEND$ is the most interesting one as it contains some local concurrency that is not allowed in FCPs (below K_j^i, L_j^i and M_j^i are fresh PIDs and $begin_j^i$ and end_j^i are fresh public names):

$$
\begin{aligned}
MSEND^i[m, n, ne, e, s, sw, w] := \\
\overline{begin_1^i}\langle m, n, ne\rangle.\overline{begin_2^i}\langle m, ne, e\rangle.\overline{begin_3^i}\langle m, e, s\rangle. \\
\overline{begin_4^i}\langle m, s, sw\rangle.\overline{begin_5^i}\langle m, sw, w\rangle.\overline{begin_6^i}\langle m, w, n\rangle. \\
end_1^i().end_2^i().end_3^i().end_4^i().end_5^i().end_6^i().HP^i\lfloor n, ne, e, s, sw, w\rfloor
\end{aligned}
$$

$$
\begin{aligned}
K_1^i := begin_1^i(m, n, ne).(\\
\tau.L_1^i + \overline{n}\langle m\rangle.n(a).([a = ack].\tau.M_1^i + [a = nack].\overline{ne}\langle m\rangle.ne(a).M_1^i) \\
) \\
L_1^i := \overline{end_1^i}\langle\rangle \; . \; K_1^i
\end{aligned}
$$

$$M_1^i := L_1^i$$

$$K_2^i := begin_2^i(m, ne, e).\big($$
$$\tau.L_2^i + \overline{ne}\langle m\rangle.ne(a).([a = ack].\tau.M_2^i + [a = nack].\overline{e}\langle m\rangle.e(a).M_2^i)$$
$$\big)$$

$$L_2^i := \overline{end_2^i}\langle\rangle . K_2^i$$

$$M_2^i := L_2^i$$

$$K_3^i := begin_3^i(m, e, s).\big($$
$$\tau.L_3^i + \overline{e}\langle m\rangle.e(a).([a = ack].\tau.M_3^i + [a = nack].\overline{s}\langle m\rangle.s(a).M_3^i)$$
$$\big)$$

$$L_3^i := \overline{end_3^i}\langle\rangle . K_3^i$$

$$M_3^i := L_3^i$$

$$K_4^i := begin_4^i(m, s, sw).\big($$
$$\tau.L_4^i + \overline{s}\langle m\rangle.s(a).([a = ack].\tau.M_4^i + [a = nack].\overline{sw}\langle m\rangle.sw(a).M_4^i)$$
$$\big)$$

$$L_4^i := \overline{end_4^i}\langle\rangle . K_4^i$$

$$M_4^i := L_4^i$$

$$K_5^i := begin_5^i(m, sw, w).\big($$
$$\tau.L_5^i + \overline{sw}\langle m\rangle.sw(a).([a = ack].\tau.M_5^i + [a = nack].\overline{w}\langle m\rangle.w(a).M_5^i)$$
$$\big)$$

$$L_5^i := \overline{end_5^i}\langle\rangle . K_5^i$$

$$M_5^i := L_5^i$$

$$K_6^i := begin_6^i(m, w, n).\big($$
$$\tau.L_6^i + \overline{w}\langle m\rangle.w(a).([a = ack].\tau.M_6^i + [a = nack].\overline{n}\langle m\rangle.n(a).M_6^i)$$
$$\big)$$

$$L_6^i := \overline{end_6^i}\langle\rangle . K_6^i$$

$$M_6^i := L_6^i$$

The initial process is now as follows:

$$\prod_{i=1}^{25} HP^i\lfloor\ldots\rfloor \quad | \quad \prod_{i=1}^{25}\prod_{j=1}^{6} K_j^i$$

5.3   Formal Verification

As outlined in the introduction, formal verification is an important motivation of this paper. It was performed as follows. First, the EFCP model of the 2×2

SpiNNaker network was automatically translated into an FCP model by the EFCP2FCP tool. Then the resulting FCP was then translated into a safe low-level Petri net using the FCP2PN tool [5]. Some small adaptations had to be done for the latter: FCP2PN requires choices to be *guarded,* i.e. each summand must start with a prefix, match or mismatch. This was achieved by inlining the calls to REC_MSEND^i and prefixing the first and last summands in the body of HP^i with τ. We also inlined the calls to L^i_j and M^i_j as an optimisation – the same effect could have been achieved automatically during the translation if rule (SeqChoice) were avoiding the creation of a new PID whenever the size of P does not exceed some pre-defined constant. The translation runtimes were negligible (<2 sec) in both cases, and the resulting Petri net contained 14844 places, 38864 transitions and 292336 arcs.

Then deadlock checking was performed with the LoLA tool,[2] configured to assume safeness of the Petri net (CAPACITY 1), use the stubborn sets and symmetry reductions (STUBBORN, SYMMETRY), compress states using P-invariants (PREDUCTION), use a light-weight data structure for states (SMALLSTATE), and check for deadlocks (DEADLOCK).

The verification runtime was 3223 sec, and LoLA reported that the model had a deadlock. In hindsight, this is quite obvious, as the model allows all the processors to become faulty, after which they stop generating new messages and the system quickly reaches a deadlock state.

6   Conclusion

The initial motivation of this research was the development of a formalism allowing for convenient modelling and formal verification of Reference Passing Systems. To that end, a new fragment of π-calculus, the Extended Finite Control Processes, is presented in this paper. EFCPs is an extension of the well-known fragment of π-calculus, the Finite Control Processes. FCPs were used for formal modelling of reference passing systems; however, they cannot express scenarios involving 'local' concurrency inside a process. EFCPs remove this limitation. As a result, practical modelling of mobile systems becomes more convenient, e.g. multicast can be naturally expressed. To this end, also a more powerful sequential composition operator ' ; ' is used instead of prefixing. The SpiNNaker case study demonstrates that EFCPs allow for a concise expression of multicast communication, and is suitable for practical modelling. Furthermore, an almost linear translation from safe EFCP to safe FCP has been developed, which forms the basis of formal verification of RPSs.

In our future work we intend to investigate the relationship between the transition systems generated by EFCPs and those generated by the corresponding FCPs, with the view to prove the correctness of the proposed translation. We would also like to evaluate the scalability of the proposed approach on a range of models and optimise the translation, e.g. by reducing the number of generated defining equations and by lifting it to non-safe processes.

---

[2] Available from http://service-technology.org/tools/lola.

References

1. Kwiatkowska, M.Z., Rodden, T., Sassone, V. (eds.): From computers to ubiquitous computing by 2020. In: Proceedings of Philosophical Transactions of the Royal Society, vol. 366 (2008)
2. Milner, R., Parrow, J., Walker, D.: A calculus of mobile processes, part I. Inf. Comp. **100**(1), 1–40 (1992)
3. Cardelli, L., Gordon, A.: Mobile ambients. In: Nivat, M. (ed.) Foundations of Software Science and Computation Structures. Lecture Notes in Computer Science, vol. 1378, pp. 140–155. Springer, Heidelberg (1998)
4. Dam, M.: Model checking mobile processes. Inf. Comp. **129**(1), 35–51 (1996)
5. Meyer, R., Khomenko, V., Hüchting, R.: A polynomial translation of π-calculus (FCP) to safe Petri nets. Logical Methods Comput. Sci. **9**(3), 1–36 (2013)
6. Milner, R.: Communicating and Mobile Systems: the π-Calculus. CUP, New York (1999)
7. Sangiorgi, D., Walker, D.: The π-calculus: A Theory of Mobile Processes. CUP, New York (2001)
8. Meyer, R., Khomenko, V., Strazny, T.: A practical approach to verification of mobile systems using net unfoldings. Fundam. Inf. **94**(3–4), 439–471 (2009)
9. Furber, S., Temple, S.: Neural systems engineering. In: Fulcher, J., Jain, L. (eds.) Computational Intelligence: A Compendium. Studies in Computational Intelligence, vol. 115, pp. 763–796. Springer, Heidelberg (2008)
10. Navaridas, J., Luján, M., Miguel-Alonso, J., Plana, L.A., Furber, S.: Understanding the interconnection network of SpiNNaker. In: Proceedings of the 23rd International Conference on Supercomputing, ICS 2009, pp. 286–295. ACM (2009)
11. Camara, J., Moreto, M., Vallejo, E., Beivide, R., Miguel-Alonso, J., Martinez, C., Navaridas, J.: Mixed-radix twisted torus interconnection networks. In: Parallel and Distributed Processing Symposium IPDPS, pp. 1–10. IEEE (2007)
12. Plana, L., Bainbridge, J., Furber, S., Salisbury, S., Yebin, S., Jian, W.: An on-chip and inter-chip communications network for the SpiNNaker massively-parallel neural net simulator. In: Second ACM IEEE International Symposium on Networks-on-Chip, 2008, NoCS 2008, pp. 215–216. IEEE Computer Society (2008)
13. Furber, S., Temple, S., Brown, A.: On-chip and inter-chip networks for modeling large-scale neural systems. In: Circuits and Systems, ISCAS Proceedings, pp. 21–24. IEEE (2006)
14. Rast, A., Yang, S., Khan, M., Furber, S.: Virtual synaptic interconnect using an asynchronous network-on-chip. In: Proceedings of Intelligence Joint Conference on Neural Networks (IJCNN2008), pp. 2727–2734. IEEE (2008)
15. Jin, X., Furber, S., Woods, J.: Efficient modelling of spiking neural networks on a scalable chip multiprocessor. In: Neural Networks, IJCNN World Congress on Computational Intelligence, pp. 2812–2819. IEEE (2008)
16. Asanovic, K., Beck, J., Feldman, J., Morgan, N., Wawrzynek, J.: A supercomputer for neural computation. In: Neural Networks, World Congress on Computational Intelligence, vol. 1, pp. 5–9. IEEE (1994)
17. Furber, S., Brown, A.: Biologically inspired massively parallel architectures computing beyond a million processors. In: Application of Concurrency to System Design, 2009, ACSD 2009, pp. 3–12. IEEE (2009)
18. Plana, L., Furber, S., Temple, S., Khan, M., Shi, Y., Wu, J., Yang, S.: A GALS infrastructure for a massively parallel multiprocessor. Des. Test Comput. IEEE **24**(5), 454–463 (2007)

19. Farber, P., Asanovic, K.: Parallel neural network training on multi-spert. In: 3rd International Conference on Algorithms and Architectures for Parallel Processing, ICAPP, pp. 659–666. IEEE (1997)
20. Wu, J., Furber, S.: A multicast routing scheme for a universal spiking neural network architecture. Comput. J. **53**(3), 280–288 (2010)
21. Puente, V., Gregorio, J.: Immucube: scalable fault-tolerant routing for k-ary n-cube networks. IEEE Trans. Parallel Distrib. Syst. **18**(6), 776–788 (2007)
22. Puente, V., Izu, C., Beivide, R., Gregorio, J.A., Vallejo, F., Prellezo, J.M.: The adaptive bubble router. J. Parallel Distrib. Comput. **61**(9), 1180–1208 (2001)
23. Gomez, M., Nordbotten, N., Flich, J., Lopez, P., Robles, A., Duato, J., Skeie, T., Lysne, O.: A routing methodology for achieving fault tolerance in direct networks. IEEE Trans. Comput. **55**(4), 400–415 (2006)

Author Index

Printed in the United States
by Bookmasters

Printed in the United States
By Bookmasters